RENEWALS 458-4574
DATE DUE

WITHDRAWN
UTSA Libraries

Organized Business Interests in Changing Environments

Globalization and Governance

General Editor: **Colin Hay**

Globalization has become the buzzword of the age, within political, business and academic circles alike. An ever-growing set of associations, connotations and mythologies have been created around this ubiquitous term and its supposed economic, political and cultural impact.

This series will engage in a critical interrogation, unpacking and disaggregation of the often underdeveloped, undertheorised and unduly homogeneous concept of globalization that pervades much of the existing literature and debate.

In examining the complex and multiple processes that constitute the dynamics of globalization, the series aims to contribute to the demystifying of the concept, challenging its logic of inevitability by putting the political back into the analysis of globalization.

The spirit of the series is international and interdisciplinary. It assesses the practices and processes of globalization in the cultural, political, social and economic spheres, examining the empirical evidence for the phenomenon, unpacking the ideological underpinnings of its discourse and discussing the prospects for the governance of globalization's effects and linkages.

Titles include:

Jürgen Grote, Achim Lang and Volker Schneider *(editors)*
ORGANIZED BUSINESS INTERESTS IN CHANGING ENVIRONMENTS
The Complexity of Adaptation

Colin Hay and David Marsh *(editors)*
DEMYSTIFYING GLOBALIZATION

Bernard Jullien and Andy Smith *(editors)*
INDUSTRIES AND GLOBALIZATION
The Political Causality of Difference

Globalization and Governance Series
Series Standing Order ISBN 978–0–333–79238–4 (Hardback) 978–1–4039–1906–9 (Paperback)
(*outside North America only*)

You can receive future titles in this series as they are published by placing a standing order. Please contact your bookseller or, in case of difficulty, write to us at the address below with your name and address, the title of the series and the ISBN quoted above.

Customer Services Department, Macmillan Distribution Ltd, Houndmills, Basingstoke, Hampshire RG21 6XS, England

Organized Business Interests in Changing Environments

The Complexity of Adaptation

Edited by

Jürgen R. Grote
Department of Public and Social Policies
Charles University in Prague, Czech Republic

Achim Lang
Department of Public Policy and Management
University of Konstanz, Germany

and

Volker Schneider
Department of Public Policy and Management
University of Konstanz, Germany

Editorial matter, selection and introduction © Jürgen R. Grote, Achim Lang and Volker Schneider 2008
All remaining chapters © respective authors 2008
All rights reserved. No reproduction, copy or transmission of this publication may be made without written permission.

No portion of this publication may be reproduced, copied or transmitted save with written permission or in accordance with the provisions of the Copyright, Designs and Patents Act 1988, or under the terms of any licence permitting limited copying issued by the Copyright Licensing Agency, Saffron House, 6-10 Kirby Street, London EC1N 8TS.

Any person who does any unauthorized act in relation to this publication may be liable to criminal prosecution and civil claims for damages.

The authors have asserted their rights to be identified as the authors of this work in accordance with the Copyright, Designs and Patents Act 1988.

First published 2008 by
PALGRAVE MACMILLAN

Palgrave Macmillan in the UK is an imprint of Macmillan Publishers Limited, registered in England, company number 785998, of Houndmills, Basingstoke, Hampshire RG21 6XS.

Palgrave Macmillan in the US is a division of St Martin's Press LLC, 175 Fifth Avenue, New York, NY 10010.

Palgrave Macmillan is the global academic imprint of the above companies and has companies and representatives throughout the world.

Palgrave® and Macmillan® are registered trademarks in the United States, the United Kingdom, Europe and other countries.

ISBN-13: 978–0–230–21665–5   hardback
ISBN-10: 0–230–21665–X   hardback

This book is printed on paper suitable for recycling and made from fully managed and sustained forest sources. Logging, pulping and manufacturing processes are expected to conform to the environmental regulations of the country of origin.

A catalogue record for this book is available from the British Library.

Library of Congress Cataloging-in-Publication Data

Organized business interests in changing environments : the complexity of adaptation / edited by Jürgen R. Grote, Achim Lang, and Volker Schneider.
    p. cm. — (Globalization and governance)
  Includes bibliographical references.
  ISBN 978–0–230–21665–5 (alk. paper)
  1. International business enterprises—Political aspects. 2. Business and politics. 3. International organization. 4. Complex organizations. 5. Organizational change. I. Grote, Jürgen R. II. Lang, Achim. III. Schneider, Volker, 1952–
   HD2755.5.O746 2008
   658'.049—dc22
                                                                2008029982

10 9 8 7 6 5 4 3 2 1
17 16 15 14 13 12 11 10 09 08

Printed and bound in Great Britain by
CPI Antony Rowe, Chippenham and Eastbourne

Contents

List of Tables vii

List of Figures viii

Preface and Acknowledgments ix

Contributors xiii

1 Organized Business Interests in Changing Environments: Introduction 1
Volker Schneider, Achim Lang, and Jürgen R. Grote

Part I: Theories and Determinants of Organizing Business Interests 15

2 From Simple to Complex: An Evolutionary Sketch of Theories of Business Association 17
Achim Lang, Karsten Ronit, and Volker Schneider

3 Between Politics, Economy, and Technology: The Changing Environments of Business Associations 42
Achim Lang, Volker Schneider, and Raymund Werle

Part II: Business Associations at the National Level 63

4 Persistent Divergence? Chemical Business Associations in Britain and Germany 65
Jürgen R. Grote

5 Business Associability in the US Chemical Industry: Private Interest Governments in Pluralist Precincts? 88
Hans-Jörg Schmedes

6 Similar Responses to Similar Pressures? Adaptation Processes of British and German Business Associations in the Information and Communications Sector 108
Achim Lang

7 Cooperation, Competition, and Mutualism in the
   US Information and Communications Sector   130
   Johannes M. Bauer and Volker Schneider

8 Complex Associations in the Dairy Sector: A Comparison
   of Development in Four Countries   153
   Claudius Wagemann

Part III: Business Associations at the European Level   177

9 Europeanized Convergence? British and German
   Business Associations' European Lobbying Strategies
   in the Formulation of REACH   179
   Arndt Wonka

10 Business Interest Associations and Corporate
   Lobbying: Which Role for Brussels?   200
   Marc Tenbücken

11 The Complexity of Adaptation: Conclusions   221
   Achim Lang and Volker Schneider

References   240

Author Index   255

Subject Index   258

List of Tables

3.1	Industry characteristics	61
4.1	Average resource allocation (in percent) and changes (frequency) of chemical business associations in Germany and Britain	80
4.2	Membership of domestic and international business associations	84
5.1	Average associational resource allocation (in percent) and changes (frequency)	99
6.1	Average resource allocation (in percent) and changes (frequency) of British and German trade associations in the I&C sector	120
6.2	Membership of international trade associations and the maintenance of a liaison office in Brussels	124
7.1	US I&C associations in the focal set (as of 2001)	138
7.2	Average resource allocation (in percent) and changes (frequency) of US business associations in the I&C sector	146
7.3	Membership of domestic and international business associations	150
8.1	Comparison of PIG structures	162
9.1	National business associations' exchange resources in EU interest intermediation	190
9.2	British and German chemical industry business associations' interaction partners in the reformulation of EU chemicals legislation.	191
10.1	Comparison of original proposal and final version	210
10.2	Relevant actors	215
11.1	Ecological relations and structural changes in comparison	224
11.2	Associational hierarchies in comparison	227
11.3	Organizational properties in comparison	231

List of Figures

2.1	Main evolutionary traits of business association theories	18
3.1	Changes in market volume and foreign trade from 1992 to 2002 (in percent)	59
3.2	Economic and technological changes affecting systems of business associations	60
4.1	Entries, mergers, and splits in the German and British associational systems	72
4.2	Ecological relations in the German and British associational networks	74
4.3	Information exchange in the German and British associational networks	78
4.4	Lobbying targets and their relevance for German and British associations (in percent)	83
5.1	Entries, mergers, and splits in the associational system	95
5.2	Ecological relations in the associational system	96
5.3	Information exchange among focal trade associations	97
5.4	Associational lobbying targets and their relevance (in percent)	102
6.1	Entries, mergers, and splits in the German and British associational systems	112
6.2	Ecological relations in the German and British associational networks	115
6.3	Information exchange in the German and British associational networks	118
6.4	Lobbying targets and their relevance for German and British associations (in percent)	123
7.1	Entries, mergers, and splits in the US associational system	139
7.2	Ecological relations in the US associational system	142
7.3	Information exchange in the US network	144
7.4	The targets of lobbying and information exchange	148
8.1	Enlarged Swiss associational system vs. shrinking British associational system	166
9.1	Ideal-type two-level arena of EU interest intermediation	181
10.1	Influence channels	216

Preface and Acknowledgments

There is a pre-history to this book to which all of us feel very much obliged. This pre-history and the story of the book itself can hardly be told other than in network analytic terms. These networks, within which both editors and authors are still moving in some respect, are spanning time and space and consist of an older and a younger generation of scholars.

Let us start with describing the scholarly communities before turning to the spaces they come from and to which some of them still continue to be attached today. Although possessing a pre-history itself, the first network of scholars was set up in the early 1980s when Philippe Schmitter and Wolfgang Streeck assembled dozens, if not hundreds, of researchers from all over the world to study the organization of business interests. Many others have occupied key positions within this network, but Gerhard Lehmbruch is certainly the one person completing a triumvirate whose reign ended toward the late 1980s and from which many guidelines for investigating that area have emanated over the years. Partly caused by changes in empirical reality, partly by an increasingly unmanageable field of study, but partly also due to the limited appeal of familiarizing oneself with the problems of dairy producers in small Swiss villages, the heyday of research into corporatist practices and associations producing an immense amount of literature both of a gray and a more accessible type ended toward the close of the decade. In the early 1990s, a network of younger scholars then started to draw attention to seemingly more acute problems of business associability essentially caused by processes of Europeanization, of internationalization, and by the end of the cold war. It could be said that, throughout the 1990s, the study of organized collective action by business, but also by labor, was much concerned with territorial levels and functional domains that had been left off the agenda of the earlier initiative. European-level arrangements of business (and labor) and global forms of private governance were studied to an extent that almost eliminated the issue of domestic forms of interest intermediation once so central to the concerns of the older generation of scholars. The two networks remained connected to each other of course, partly overlapped, and eventually created quite some multiplexity and synergy. Members of the first network, the above triumvirate in particular, remained active in that field of inquiry and, occasionally, bothered younger scholars with much finger-wagging about the stickiness of domestic institutions and the inertia of organizations that often had hardly changed very much since the eighteenth century or so. The role of bridges or cut-points between the two research structures, however, was filled by an intermediate generation of scholars, of which two of the editors of this volume form part to some extent. Although later active in studying international collective action, Schneider has been more deeply involved in the first network with a number of important contributions to the flagship series on corporatist research (Sage), while Grote has been more concerned with European issues right from the start, with the problem of size, and with territorial forms of interest intermediation.

This present volume is a second attempt to put the issue of domestic business associability back on the agenda (for the first attempt see Streeck *et al.*, 2006). It springs out of a research project funded by the German Science Foundation (DFG), first devised, with the help of Philippe Schmitter, at the European University Institute and then carried out by Schneider and Grote at the University of Konstanz. This is where space comes in. Although we do not wish to downgrade the relevance of other institutions both at home and abroad, the more centrally positioned knots connecting both the older and the more recent network of scholars can in fact be counted on one hand. This spatial network is made up of the EUI, the University of Konstanz, the Social Science Research Center in Berlin (WZB), the Max Planck Institute for the Study of Societies (MPI), and the Mannheim Centre for European Social Research (MZES). Schmitter and Streeck, before moving back (or forward) to the MPI and the EUI respectively, had started their project on the Organization of Business Interests at the WZB, while Gerhard Lehmbruch, at that time, held a chair in political science at the University of Konstanz. Schneider and Grote had been at the EUI – by now the European PhD machine par excellence – for quite some time before moving back (or forward) to the MPI and the MZES respectively. In that latter institute, another key person active in the study of organized collective action was Beate Kohler-Koch, with whom Grote collaborated in the mid-1990s although on a slightly different topic. After completing his habilitation at the University of Mannheim, Schneider then took up the Lehmbruch chair at the University of Konstanz, while Grote later joined him as assistant professor, research associate, and stand-in chair. While both had Schmitter among their supervisors in Florence, they now started to draw younger colleagues into the network. Most of these, after having obtained their doctorates at the University of Konstanz, the EUI, or the MZES, have contributed to this present volume. Achim Lang, after some time spent at Darmstadt University – a place being least approximate to the MZES both geographically and in terms of further network connections – is now assistant professor at Konstanz. Claudius Wagemann, having graduated from Konstanz and having spent some time at the MPI, obtained his PhD at the EUI and is now employed by the Italian Institute of Human Sciences (SUM) in Florence. Arndt Wonka, after having worked in Konstanz on the European lobbying strategies of British and German associations, then moved to the MZES where he completed his dissertation. Hans-Jörg Schmedes also obtained his PhD at Konstanz before moving into the heart of interest conflicts, the German Bundestag. Another PhD holder of the University of Konstanz, Marc Tenbücken, also worked and published on European lobbying and then moved into consultancy. It is, in particular, Achim Lang, Hans-Jörg Schmedes, and Arndt Wonka who have for many years helped to get the project off the ground, collect the information, process the data, and come up with the results.

Yet, the spatial network story does not finish here. Raymund Werle, who has for many years collaborated with Schneider at the MPI, is still working at that institute and has paid frequent visits to Konstanz both on a personal and a professional basis. The same is true of Karsten Ronit, together with Johannes Bauer the only non-national in this group of business interests fanatics. Whether they are less teutonic, though, is questionable. Ronit spent several years at the University of Konstanz as assistant professor and, before and after, co-edited more than a couple of volumes with both Schneider and Grote.

Finally, to complete this brief network-analytic account, it should be said that the ties connecting most of us, as well as the members of the older and the more recent network, are strong, not weak. Paraphrasing the title of Marc Granovetter's seminal article, we are convinced that our network can be characterized by a 'Strength of Strong Ties'. Such ties, habitually, are thought to result in encapsulation, incestuous breeding, and a loss of information, thus ultimately resulting in gridlock of all sorts. By opening up the field of collective action research and including insights from organization theory, theories of evolution, and network analysis – or, in other words, by engaging in a process of varying our analytical lenses and then selecting the most appropriate ones – we have hopefully avoided the sort of inertia of which the study of business associability has sometimes been accused.

Many people and institutions have helped to make this endeavor possible. Institutionally, we have been assisted by a generous grant received from the German Science Foundation (DFG). The Fritz-Thyssen Foundation has supported us with funds used to organize workshops and conferences from which our first volume originated. The MPI has granted us hospitality for several of our meetings and the same can be said of the Institute of Advanced Labour Studies in Amsterdam. The University of Konstanz has co-financed another workshop taking place in the most Mediterranean place Germany has to offer – the castle of Meersburg, overlooking the lake of Konstanz. Grote, in particular, wishes to mention the support of the Marie Excellence Grant program of the European Commission and the support received by colleagues at the Centre for Social and Economic Strategies (CESES) at Charles University in Prague.

Personally, we owe a lot to the doyen of modern interest group research, Philippe Schmitter. Remaining in the shadows – though not (always) of hierarchy – he has actively encouraged us to embark on our project, has contributed first important thought pieces that have guided us in the initial steps of inquiry, and has always followed up the progress we have made during all these years. Special thanks also go to colleagues who have joined us during phases of our project. Dirk Lehmkuhl contributed much to our discussions on the adaptation of interest systems to the challenges of Europeanization and has even presented papers on that issue. Although not directly involved in this more Konstanz-based network, Wolfgang Streeck has critically accompanied our progress in the various Florence, Köln, and Amsterdam meetings. Most of all, however, we wish to thank the representatives of members in our samples: hundreds of CEOs of business associations visited by us in Washington DC, London, Brussels, Frankfurt and Berlin, Bern and Vienna. More than a handful of leading representatives of the German VCI even visited us at our Meersburg workshop, wondering how stimulating a discussion could be that directly concerned their everyday business. Most wholeheartedly, we wish to thank our co-editor, Achim Lang, who, after Grote's departure to Central Europe, has been particularly active in carrying out most of the editing tasks and bringing the data into line in such a way that it is comprehensible to the interested reader. Without Achim, this volume might never have seen the light of the day.

Contributors

Johannes M. Bauer is a Professor in the Department of Telecommunication, Information Studies, and Media at Michigan State University. He is also the Co-Director of the Quello Center for Telecommunication Management and Law at Michigan State University. Dr. Bauer joined Michigan State University in 1990 after receiving his doctorate in economics from the Vienna University of Economics and Business Administration, Vienna, Austria. From 1993 until 1998, he directed the Institute of Public Utilities and Network Industries at the Eli Broad Graduate School of Management at Michigan State University. Dr. Bauer taught and researched as a visiting professor at the Delft University of Technology, the Netherlands (2000–2001) and the University of International Business and Economics in Beijing, China (2002). His work is published in the leading journals in the field, including *Telecommunications Policy*, *Information Economics and Policy*, *Communications & Strategies*, *Telematics & Informatics*, and *Info*.

Jürgen R. Grote holds the Marie Curie Chair in Public Policy Analysis at Charles University in Prague (Czech Republic). He received his PhD from the European University Institute in Florence (Italy) and has been working as research fellow (EUI-Florence; Darmstadt University of Technology, Germany; Mannheim Centre for European Research, Germany), and as assistant professor and stand-in-chair (University of Konstanz, Germany). He has written on organized collective action by business associations, governance, policy networks and network analysis, regional politics, European integration, and Europeanization. He is currently working on problems of transition and consolidation in the Visegrad countries with a focus on globalization and Europeanization. He has edited a number of books, including *Organized Interests and the European Community* (with J. Greenwood & K. Ronit, London/Newbury Park, CA: Sage, 1992), *Participatory Governance. Political and Societal Implications* (with B. Gbikpi, Opladen: Leske + Budrich, 2002) and *Governing Interests: Business Associations Facing Internationalization* (with W. Streeck, J. Grote & J. Visser, London: Routledge, 2006).

Achim Lang is Assistant Professor at the University of Konstanz (Germany). He studied public policy and management at the University of Konstanz and the Universidad Complutense de Madrid (Spain). He holds a PhD in political science for his study on the evolution of sectoral business associations. Achim Lang has held research positions at the University of Konstanz, the University of Cologne, and the Darmstadt University of Technology. He authored *Die Evolution sektoraler Wirtschaftsverbände. Informations- und Kommunikationsverbände in Deutschland, Großbritannien und Spanien* (Wiesbaden: VS, 2006).

Karsten Ronit is Associate Professor at the Department of Political Science, University of Copenhagen (Denmark). He has published on private organizations, in particular business interest associations, and their political activity at domestic and international levels. Karsten Ronit edited *Organized Interests and the European Community* (with J. Greenwood & J. R. Grote, Beverly Hills, CA: Sage, 1992), *Evolution of Interest Representation and the Development of the Labour Market in Post-Socialist Countries* (with O.K. Pedersen & J. Hausner, Bonn: Friedrich Ebert Foundation, 1995) and *Private Organisations in Global Politics* (with V. Schneider, London: Routledge, 2000). He has also published in a number of international journals.

Hans-Jörg Schmedes is Parliamentary Advisor to Peter Friedrich, Member of the German Parliament, in the German Bundestag in Berlin. Previously, he worked for the European Commission's Health and Consumer Protection Directorate-General in Brussels (Belgium). Furthermore, he participated in several election observation missions on behalf of the Organisation for Security and Co-operation in Europe (OSCE) and the European Union (EU). He studied public policy and management at the University of Konstanz (Germany) and at York University in Toronto (Canada). Hans-Jörg Schmedes holds a PhD in political science from the University of Konstanz. He has recently published *Wirtschafts- und Verbraucherschutzverbände im Mehrebenensystem* (Wiesbaden: VS, 2008).

Volker Schneider is a Professor of Political Science at the University of Konstanz, Germany, where he holds the Chair of Empirical Theory of the State. He received a PhD from the European University Institute in Florence (Italy), and he was research fellow at the Max-Planck-Institute for the Study of Societies in Cologne (Germany) between 1986 and 1997. He has written on policy networks, politics and policy of technology, government–business relations, and the evolution of governance structures. Over the long term he is working on state structures and public policy in a systemic and relational perspective, combining complexity, governance, and network theory. Currently he is completing cross-national comparative research projects on the retreat of the state from public infrastructures and the role of business associations in politics and economic governance. He has edited several books. Among them are *Governing Interests: Business Associations Facing Internationalization* (with W. Streeck, J. Grote, & J. Visser, London: Routledge, 2006) and *Private Organisations in Global Politics* (with K. Ronit, London: Routledge, 2000).

Marc Tenbücken is co-founder and executive director of the political intelligence company *Content5* in Munich. He studied public policy and management at the Universities of Konstanz, Geneva, and M.I.T. Marc Tenbücken worked as a consultant for Roland Berger Strategy Consultants. Subsequently, he became a junior research fellow at the University of Konstanz from which he holds a PhD in political science. He authored *Corporate Lobbying in the European Union* (Frankfurt: Peter Lang, 2002) and co-edited *Der Staat auf dem Rückzug. Die Privatisierung öffentlicher Infrastrukturen* (with V. Schneider, Frankfurt: Campus, 2004).

Claudius Wagemann is Scientific Secretary of the PhD Programme of the Italian Institute of Human Sciences (SUM) in Florence. He studied public policy and management at the University of Konstanz (Germany) and holds a PhD from the European University Institute in Florence (Italy). Claudius Wagemann worked as a research fellow at the Max Planck Institute for the Study of Societies at Cologne (Germany). He has published *Das Bild der SPD im Bayernkurier* (Wiesbaden: DUV, 2000) and edited *Qualitative Politikanalyse* (with J. Blatter & F. Janning, Wiesbaden: VS, 2007).

Raymund Werle is principal research associate with the Max Planck Institute for the Study of Societies at Cologne (Germany). He received a Diploma (MA) in Economics and Sociology and a PhD in Political Science. He was educated at the Universities of Bonn, Cologne, Mannheim, and at the State University of New York at Stony Brook (postgraduate DAAD fellow). Raymund Werle has held research and teaching positions at the Universities of Bielefeld, Mannheim, and Heidelberg, and at the Research Center on Nuclear Energy in Karlsruhe. He has authored and edited several books. Among them are *Coordinating Technology. Studies in the International Standardization of Telecommunications* (with S. K. Schmidt, Cambridge, MA/London: MIT Press, 1998), *Gesellschaftliche Komplexität und kollektive Handlungsfähigkeit* (with U. Schimank, Frankfurt am Main: Campus, 2000), and

Gesellschaft und die Macht der Technik: Sozioökonomischer und institutioneller Wandel durch Technisierung (with U. Dolata, Frankfurt am Main: Campus, 2007).

Arndt Wonka is post-doctoral researcher at the Bremen International Graduate School of Social Sciences (BIGSSS). He received a MA in Political Science, Sociology, and Law from the University of Konstanz (Germany) and his PhD from the University of Mannheim (Germany) and previously was a post-doctoral fellow at the Institute for Advanced Studies in Vienna (Austria) and a post doctoral researcher at the Mannheim Centre for European Social Research (MZES), to which he is still affiliated as co-director of research projects. Arndt Wonka edited *Governance in Europe: The Role of Interest Groups* (with A. Warntjen Baden-Baden: Nomos, 2004) and published *Die Europäische Kommission. Supranationale Bürokratie oder Agent der Mitgliedstaaten?* (Baden-Baden: Nomos, 2008) as well as articles on legislative politics in the EU and the European Commission in the *Journal of European Public Policy*.

1
Organized Business Interests in Changing Environments: Introduction

Volker Schneider, Achim Lang, and Jürgen R. Grote

During the last few decades the environment of political systems in advanced industrial society has changed dramatically. Growing international expansion of economic transactions, in large part driven by a revolution in communication technologies, has led to an unprecedented degree of mobility in capital, goods, and services. It has also caused national polities to be increasingly dependent on political and economic processes that are beyond their immediate control. Although this did not lead to the end of the nation state as some alarmist accounts predicted, it undoubtedly resulted in a change within power structures and the division of labor in political systems. A growing strand of literature argues that control is increasingly being transferred to the international level and that private actors such as trade associations, multinational corporations, and social movements are gaining in importance within political processes.

An important question is how this deep structural change has affected the political subsystem of interest intermediation based on interest associations, including the role and status of these organizations within the political system, as well as their general contribution to social and political order. Today interest organizations, and business associations in particular, are acknowledged as important components of political systems. This has not always been the case, since interest associations are quite peculiar objects of political research. Despite their continual increase in number and significance in almost all social areas – from the local up to the inter- and supranational level – these distinct forms of political organizations are still controversial in a normative sense, and analytically they only started to gain in importance during the final three or four decades of the twentieth century. Traditional political science concentrated on institutions such as governments, parliaments and parties. Other forms of interest representation such as business associations and social movements, on the other hand, entered the analytical spectrum in the second half of that century. Accordingly, only a few constitutions in the world explicitly recognize these groups as legitimate participants in the political process.

What is the reason for this analytical deficit? A major obstacle seems to be, first, the sheer number and diversity of associations. The wide perimeter of organizational populations in the world of associations renders analysis much more difficult than is, for instance, the analysis of party systems. The number of interest groups within large industrial nations and on the international level is difficult to estimate. A systematic empirical analysis of this specific organizational field is thus more difficult than in any other area of political organization.

Interest associations are also separated from parties by a normative barrier. While the participation of parties in the political process is, for the most part, formally anchored in constitutions and special laws, the activities of associations are generally considered as belonging to the informal or even opaque side of politics. Unlike with parties, there is a rather limited consensus on the role of associations in the political process. Here we find an entire spectrum of attitudes. First, one would expect the conservative and neoliberal perspectives to be juxtaposed in the issue space. On the question of associations, however, they are quite close to each other and generally tend to evaluate the participation of these organizations as negative. The conservative view reduces the political system to the state and considers it to be the sole bearer of public responsibility, whereas the participation of social interests is conceived rather more as a nuisance. As defenders of partial interests, associations infringe on the sovereignty of the state and the realization of the common good. The neoliberal perspective dominated by economists, in contrast, views the ideal society as coordinated by market relations, and associative forms often appear as collusions of 'rent seekers' (Tollison, 1997; Buchanan et al., 1980).

A middle position is inspired by political sociologists and political scientists and could be designated as the 'state–society–synergy' perspective (Evans, 1997). This admittedly includes an enormous reservoir of approaches, in which the creation of social order is not conceptualized through the market and state alone, but is also supported by a broad spectrum of coordination and self-regulation mechanisms beyond the market and the state (Streeck & Schmitter, 1985a). From this perspective, associations are constitutive components of political systems. They mobilize important resources and support in the political process by participating in the formulation and implementation of public policies. These participatory structures create heterogeneous 'policy networks', in which private and public actors communicate and tackle problems in a cooperative manner (Kenis & Schneider, 1991; Ronit & Schneider, 1997). In such contexts the role of associations is not restricted to the articulation and aggregation of interests alone, as suggested by traditional political perspectives. In addition, interest associations participate in policy making and co-regulation in order to mobilize complementary resources and cooperate in policy implementation. In some areas they even take over complete responsibility for self-regulation. Depending on the specific character of a political system, interest associations are more or less active during various phases of the policy cycle, from the issue definition and agenda setting of a political matter to the formulation and implementation of a political program.

Research questions and approach

A central assumption of this book is that national political systems and their associational subsystems face changing environments and increasing pressure to adapt. This perspective raises two important questions. First, what are the nature and pattern of these changes to which political systems have to adapt? Are changes slow and incremental, or do we encounter rapid and deep transformations (Pierson, 2003)? Second, what long-term impact do these changes have on political systems, and how do associational subsystems adapt to the transformations? Are systems transforming to completely new configurations, or are changes and transformations more incremental?

The first question is answered in the political and social sciences literature by a broad spectrum of approaches that may be described by polar extremes. On the one hand there are, 'great transformation' or 'deep impact' ideas, portraying recent changes as severe environmental shocks, 'hitting' and transforming national systems profoundly. At a very general level there is a strand of globalization literature that even predicts the demise of the nation state and consequently a 'power shift' toward international organizations (for instance toward the EU) and also toward multinational companies. In summarizing these changes Juergen Habermas, for instance, expects the emergence of a 'post-national constellation' (Habermas, 2001), while Ulrick Beck proclaims a new phase of modernization transcending the nation state toward a cosmopolitan order and creating completely new forms of politics (Beck *et al.*, 2003).

At the level of middle-range theory, there is a vast literature on Europeanization that also uses the 'meteorite impact' metaphor, observing massive pressures on national political systems to adapt to new supranational political structures that were created by the process of European integration. Here, the European Union is seen as a completely external and autonomous environment – like a massive alien force – which is 'hitting' the political systems of its member states (Börzel & Risse, 2000). Units of adaptation in this debate are mostly policy sectors; however, some scholars also study restructuring at the level of national administrations, party systems, and associational orders (Featherstone & Radaelli, 2003).

If these global and European 'deep impact' diagnoses are true, we clearly must expect a profound transformation of political systems, their nation states and their business associations. Whereas globalization literature emphasizes the emergence of large firms and multinational companies as political actors undermining the intermediating role of interest organizations, in the Europeanization literature it is presumed that national nodes and channels of interest intermediations are successively shifted and replaced by European interest organizations in European policy making.

At the other extreme there is a literature in which current changes only express minor fluctuations around a secular trend of slowly increasing functional differentiation, specialization, and transnational extension of social relations. This stream of thought is best described by differentiation and modernization theory (Alexander & Colomy, 1990) which has two major implications. The first is that change is incremental and piecemeal, the second is that transformations are similar in all countries, at least in political systems at the same level of social and economic development. In such a perspective we would expect, despite slowly growing international and regional layers of political systems, that national business associations will still play an important role in political systems and that their structures and functions would only show some minor adaptations.

These two main perspectives thus imply quite different trajectories of systems adaptation. In this book we will explore these questions through empirical case studies. We trace these transformations not only at the system level of associational orders, but also at the organizational level of associations with respect to their structures and strategies. Our goal is to find out how changing environments will affect the role and position of business associations in the political system and the policy process, and how these changes are related to the internal structures and strategies of business associations. Are there differences between sectors and countries? Do these changes enhance or weaken the capacity of formally organized interest groups to coordinate firms in their relevant sectors? Do they strengthen associations in their role to advance their members' interests by lobbying and other forms of interactions with political actors (above all governments) in national and international political systems? How do associations respond and eventually adapt to these global transformations? Has this led to changes in lobbying and coordination strategies, for instance to an increasing importance of inter- and transnational actors as lobbying targets? How do structural changes in associational systems relate to these transformations? Are some national associational systems more successful at coping with these challenges?

An important goal is the consideration of these questions and the exploration of adaptation processes by means of complexity theory. We consider these changes as neither discrete and holistic in a 'deep impact' sense, nor as particular and piecemeal from the modernization perspective. In some countries and sectors associational systems have encountered deep transformations, whereas in other countries adjustments were far less dramatic. Besides variants of complexity, our major findings are also compatible with historical institutionalism and central propositions of the varieties of capitalism debate. Change does not happen everywhere in the same way, and it does not affect everything in the same manner. We are able to depict a broad spectrum of adaptation processes in a number of countries, sectors, and organizational levels, conditioned by different structural and historical settings.

Our interpretation is inspired by variants of complexity theory. The approach is anti-monistic and anti-holistic, because it emphasizes that adaptations unfold differently at different levels of organizations and their environments. At the same time it is anti-particularistic or anti-individualistic, since it emphasizes the systemness and nestedness of these processes. There are interdependencies in changes and adaptations at various levels and domains. In other words, such a 'complex associations theory' treats interest associations as political subsystems with adaptive capacities, as emphasized in the 'complex adaptive systems' literature (Holland, 1992; Anderson, 1999). From this perspective interest associations are particular organizational species that are embedded in ecological hierarchies, where the highest level is the organizational community. At the community level, populations of business associations co-evolve and co-adapt with other organizational populations such as governmental institutions, administrative agencies, parties, and so on. The complex as a whole is conceived of as an organizational ecosystem, in which the constituent units form a complex web of interdependencies based on resource exchange, cooperation, and competition. Interest associations are oriented toward organizational domains, and acquire financial, personnel or other types of resources from governmental bodies or from their members. Resources are transformed into outputs, including services for members and lobbying activities directed at governmental bodies.

At the organizational level, adaptation takes place when organizational properties of business associations are adjusted in order to meet new environmental demands. Demands arise from changes in the composition and structure of the policy arena in which a business association is operating and in the economic branches it represents. Such changes include the Europeanization and internationalization of governance activities. Transformations in the market structure, such as growing competition at global and European level and intensified international trade, can trigger changes in organizational properties by way of altering the composition of member firms. Internal pressure may in part be induced by external developments, but it essentially affects how individual firms and members perceive and react to the performance of 'their' association. Both pressures have had and still have a substantial impact on the organizational structures and activities of business interest associations. The prime objective of the book is therefore to disentangle these different adaptation processes and identify their relative importance. In Chapter 2 we will show in detail how this new perspective is related to theory development with respect to the role of interest groups and business associations in political systems.

Contributions to the theoretical and empirical debates

As the previous section made clear, the book contributes to various theoretical debates. With respect to the debate on the nature of recent changes and transformations, we provide ample evidence that 'deep impact' perspectives vastly exaggerate and that changes are not simple and unidirectional. At the empirical level, changes appear more complex and differentiated. Our findings show that stability and incremental adaptation coexist. However, we also find large ruptures and deep restructuring in some sectors and countries. One major finding is that there is no single logic of adaptation, but rather a variety of responses to how business associations cope with changing environments. In addition, adaption pressure varies according to national and sector contexts. This seems determined to a large degree by historical embeddedness in societal and economic structures.

The book depicts the complexity of adaptation in detail. The responses of organized business interests to Europeanization and globalization in the chemicals industry, the information and communications sector, and the dairy industry – all representing great differences in terms of economic life cycles – are systematically analyzed. A deviant case from the automotive industry is also included. The main focus is on associational development in three countries, namely the US, the UK, and Germany. The book also considers exceptional and deviant developments in the Swiss dairy industry, which enrich our understanding of different forms of interest intermediation.

Within the specialized literature on organized business interests, the analysis contributes to a third wave of studies, in which the focus of interest group research has moved to change and adaptation. The first wave of interest group literature stems from the 1960s. It established this new research field on the agenda of political science and emphasized the importance and specific functions of interest associations within modern political systems. Key contributions at this time were made by Truman (1968 [1951]), Beer (1956), and Ehrmann (1957). This first wave was strongly shaped by structural-functionalist systems theory, and was the subject of an in-depth review by Gabriel Almond (1958). A second wave emerged during the late 1970s and was heavily driven by the debate on neocorporatism (Schmitter & Lehmbruch, 1979; Lehmbruch & Schmitter, 1982; Cawson, 1985b; Streeck & Schmitter, 1985b), emphasizing the variety of associational systems at national level, their multilevel nature, and their specific contribution to societal governance. Excellent reviews of this literature can be found in Czada (1994) and Molina and Rhodes (2002). The third wave started in the early 1990s, emphasizing changes and restructuring in the face of Europeanization and globalization. Whereas the vanguard of this literature pointed to the emergence of a European political system and the coevolution of interest associations at the European level (Greenwood *et al.*, 1992b; Streeck & Schmitter, 1994), a subsequent group of studies pointed to the emergence of global structures of associative interest intermediation (Greenwood & Jacek, 2000; Ronit & Schneider, 2000). During the late 1990s this debate became increasingly general. One consideration was how this new political layer would affect national systems of interest intermediation. In other words, the question arose of if and how Europeanization and globalization were adding particular pressure for change and transformation.

A recent group of literature compares different systems of business associations and their strategies of adaptation (Grant, 2000; Greenwood, 2002, 2003; Streeck *et al.*, 2006; Traxler & Huemer, 2007). Contributing to this particular debate is one of the main preoccupations of this book. In addition, substantial insights are added to the current debate on varieties of capitalism, which highlights path-dependent adjustments due to historical contingencies. Simultaneously, national idiosyncrasies from supranational processes such as Europeanization and globalization are disentangled.

Methodologically, quantitative and qualitative approaches are combined. Most of the case studies presented in this volume perform quantitative surveys (on the basis of identical questionnaires) with all major business associations of the respective sectors. The questionnaire that was used includes questions about the development and change of lobbying, service activities, and the networks in which associations are embedded. Network questions referred to reputation, information exchange, and competition between associations in the sector. These network data describe the setting of associations in terms of density, cohesion, actor centrality, hierarchy, and other characteristics. The country studies employ innovative visualization tools from social network analysis.[1]

Overview

The book consists of three parts. The first part highlights the theoretical background in interest group research. Subsequent parts describe the empirical findings and theoretical interpretations in view of the conceptual framework of the book. Chapters in Part II of the book deal with business associations at the national level, and two chapters in Part III analyze business associations at the European level. A concluding chapter summarizes major findings and formulates some generalizable observations.

In Chapter 2 Achim Lang, Karsten Ronit, and Volker Schneider outline the inputs of various streams of theory development into a complexity perspective. An overview of the major theories of associations and associational systems is given, and it is demonstrated that theories of business associations and associational systems have developed from rather simple membership-centered perspectives to more complex approaches including a variety of causal factors. We outline the contribution of traditional theories and approaches such as Marxism, pluralism, new political economy, the corporate actor theory, (neo)corporatism and system theory. In addition, new approaches in interest group studies within the European integration, international governance, and organizational ecology literature are highlighted. Chapter 2 also summarizes a theory of complex associational systems, which is seen as a synthesis of the two logics theory of associations, the multilevel governance approach, and the population ecology perspective. The new synthesis takes the variety of business association types, the diversity of relations between them, and their involvement at different governance levels into account. Moreover, adaptation to environmental forces is not solely explained by means of a simple one-factorial best-fit model, but also includes endogenous factors.

Chapter 3 is coauthored by Achim Lang, Volker Schneider, and Raymund Werle and focuses on political, economic, and technological constraints that pull and push associational adaptation processes in different directions. It is observed that political constraints have been given priority in explaining associational behavior and inter-associational structures, whereas technological and economic determinants are still widely neglected. The chapter reviews the existing literature on political, technological, and economic factors and their effects on associational systems, and sketches some impact scenarios of technological changes on the associational behavior and inter-associational structures. Finally, the last section compares the economic sectors in agriculture, chemicals, and information and communications in order to hypothesize likely adaptation processes of business associations operating in these sectors.

In Chapter 4 Jürgen Grote compares chemical business associations in Britain and Germany. It is stressed that the internationalization of markets and the Europeanization of politics have led to changes in the composition of the associational landscapes in both countries. Innovations in biotech and life sciences triggered population dynamics such as increased competitive relations and declining hierarchical coordination. Political factors, especially European integration, have led to a broadening of lobbying activities, at the European as well as the domestic level.

In Chapter 5 Hans-Jörg Schmedes explores the adaptation of business associations in the US chemical sector. The chapter provides an empirical account of organizational change processes for the last two decades and shows to what extent these changes can be traced back to changes in the associational environment. It is emphasized that serving members' interests lies at the center of associational activities. However, in order to reduce this dependence, some associations diversify by using additional income sources. Economic consolidation processes have particularly affected the number and composition of members, forcing associations to adapt to this new situation. This chapter also identifies structural arrangements and associational policies that do not correspond to the pluralist image of associational structures in the US. This is the case for the network position held by the American Chemistry Council, as well as for its role as advocate for a considerable part of the industry. The existence of associational programs that clearly correspond to the definition of private interest governments is in sharp contrast to any theoretical assumptions on the associational system of the US.

In Chapter 6 Achim Lang compares adaptation processes within British and German business associations in the information and communications sector that have been exposed to fundamental changes in their environment. The author concludes that processes of Europeanization and globalization have initiated similar adaptations within the British and German associational systems. High growth rates and technological innovations have led to an increase in the organizational population, while Europeanization has brought about more lobbying activities at the European level. Aside from these similarities, both associational systems adopted different evolutionary paths that have been driven by endogenous factors. The low integration of the British associational system in particular has led to the dominance of the logic of membership, in which narrow preferences of the member firms prevail. The German associational system, on the other hand, is highly integrated due to external enforcement of a hierarchical structure and counteractions set forth by potential losers from vertical integration.

In Chapter 7 Johannes Bauer and Volker Schneider analyze the development and adaptation of business associations in the US information and communication technology sector. The chapter explores the structure of and relations among these associations and relates them to changes in their economic and political environments. Various aspects of inter-organizational relations and the positioning of the different associations in these networks are described. The last section of the chapter extends the relational analysis to the lobbying and influence level, in order to show the variety of strategies and the major targets of influence. A pivotal finding is that there was a great deal of stability and only partial change during the last decade. In structural terms, the chapter provides evidence that the American system of business associations only partially resembles the much-cited pluralistic market for influence, but exhibits frequent cooperation and 'mutualism' among business associations. Additionally, interest representation centers around a small fraction of these business associations, which make up a sort of elite pluralism. The chapter also demonstrates that US associations frequently invest in supranational lobbying activities, for the most part in Brussels.

In Chapter 8 Claudius Wagemann considers associations in the dairy sector. He examines changes in organizational communities, organizational populations, and individual associations in the dairy sector of four countries, namely Austria, Britain, Germany, and Switzerland. Developments in this sector give some important insights into complex adaptation processes within organized business. Up to the 1990s, the dairy sector in most countries was regulated as a 'private interest government' (PIG), which has also been described as 'the most advanced form of neo-corporatism' (Traxler, 1985: 150). While it has been exposed to enormous changes at the European and global level, it is still embedded in national niches. The chapter shows that associational systems featuring monopolistic interest representation and intermediation as well as clearly defined associational hierarchies have not survived the economic and political perturbations in the dairy industry. In contrast, less centralized associational systems were able to retain their structures due to higher internal flexibility.

In Chapter 9 Arndt Wonka studies the European lobbying strategies of British and German business associations in the formulation of REACH, a recent European policy program regulating the chemical industry. The chapter highlights the procedural characteristics of national business associations' European lobbying strategies. The author's findings show that national business associations tend to influence private and public actors from their national context, as is the case with MEPs. The configuration of national systems of business associations influences the European lobbying strategies of national business associations. As a result, pluralist or corporatist features of national systems of interest intermediation are extended to EU interest intermediation.

In Chapter 10 Marc Tenbücken is concerned with corporate lobbying at the EU level. He discusses the role of business interest associations (BIAs) in the lobbying strategies of multinational companies (MNCs) during the decision-making process of the Directive on end-of-life vehicles. The Directive was subject to immense direct lobbying by the automotive industry, which successfully managed to modify the original Commission proposal. The author's major argument is that in 'emergency' situations MNCs change their strategy from associational to direct lobbying. At the same time, MNC shift their attention from European to national influence routes. Thus, in emergency situations MNCs tend to bypass national and supranational BIAs. As a result, the positions of the European BIA and the national sectoral BIA are severely weakened.

In the concluding chapter Achim Lang and Volker Schneider summarize three major findings of the overall comparative endeavor. First, economic and technological factors do matter. In almost every study in this book these factors are the driving forces of changes in the behavior and structures of business associations, although their impact is indirect in nature. Economic and technological factors lead to changes in the make-up of sectors and branches and thus alter the membership base of business associations. In reaction to these market forces, business associations adapt their internal strategies to external changes. In some instances the entire composition and structure of the associational system are adjusted. It is the main characteristic of business associations to be an institutionalized form of collective action, which makes them highly dependent on their member firms' financial, personnel, and informational resources. Business associations are thus vulnerable to economic and technological changes. Political institutions (and societal developments) continue to remain important factors, but political scientists often overestimate their impact, which is mainly limited to different lobbying and access strategies.

Second, adaptation involves multiple levels and components of associational systems. External factors exert adaptation pressure on the domestic associational systems, which can be absorbed through changes within an association; that is, by modifying the internal division of labor or by altering the production of public and private goods. When there are multiple and intense pressures, the composition of the associational system and the inter-associational relations may equally be affected. Moreover, neither system level is independent of the other. External pressure may therefore lead to interdependent adaptive changes if, for instance, newly founded associations bring in different lobbying styles and techniques, thereby out-competing the established associations. These in turn then have to adapt to those within-system changes as well. Inter-associational relations are not restricted to a simple dichotomy of cooperation–competition, but equally include compound forms and combinations.

Third, the lobbying and access strategies of business associations have to be seen in a refined perspective. Lobbying has long been viewed as an attempt to influence a specific and clearly definable policy outcome. This book adds a more strategic perspective to the spot market of lobbying. Business associations increasingly adopt a long-term perspective and try to create an environment that is generally favorable to their forthcoming lobbying activities. We call this strategy 'political gardening', including the whole set of efforts in which business associations have to invest in a general shaping of the political landscape to reap the harvest in successive lobbying attempts. This includes permanent PR activities, political marketing, and the ongoing attempt to create an atmosphere that is generally conducive to their interests (societal lobbying). The chapter concludes by outlining a number of suggestions in that regard that are thought to be important for future endeavors along similar lines of inquiry.

Note

1. The network diagrams are produced by *visone*, a specialized program for network analysis and visualization developed by Ulrik Brandes and his group at the University of Konstanz, Germany (see also Brandes *et al.*, 1999).

Part I
Theories and Determinants of Organizing Business Interests

2
From Simple to Complex: An Evolutionary Sketch of Theories of Business Association

Achim Lang, Karsten Ronit, and Volker Schneider

Laments about the poor state of theory development in interest representation and associability are widespread (Knoke, 1986; Baumgartner & Leech, 1998). Despite the prevalent agreement on this matter, some scholars have only recently taken up the responsibility of investing in theory development and building a more compelling theory under the label of 'neopluralism' (Lowery & Gray, 2004; McFarland, 2004). However, their focus rests quite narrowly on economic, pluralist, and ecological approaches that share basic assumptions about the causal mechanisms of interest group activities, but on the whole cover a particular part of the theoretical landscape. Furthermore, their attempt does not distinguish between different interests or differing group characteristics. For the purposes of this volume their approach to theory development seems rather skimpy and too abstract to begin the endeavor. Therefore we will concentrate more specifically on theories and approaches that focus on organized business interests, a field where further theory development is also needed.

In our opinion, a new kind of systems theory is able to conceptualize associational interest representation and intermediation by business in complex political settings and to explain their adaptation toward new political and economic challenges. Thus, theory building moves from simple to complex.[1] New kinds of systems theory have evolved over the last decade, and some elements found here are useful in the context of analyzing organized business and enriching existing traditions in the study of business associations. These new approaches combine basic elements of system theory with actor-centered approaches such as the idea of the social embeddedness of actors, or emphasize structural interdependencies in processes among social actors and their environment. Ecological approaches in organization theory, for instance, apply an 'ecosystem' approach to social reality that emphasizes the interdependencies and the multiplexity of relations between the constituent entities of these systems as well as their adaptation to changing environments (Baum & Amburgey, 2002). Complexity theory in sociology and political science highlights emergent structures from local interaction and complex evolution and adaptation patterns that vary across time, space, and level.

A common feature of these different approaches is a multilevel perspective on society in which social processes cannot be reduced to some few basic principles shaping action and social evolution. In contrast, explanations have to take into account that social processes are nested and differentiated, thus leading to multiple mechanisms and forces shaping social action.

Figure 2.1 indicates the main paths of theory evolution. Not all links and schools of thought are established in this figure. However, the scope

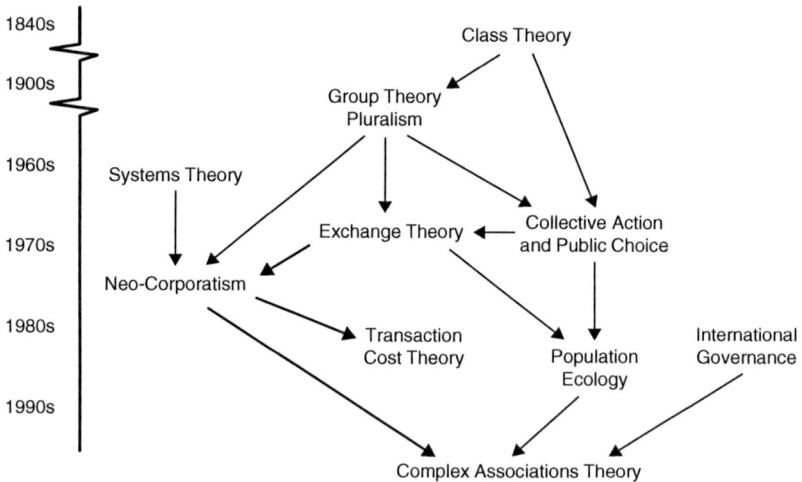

Figure 2.1 Main evolutionary traits of business association theories

Note: The arrows indicate a theory's influence on subsequent theoretical developments regarding organized business. Influence denotes either an opposing perspective such as the pluralists' denial of objective interest in class theory, or a restatement and recombination of arguments in subsequent theoretical perspectives such as the inclusion of various external constraints under the notion of 'selection forces' in population ecology. There has been a historical development of theories that can be synthesized into complex association theory, although it is noteworthy that theories have not simply replaced each other but coexist.

of represented theories goes far beyond textbook standards and indicates the richness as well as the inconsistency of the field. Theory development has, at its best, contributed to some kind of collective evolution and learning process in which the answers have become increasingly differentiated and multifaceted. However, theory development has not been a straightforward process of accumulation of knowledge. Previous achievements have sometimes fallen into oblivion, and there is also much mutual neglect and reinvention of old ideas.

Accordingly, the following sections deal with central propositions of each theory cluster and the way in which these 'schools' and their classic contributions are related to each other. We seek to extract those parts of the theories that can be utilized in further research and be synthesized into theories emphasizing organizations as complex units of action. In a second step we will rearrange these extractions so as to fit them into these new system theoretical approaches mentioned above.

From objective to subjective interests: Associability of classes, groups, and utility-maximizing actors

While the political relevance of organized groups had already been observed by classical philosophers (e.g., Althusius, Hegel, de Tocqueville), theories on the formation of large voluntary organizations like trade unions or business associations are a rather modern phenomenon. Karl Marx was the first to provide a systematic account of the operational principles and dynamics of this new economic system, and he tried to explain how and why capitalists and workers associate and enter the political arena as organized political actors. Theories challenging Marxist assumptions developed in the twentieth century and provide the basis for bottom-up or micro explanations of associative action that conceptualize associability as primarily membership driven. This section scrutinizes their basic arguments and propositions.

Class theory

It is no surprise that Arthur Bentley, who generally is considered to be the founding father in the study of interest groups, considered Marx as the starting point of theories of interest group activity (Bentley, 1967 [1908]: 465–8). Marx advanced a materialist conception focusing on the class divisions in societies that are inherent in economic structures and the various political conflicts emanating from these structural tensions. Classes are groups of individuals based on objective properties: They share the same position in a mode of production; that is, they have similar material relations to the means of production. The dominant class controls production tools, whereas dominated classes get access only through the exchange of labor in various forms. In Marx's perspective, the economic development of human societies is characterized by the evolution and subsequent replacement of varying modes of production, from ancient societies based on common ownership to class-based societies such as slavery, feudalism, and capitalism. Each mode of production is accompanied by specific forms of ownership that determine if and how class divisions emerge in societal development.

Modern capitalist society, so goes the theory, is based on two major classes: workers and capitalists. The dominant position of capitalists in this mode of production is derived from their control over the means of production. Workers get access to their means of subsistence through employment contracts in which they exchange control over their paid wage labor. The workers thus form trade unions as permanent associations that necessarily get more and more political (Marx, 1966: 168).

In this view, the association of business emerges as a reaction to the organization of the working class, but apparently with fewer problems of collective action, because capital seems to be 'always united'. However, this perspective never developed into a theory on business collective action in the context of formal business interest associations.

Marixst theories have been taken up by numerous scholars. Most, however, have only given a fairly abstract exposé of the organization of business. In such a context, Claus Offe and Helmut Wiesenthal have refined Marx's theory of class antagonism, sketched the inherent logics of collective action within the different classes, and outlined their consequences for the organization of interests. Accordingly, trade unions organize workers' interests that cover the entire range of needs and wants of the working class, whereas business associations are confronted with a small interest spectrum that primarily includes expected costs and returns of their member firms (Offe & Wiesenthal, 1980: 75). Furthermore, business associations are only one form of collective action that capital may employ. The firm is itself a form of collective action, because as a legal person it can accumulate resources in ways unavailable to physical persons, and it can be used to take up direct political action. Informal cooperation beyond an associational framework is another strategy for coordinating collective action between capitalists.

Organized interests depend on their capacity to generate the members' *willingness to pay*, which, according to Offe and Wiesenthal, is rather unproblematic. First, trade and employers' associations may provide a variety of services on which especially small firms are highly dependent and which can seldom be obtained in the free market. Thus firms are offered an incentive to become and remain members of associations. Secondly, willingness to act is relatively uncomplicated because capital is already in a powerful position vis-à-vis trade unions and the state. This mainly has to do with the second imperative to generate the members' *willingness to act* (*ibid*.: 80), which fully applies to trade unions but not to any form of capitalist collective action. Trade and employers' associations particularly do not rely on the ability to develop a potential for sanctioning, because the 'decisive power remains with the individual firm and its strategic choices' (*ibid*.: 83).

In summary, Marxist or Marxist-inspired class theory conceives of organized business interest as primarily membership driven and based on objective interests derived from the actors' position in the social structure. Business associations provide services to their members, influence government bodies, and negotiate labor relations. However, the fundamental power of the capitalist class remains at the discretion of the member firms. The greater interest homogeneity compared to the multiple interests of the working class and the smaller number of capitalists lead to a community of comparatively few business associations.

Pluralist group theory

The beginning of modern pluralist thinking can be traced back to the landmark study *The Process of Government* by Arthur F. Bentley in 1908. In his work Bentley rejects the Marxist idea of objective interests underlying the capitalist and proletarian classes, which appears to be solid and firm in theory but resists empirical verification (Bentley, 1967 [1908]). He therefore introduced a political process theory in order to capture the questions of power and the involvement of multiple groups in policy making (McFarland, 2004: 4). Bentley viewed group formation as the result of interest-guided actions by individuals. The mutual attempts of the different groups to influence and affect one another's behavior lead to a balance of interests through the equilibrium of pressure groups. The political process is thus characterized by permanent pressures and counter pressures of the different groups involved (Bentley, 1967 [1908]: 258).

More than four decades later, David Truman continued this line of argument in his book *The Governmental Process* (1968 [1951]). He was particularly concerned with interest group interaction and pressures, which, in his view, are lessened by overlapping memberships facilitating the attainment of equilibrium in an interest group system. The underlying idea of Truman's group concept was that these social units produce uniform behavior. A group does not necessarily depend on similar properties of its members but on their relationships to one another (Truman, 1968 [1951]: 24). Nevertheless, most groups are formed around certain common characteristics of their members. The notion of interest groups then refers to groups that, on the basis of their similar properties, make demands on other societal groups. A political interest group directs its claims to government or other political institutions (*ibid*.: 37). The diversity of interest groups thus reflects the complexity of social structure as a whole. Truman states that potential interest groups will be formed if their interests are affected in the political process. These newly formed groups, then, try to access the political process and influence government bodies in order to push through their interests.

Pluralist group theory tends to perceive business interest associations as relatively privileged compared to other groups, for the reason that business associations have sufficient capacities to influence the political process or to provide financial assistance for politicians for their electoral campaigns. However, 'this influence is contingent on factors such as the level of public scrutiny, countermobilization by other interests, and the preferences of elected public officials' (Witko & Newmark, 2005: 357; see also McFarland, 2004).

McFarland summarizes the major contribution of political process and group theory in the pluralist tradition (McFarland, 2004: 4–5): A large number of actors have causal impact on the policy-making process and policy outcome. These actors are commonly viewed as groups and individuals that represent group interests. Interests do not only refer to objective structural positions in the social structure, but can be related to all kinds of subjective motives. The different groups interact and affect one another's interests and behavior. The different groups take action in order to pursue their interests, and those interests can change in the course of the interaction. Thus, new and exciting steps were taken in the pluralist approach to understand business political action in relation to political processes and institutions, but only occasionally was direct reference made to business interests.

Collective action and public choice

In the late 1950s Anthony Downs presented an economic explanation of the democratic processes within political systems. He interpreted party competition and voting behavior as driven by utility-maximizing voters and political entrepreneurs who rationally choose between competing policy programs. Downs also mentions interest groups as a vital factor in the information-collection process of political parties acting under uncertainty (Downs, 1957). However, he never elaborated a theory of collective action or pressure politics.

This task was taken up by Mancur Olson in his seminal book *The Logic of Collective Action* (1970 [1965]), where the formation and behavior of interest groups are explained by utility-maximizing and rationally acting individuals. Olson criticizes the assumption of group theorists and Marxists that individuals with common interests would inevitably organize and take up political action to pursue that interest. He demonstrated that in large groups free-rider behavior dominates because non-members cannot be excluded from the gains that collective action produces. However, if an association is able to provide positive inducements that are restricted to its membership – 'selective incentives' in Olson's language – then the net benefit of being a member is higher than that of being excluded.

Small, inclusive groups focusing on narrow interest domains are likely to provide collective goods without depending on selective incentives. In small groups at least some members will realize that their individual gain from having the collective good exceeds the cost of providing some quantity of that collective good (Olson, 1970 [1965]). This is very important in the case of business interest associations, because many industries consist of a relatively limited number of firms and hence can be characterized as small groups.

Economic explanations of political action, its distributive effects, and social costs entered the research agenda in the 1960s under the topics of public choice and rent seeking. In this strand of literature, policy outcomes mainly result from interest groups' efforts to exert pressure on governmental activities through money and information (Austen-Smith, 1997), a perspective which is particularly relevant for resourceful organizations such as business groups. In this context lobbying mainly refers to the strategic transmission of information between interest groups and governmental bodies, and involves also the collection and verification of information. Policy makers usually act under uncertainty with respect to the political, social, and economic consequences of their legislative activities. Interest groups in control of this resource can bring in their stake in the decision-making process. Business interests thus have a clear advantage regarding group size and resource procurement. Leech (2006), for example, analyzes interest representation strategies of different categories of interest groups and concludes that organized business interests have a significantly higher lobbying frequency than groups representing social welfare interests.

In summary, the collective and public choice approaches offer a formally rigorous upgrade to group theoretical accounts of the political process. Political outcomes are determined to a large extent by interest group competition. Interest groups merely provide services to their members and lobby government bodies. However, differences in group size and external circumstances (deadweight costs) have major effects on collective action. Organized business interests occupy a privileged position within this economic perspective, since they represent rather exclusive member groups and are thus less vulnerable to free-rider effects and changes in deadweight costs.

Exchange theory

In the 1960s and 1970s Peter Blau (Blau, 1964) and James S. Coleman (Coleman, 1972, 1974), among others, introduced exchange theory in the social sciences, which entered the interest group and business association agenda from two different directions, namely political entrepreneurship (Salisbury, 1969; Moe, 1980) and corporate actor theory (Coleman, 1974, 1994 [1990]).

Robert H. Salisbury is among the first to pick up this new intellectual strand in the social sciences. He points out some inconsistencies and blind spots in the arguments of Truman and Olson regarding entrepreneurial aspects in the formation of interest groups. Salisbury proposes to center the theoretical argument in the 'exchange relationships between entrepreneurs/organizers, who invest capital in a set of benefits, which they offer to prospective members at a price-membership' (Salisbury, 1969). The political entrepreneur initiates the formation of interest groups and associations by investing his capital in a set of benefits that may include material, solidary, and purposive incentives.[2] Salisbury demonstrates that associations seldom come out of nothing but have a kind of predecessor. In our case, some new business associations may have been subdivisions of older or enveloping associations. These new associations are organized by political entrepreneurs who ultimately decide to split from the mother organization, or build a now one when the old is defunct. Even entirely new business associations are commonly led by experienced political entrepreneurs who have already done the job before.

Terry M. Moe (1980) develops the entrepreneurial perspective on interest groups further. He assumes that the political entrepreneur is bounded rational, self-interested, and the leader of the group. 'He takes action to enroll members, to design, sell, and distribute packages of benefits' (*ibid.*, 37). The entrepreneur furthermore distributes tasks to organizational members and manages exchange relationships with external organizations. The entrepreneur's political activities comprise the management of exchange relationships with governmental bodies and non-governmental organizations that operate in the political system.

A somewhat different perspective is provided by James S. Coleman and his corporate actor theory that centers on resource exchange and resource pooling (Coleman, 1972, 1994 [1990]). According to Coleman, corporate actors are entities that at least consist of various principals and an agent. Corporate actors are based on multilateral exchange relations whose characteristic feature is that various individuals (or various corporate actors) pool resources in order to make use of them collectively. These individuals or principals set up a constitution for the corporate actor in which certain rights are delegated to a central authority that acts on their behalf. However, for controlling the agent's actions the principals have to set up organizations within the corporate actor in order to pool resources for the supervision of the central authority (Coleman, 1994 [1990]).

Coleman's account of social contract theory is embedded in a system of political exchange in which the party machine may act as an intermediary between business, legislators, and voters in order to facilitate the exchange of money, legislation, and votes. Each actor strives to control certain outcomes within the political system. These outcomes can be reached by exchanging resources held by some actors (at the market price). The actors who control (scarce) resources find it easier to control these outcomes, thus exerting power within the political system (*ibid.*: 133–5). In the case of business interests, their main exchange currencies are money and jobs that may be traded against favorable legislation.

To sum up, the different versions of exchange theory center on the exchange relations between 'individuals' and corporate actors within the political system. In this perspective business associations are set up by political entrepreneurs who offer potential members certain goods in exchange for membership dues. These corporate actors, however, show tendencies of self-interested behavior that may be counteracted by the members. The political system is conceptualized as a political market where goods are exchanged in order to control certain events and outcomes.

Associability upside down: Functional needs and institutional constraints shaping associational systems

A common feature of the theoretical perspectives we have discussed up to this point is that the political process by which interests are articulated and transformed into collective action essentially is a bottom-up process. Interests are derived from individuals or groups that share similar positions in the social structure or just common subjective preferences in a specific situation. Actors with common or similar interests try to realize these interests through collective organization. A different perspective is applied by systems theory and neocorporatism, in which business interests and their representational forms reflect the functional needs or constraints of the political system.

Systems theory

An initial systemic theory of political processes was provided by Easton in the 1950s. However, his perspective was too abstract and coarse grained to acknowledge the role of specific political actors such as specifically organized groups. More influential – at least in interest group theory – was Almond's structural functionalist approach in comparative politics, in which he emphasized the role structures and action orientations of political actors such as parties and interest groups. These actors fulfill political roles or functions shaped by the overall political system. The concept of the political system 'covers all patterned actions relevant to the making of political decision' (Almond, 1956: 393), and he emphasizes that 'system implies a totality of relevant units, an interdependence between the interactions of units, and a certain stability in the interaction of these units'. Essentially this implies a holistic perspective where the functions of various actors and structures are affected by the macro structures of overall systems.

This basic idea was more clearly outlined when Almond applied his approach to the comparative study of interest groups (Almond, 1958). In this perspective, all political systems – traditional and modern – basically fulfill the same functions; that is, to transform political inputs (demands and support) via interest articulation, interest aggregation, policy making, and policy implementation into political outputs. Which acting components in the system are responsible for the various tasks and roles depends on the structural differentiation of the system. In traditional systems with low degrees of differentiation, components such as political parties, interest groups, legislatures, executives, bureaucracies, and courts interpenetrate each other and fulfill multiple functions. In modern systems in contrast, each component has its specific role in the overall division of political labor: interest groups articulate interests; parties and legislators aggregate these demands; and legislators, bureaucracies, and courts make and implement public policies.

The role, structure, and behavior of interest groups are thus not given, but depend on the particular differentiation and structuring of the overall political system. Political macro structures like the constitutional distribution of powers, the organization of the legislature, the electoral system, and the party system define various roles and micro structures, on which interest group behavior in the political process is based. For instance, the American system of federalism and separation of powers creates a different 'target structure' for interest groups than the British parliamentary–cabinet system.

Almond's general and abstract approach does not provide for a specific theory of economic interest groups. Business associations are part of the interest group system and can be distinguished from other forms of associational groups by their explicit representation of particularistic interests, by their full-time professional staff, and by their statutory procedures for internal decision making (Almond & Powell, 1966). However, the membership base of these associational groups makes them both more resourceful and recognized as more legitimate in society compared to other groups.

In summary, systems theory primarily assigns organized business interests specific roles and functions in the policy process that depend on the degree of differentiation of a given society. Accordingly, in modern societies these dimensions cover interest articulation and to some extent interest aggregation. The latter includes the mobilization of members and internal processes of decision making, while the former consists of lobbying strategies and interest intermediation.

Neocorporatism

The concept of corporatism was rediscovered by Philippe C. Schmitter and Gerhard Lehmbruch in the 1970s and subsequently led to a paradigm shift in political science (Almond, 1983; Czada 1994). Schmitter and Lehmbruch both observed highly organized and functionally differentiated systems of business interests in Latin American and South European dictatorships as well as in democratic European states, which by no means resembled US-style pluralist markets for representation but rather exhibited monopolistic features of interest representation and intermediation (Schmitter, 1979; Lehmbruch & Schmitter, 1982). Neocorporatism primarily focuses on two aspects of an associational system: its function within the political system on the one hand and its structure on the other.

Initially, an important part of the corporatist research agenda aimed to provide an explanation for tripartite agreements between government, employers, and unions and their effects on macroeconomic variables. 'Tripartite national policies agreed between government, employers and trade unions were to safeguard macroeconomic objectives such as low inflation, low unemployment, a stable exchange rate, and a high growth while respecting the rights of unions and employers to free collective bargaining' (Streeck & Kenworthy, 2005). Soon neocorporatism extended its scope from macroeconomic policies to forms of meso- and micro-level governance. Empirical findings at these governance levels conclude that interest intermediation involves a large number of actors with multilayered interactions and thus exceeds the original neocorporatist theorizing[3] (Cawson, 1985b; Schneider, 1985, 1992).

The structure of corporatist governance arrangements is the second pillar of neocorporatism. Four dimensions of organizational properties can be distinguished – domains, structures, resources, and outputs – that capture the essence of associational structure and behavior (Schmitter & Streeck, 1999 [1981]). Domains specify the scope of interests that a business association represents; intra-organizational structures indicate the horizontal and vertical diversification within business associations, thus outlining the division of labor and the hierarchical levels; resources include primarily financial and personnel inputs; and outputs comprise all goods produced by a particular business association. Typically, associations provide political interest representation and service goods.

The organizational dilemma that business associations have to face is that they must be structured in such a way as to offer incentives to their members in order to extract sufficient resources for their survival, as well as to public authorities in order to gain access and exercise influence (*ibid*.: 19). In an exchange model Schmitter and Streeck distinguish the logic of influence and the logic of membership on which the structure and behavior of business associations are dependent. The dominance of any logic leads to distinct organizational properties and structuring of the whole associational system. In simple terms, the dominance of the logic of membership yields a pluralist system of business associations, while the logic of influence leads to corporatist patterns (*ibid*.: 54). The proposition is straightforward: Corporate members of business associations are mainly interested in undistorted interest representation and thus prefer associations with a narrow and small interest domain. Consequently, these associations are internally simple because internal differentiation is not needed to meet different member demands. Business associations have one key supplier of resources: their member firms. In turn, business associations are able to offer them interest representation, which is also the major good provided for public authorities and other political institutions. Opposite effects originate from the logic of influence. Public authorities favor interaction with a few business associations that represent multiple interests and thus create incentives for their formation. Among these incentives are institutionalized access to the decision-making process or state recognition and licensing. Business associations equipped with these political resources may offer them to their members and receive compliance in their turn. Under these circumstances the internal and external organizations of interests are functionally differentiated and there exists an integrated and hierarchically ordered system of business associations.

In summary, the neocorporatism approach provides a more top-down focused theory of collective action in which the state is a driving force of associability.[4] Public authorities provide incentives that may be 'sold' by business associations to their member firms in exchange for compliance and more autonomy. The autonomy from the narrow interests of their members may subsequently be invested in tripartite macroeconomic agreements that involve compromises and consensus among the participants.

Applications of grand theories and new forays

The late 1980s saw the perpetuation of the pluralism–corporatism debate and some applications of grand theories from other scientific disciplines, such as the biological theory of evolution (Mayr, 2001). However some of them, especially the transaction costs perspective, make a bare living as niche theories and are only occasionally mentioned in studies on business interest associations. Nevertheless, they provide useful insights that enrich our understanding of associational structure and behavior and should be synthesized with some of the useful parts of the research dealt with above. In the 1980s and 1990s organized business interests also became an integral part of theories of international and European governance, in which they perform self-regulatory functions or promote the development of international governance arrangements.

International governance: International political economy and European integration theory

The last three decades have seen an immense growth in international policy making at the European as well as the global level. Both phenomena eventually entered the scientific debate under the heading of international political economy (IPE) and European integration theory, which emerged as new paradigms in the 1960s and 1970s and reached adolescence in the following decades through consolidating themselves as disciplines or subdisciplines within the broader framework of international and transnational relations (IR).

The study of international political economy must be seen in the context of international affairs that have been dominated by various realist schools in international relations emphasizing the role of states and public authority. Major emphasis has been put on the multifaceted relations between the two modes of governance: state and market. As major actors in the economy and in business, multinational and transnational corporations were wheeled in early on, adding an important component of private diplomacy to global politics (Stopford & Strange, 1991). However, the political actions of business are not reducible to the behavior of single, even powerful global corporations, but must also include collective forms of interest articulation.[5]

A more varied understanding of business has also gradually given rise to new studies on self-regulation and collective agreements under the auspices of business interest associations. Thus, it is recognized that business establishes norms and rules that replace or complement traditional public regulation in the international realm. Important examples of 'private authority' are provided across many industries (Cutler et al., 1999). This line of research is part of the ongoing discussion in IR in which governance mechanisms are not exclusively interpreted as matters of conflict and cooperation between states, but increasingly also private actors. Indeed, some of these norms and rules emerge through collective action in business interest associations, but this literature has also shown that collective action can take a plethora of forms.

Research on European integration is an integral part of the international governance perspective and, due to the high degree of institutionalization of EU policy making, has interesting implications for the debate on business associability. Reviews of European integration research consider three major strands in theory building (Marks et al., 1996): neo-functionalism, intergovernmentalism, and multilevel governance. Neofunctionalism was the first theory to explain European integration, and within this framework interest groups have always played a major role because interest group formation at the supra-national level may become a substitute for popular identification with the emerging political institutions (Streeck & Schmitter, 1994).

It was expected that the political spillover of supra-national competencies and jurisdictions to new policy areas would lead to a reorientation of interest groups toward the EU institutions and to a decline of national political arenas (Eising, 2004). Intergovernmentalism, in contrast, is an offspring of international relations theory that was tailored to the new research area. In this setting interest groups, often receiving scant attention, remain focused on the national level. Proponents of the multilevel governance approach emphasize the network-like structure of EU policy making, where European as well as national institutions share important powers and where a large number of public and private organizations are involved. Multilevel governance discards the idea that interest groups are restricted to either the national or the European arena (*Marks et al.*, 1996; Greenwood, 2003).

In sum, international governance focuses on the state–business interactions and interdependencies in multilayered political systems. The complex architecture of international bargaining arenas has attracted a great variety of actors that seek access via different influence routes. As a result, competition for influence has become more intense. Furthermore, associations at the international or European level have been established, which eases coordination between associations at national levels as well as increases competition within multilayered systems. Finally, the international governance literature has not only been concerned with interest articulation in an international political setting, but also stresses the contribution of business associations to societal order through self-regulation.

Population ecology

Population ecology applies biological concepts and categories directly to organizations. Michael Hannan and John Freeman were the first to fully adapt the natural selection model from biology to organization theory (Hannan & Freeman, 1977). The central proposition is that environments differentially 'select' organizations for survival on the basis of fit between organizational form and environmental characteristics (Scott, 1998). Changes in the populations of organizations therefore mirror the effects of the evolutionary processes of variation and selective retention (Aldrich, 1999). Variations occur when new organizations are founded and bring new organizational forms to the population, or when organizations deliberately or accidentally change their composition or behavior. In the competition for scarce resources some organizational forms prove more successful than others, and thus are selected positively by environmental factors. Over time more successful organizational forms have a higher survival rate and become more frequent within the population. Features of successful forms of associability and political representation are thus retained because populations come to be composed of them

(Baum & Amburgey, 2002). This is also relevant in the further development of large and encompassing organizations that grow out of the more fragmented patterns of the pluralist models.

Natural selection models of founding and mortality rates were first applied to business associations during the late 1980s and early 1990s and have become a research field in the US. Aldrich and Staber (1988) and Aldrich *et al.* (1994) investigated the impact of political and economic variables on the composition of the US trade association population. Although these findings cannot necessarily be transferred to other countries where more stable patterns exist, they are of experimental value and are still useful in analyzing these dynamic processes. Analyses showed that economic growth increased associational foundings, while government actions had no or mixed effects on the vital rates in the population of trade associations. Increasing labor union activities, in contrast, led to mergers between business associations. Within-population dynamics also have major impacts on the composition of trade association populations. Density affects the merger and disbanding rate. Transformations of trade associations occur infrequently and are triggered by internal heterogeneity (Aldrich *et al.*, 1994).

Gray and Lowery (1996, 1997) found that interest groups act in well-defined niches that are made up of attributive and resource dimensions specifying the environmental factors that bear on the interest group's survival. Niche overlap between several associations or populations leads basically to a partitioning of that niche. Gray and Lowery emphasize that this may be achieved by two mechanisms. First, two associations with overlapping interest domains compete over the share of overlap until this share is partitioned so that the overlap has been removed. Associations and populations of associations thus become dissimilar over time. Secondly, associations actively cooperate to find a consensus over the partitioning of the overlap. Similar to Aldrich *et al.* (1994), Gray and Lowery found 'that interest group niches – and thus the structure of interest group communities – are more strongly determined by the internal needs of organized interests than by their patterns of interface with government' (Gray & Lowery, 1996: 108).

To sum up, population ecology models the effects of environmental factors, mainly (macro) economic development, legislative activity, and population structures on population dynamics and associational behavior. Empirical studies show that within-system cooperation and competition have larger effects than exogenous variables. However, different types of associations may display different forms of adaptation. In the case of business interest associations there is surely a tendency to attribute great importance to the internal life. Membership includes not only competitors in the marketplace but also firms of different sizes. Such asymmetries in resources and power may have a strong bearing on associations.

Transaction cost theory

Transaction cost theory is a well established subdiscipline in economics and has received widespread attention among scholars of institutional economics, contract law, and organization theory. Transaction cost theory considers the fact that microeconomic analysis of economic activity centers exclusively on intra-firm activities and market mechanisms, and has so far neglected the importance of exchange relations among market participants (Williamson, 1991). It focuses on these exchanges of goods and services as the basic elements of economic activity. In essence, exchange relations add additional transaction costs to the production costs of products and services. Transaction costs may arise before and after transactions have taken place. Therefore transaction cost theory distinguishes between ex ante and ex post transaction costs. Ex ante transaction costs contain information, negotiation, and contracting costs that lead to a contractual act. Ex post transaction costs include enforcement and arbitration costs (Ebers & Gotsch, 1999).

Transaction cost theory compares discrete structural governance alternatives in relation to the costs they pose on economic transactions in different environments, especially under conditions of uncertainty. Exchange relations are governed by three 'generic forms of economic organization – market, hybrid, and hierarchy' (Williamson, 1991: 269). These forms are characterized by different governance mechanisms and by varying capacities to adapt to environmental turmoil. Business associations, in this perspective, are seen as hybrid organizations integrating principles of governance typically known from government, market, and community (Streeck & Schmitter, 1985b). In an associative mode of governance, firms in an industry become organized by pooling resources and by delegating rights and powers to a central organization with permanent staff in order to promote members' interests. The association may also regulate intra-industry competition and may order relations between industry members and their customers and suppliers (Schneiberg & Hollingsworth, 1998). However, these activities are not found across all business interest associations, and the power conferred on associations is highly varied.

Within the framework of transaction cost theory, associational governance is less rooted in property rights and contract law and more in collective self-regulation (Schneiberg & Hollingsworth, 1998) when intra-industry competition is high or the industry's supply or demand side faces considerable market power (Van Waarden, 1987). Associational governance is a means of lowering industries' ex ante transaction costs through collective and sometimes binding agreements. These agreements regulate competitive relations between the members of the association and thus influence the price mechanism or other aspects of performance in the whole industry (Schneiberg & Hollingsworth, 1998).

To sum up, transaction cost theory elaborates a framework in which different modes of economic governance can be assessed. An associative order is a form of collective self-regulation within and between industries that aims to lower transaction costs. Associative economic governance relies on cooperation between industry members and between associations of different branches in order to achieve binding agreements. Therefore, regulatory tasks have to be delegated to business associations that (in)formally coordinate the behavior of firms.

Towards a new synthesis: Complex associative action theory

In previous sections of this chapter we sketched major lines of theory development in interest group and associative action research. Most of these theories originated in different scientific disciplines, in different cultural settings, and they interpreted associative action in different vocabularies. They have long resisted attempts to develop a more encompassing theory that is able to integrate if not all, then some of the above approaches to explain collective action and interest group behavior. However, the overview should also have made clear that research in this area provides a rich mosaic of findings that seems to be disposed for a substantive advancement in theory building. Attempts at this have recently been made by Lowery and Gray (2004) and McFarland (2004), who cover a wide range of theories – particularly pluralism, public and collective choice – in their overviews. Unfortunately, they focus exclusively on the North American discourse in interest group politics and pay scant attention to other strands of literature, such as neocorporatist research or systems theory.

Nonetheless, we take up the suggestion by Lowery and Gray to merge evolutionary thinking and interest group theory into a more persuasive perspective (Lowery & Gray, 2004). In this perspective our crucial stimulation is derived from neocorporatist research and the latest advances in organization theory, namely organizational ecology and complex adaptive systems. These theories provide for a meta-theoretical basis on which we will put the building blocks of the more traditional interest group and associative action theories. In the following paragraphs we provide a sketch of how this synthesis of various theories might look. Of course, we do not yet intend to provide a fully elaborated synthesis, which is far beyond the scope of this volume. However, it should suggest a reasonable alternative to neopluralist theorizing and offer an integrated approach to the study of business associations.

A useful integration and systematization of the complex system perspective has been provided by the so-called CESM model of philosopher of science Mario Bunge (2003). In his perspective the most elementary description of a system is the identification of its various components C, its differentiation and embeddedness in an environment E, and multiple structures including various relations among components (endostructure) and between components and their environment (exostructure) S. However, a description of a system based on components, environment, and structures would still be incomplete if the various mechanisms M and processes that make a system 'tick' are not singled out. A further important point is that every system is nested in other systems of higher order, and is composed of systems at lower levels. Hence, systems vary in their compositional, structural, ecological, and 'mechanismic' complexity.

Organizational ecology theory is a progeny of population ecology theory that has incorporated the central evolutionary categories and concepts, but rejects the premise that organizations are unable to transform their behavior and structures deliberately. Another feature of organizational ecology is that the population perspective is abandoned in favor of a multilevel evolutionary perspective where the evolutionary process takes place at different organizational levels. Accordingly, organizational ecology theory differentiates between properties of the organizations and inter-organizational relations that adapt to exogenous factors to which organizations and populations of organizations are tight by their exostructure (Baum & Amburgey, 2002; Galunic & Weeks, 2002).

The organizational properties of business associations are studied as core elements in all theories of organized business interests. In some way all the above-mentioned theories focus on interest representation and interest intermediation functions as the core properties and modus operandi of this associational form. However, only some theories conceptualize the relationship to member firms and the various strategies to extract sufficient resources. *New political economy* states that the capacity of resource extraction varies with group size. Smaller groups will find it easier to attract and retain members than larger groups, which in turn rely on providing club goods as selective incentives to their members. Similarly, *class theory* asserts that trade and employer associations are comparably more capable of providing private goods to their members than are trade unions, for the reason that they may offer expertise that can not often be obtained in the free market. In contrast, *neocorporatism* focuses on other entities than member firms. Public authorities in particular may provide business associations with sufficient material and moral support so that associations are able to gain strategic autonomy vis-à-vis their members.

The evolutionary process of business association systems can roughly be divided into variation and selective retention processes (Campbell, 1969). Variations occur when system properties such as influence strategies or membership services are incorrectly replicated or deliberately changed. Over the course of time, some variants prove more beneficial to the association than others in coping with a challenging environment. Thus managers inside the organizations select them positively. Likewise, external actors such as members of associations or government regulators select those organizations within a population that possess favorable properties. Firms may decide to join or leave associations, and government agencies may decide to recognize or ignore certain business associations. According to organizational ecology thinking, competition is the driving force behind the selection process.

Whether business associations change their internal structures or procedures is also dependent on environmental adaptation pressure and selection mechanisms. The selection and adaptation forces reside within the so-called exostructure, which transports environmental changes into the associational systems. A glimpse at different theoretical approaches illustrates these mechanisms. Traditional *class theory* views business as a second mover, which hardly needs collective action since its power resides within the individual firm. Capital establishes business associations as a reaction to pressures by the labor movement, and thus the adaptational pressure arises when, for example, a trade union is established that threatens the capital-accumulation process. The selection mechanism proceeds in such a way that better-adapted business associations that cope better with the trade union challenge will, at least in the long run, find it easier to extract sufficient resources from their targeted member population, and thus are more likely to flourish and survive. *Pluralism*, in contrast, is less restrictive in its assumptions about business association behavior. It assumes that groups set up collective action as long as any common group interest is attached as a result of state interventions or actions undertaken by other groups. Again, the selection mechanism operates by means of resource procurement. Business associations with more common interests and with better lobbying strategies will recruit more members than will less successful ones.[6] Moreover, the members' demands of undistorted interest representation lead to the establishment of rather small associations that focus on narrow interest domains. Similarly, *organizational ecology*, *choice/collective action theories*, and *exchange theories* view resource dependencies as the main selection mechanism that decides whether the associational lobbying or service strategy meets external demands. *Transaction cost economics* departs from this view, since business associations provide a hybrid mode of governance that allows for (in)formal communication between market participants. As Williamson (1991) clearly points out, the governance mode with the lowest transaction costs will be chosen and thus be selected positively due to market pressures.

Top-down theories, however, locate selection forces within the political or governmental system. Functionalist *system theory* scrutinizes functional requirements of higher system levels as drivers of associative action. In the case of business associations, the interest articulation function makes them indispensable elements of the political system. Selection, then, takes place if system demands are insufficiently implemented. As a result, the articulation function will be supplied by other subsystems such as firms or movements. *Neocorporatism* stresses the importance of institutionalized participation in political decision making, which gives business associations some autonomy from member interests and demands and allows them to implement public policy. Under these conditions, business associations are able to develop encompassing interest domains that secure resource procurement from members. In corporatist political arrangements it is clearly state intervention that acts as a selection mechanism.

However, it is important to stress that the evolutionary process does not necessarily lead to a homogenization of associational forms. Even when business associations face the same selection pressure, such as internationalization of their members or increased international regulation, they need not become similar over time. This is because business associations interact with other associations in their population and this 'interaction causes replication to be differential' (Hull, 1994: 627). In consequence, the type and strength of the relations between business associations (endostructure) influence the intensity of the exogenous selection pressure (exostructure). Business associations within highly competitive populations face similar and intense selection pressures, while associations within cooperative populations, in which resource partitioning and resource pooling dominate, are less exposed to environmental selection forces (see Gray & Lowery, 1996) or find it easier to provide better-adapted answers to environmental challenges. This is important in understanding for instance the different patterns of associability and business political action in North America and in Western Europe. Cooperation and information exchange furthermore facilitate the transmission of successful strategies of business associations and can thus be seen as mechanisms of cultural transmission that alter the pace of the evolutionary process. In particular, better-adapted and more successful organizational properties tend to diffuse faster within cooperative populations.

The fact that the interaction structure mediates selection pressure has been conceptualized by complex adaptive systems theory and by recent accounts in organizational ecology. Interactions are part of the relational level of business association systems (endostructure). Brittain and Wholey (1988) distinguish six different relations, including symmetric relations such as full competition in which both organizations compete, as well as asymmetric cooperation and competition, in which one organization competes/cooperates while the other behaves neutrally.

Many associational systems are not only integrated by these kinds of relations but are coordinated by means of information exchange. In particular, *neocorporatism* stresses the importance of internal coordination between independent associations or between affiliates within an umbrella or peak association (Streeck, 1989), which may serve for broader economic agreements between capital, labor, and the state. In these instances, associational systems act as a cohesive whole in which different parts are assigned different tasks. *Transaction cost theory* primarily views an associative order as a hybrid mode of economic governance that aims to reduce transaction costs by (in)formal agreements and information exchange.

To sum up, our sketch of a complex association theory builds on existing theories of business associability. We differentiate between two system levels – organizational properties and inter-associational relations – which are exposed to environmental constraints and demands in a wider political context where governmental institutions are included. The adaptation process to the associational environment, however, is not a linear process due to the interdependencies between organizational properties and inter-associational relations. In particular, the latter alter the direction and pace of the adaptation process.

Conclusion

In this chapter we have sketched the main theories of collective and associative action and have integrated them under the umbrella of the latest advances in general organizational research, namely organizational ecology and complex adaptive systems theory. Our aim was to outline a new approach to business association thinking that contributes to the dissolution of traditional boundaries between economic, political, evolutionary, or sociological ways of dealing with associative action. We therefore introduced these variants of organization theory in order to provide a macro-theoretical 'platform' (Galunic & Weeks, 2002) for adding major insights from existing business association theories.

In a first step we distinguished between two levels of organized collective action. *Organizational properties* include domains, structures, resources, and outputs of business associations. Associations acquire financial, personnel, or other types of resources from their members or from public authorities and transform them into outputs within functionally diversified and hierarchically integrated structures. Outputs predominantly include services for members and political activities directed toward public authorities or other societal and political actors, such as trade unions, consumer organizations, or environmental movements. At the level of organizational properties, adaptation takes place when the organizational structures and processes of business associations are adjusted in order to meet new environmental demands. New environmental demands arise from changes in the composition and structure of the political system in which business associations operate, or from transformations within the economic sectors that the associations represent. Changes in the political system include, for instance, the Europeanization and globalization of governance activities. Transformations in the market structure, the intensity of competition, and foreign trade are examples of environmental forces that trigger changes in organizational properties through altering the composition of member firms and their strategic orientation.

The *relational level* contains interactions among business associations and the emerging properties resulting from these interactions. We distinguish three basic types of relations – competition, cooperation, and exchange – that have differing mediating effects on the adaptation process. Business associations embedded in a highly competitive population face comparably intenser adaptation pressures. In competitive populations business associations tend to build up separate niches. As a result, business associations within a population become dissimilar over time.

Cooperation, on the other hand, provides the basis for the diffusion of well-adapted organizational properties that may be implemented by copying successful associations. In consequence the population gets similar over time.

Adaptation arises from environmental constraints and demands that affect resource procurement and utilization. Bottom-up theories of business associability, such as public choice or exchange theory, model members as the main selection force that may exit unsuccessful associations or voice their discontent. In contrast, top-down theories, such as neocorporatism, view associational systems as primarily driven by government concessions such as institutionalized access to policy making. Adaptation pressures shape the strategic options of business associations but do not determine it. The direction and pace with which business associations explore their strategic options are dependent on the inter-associational relations that guide the search for better-adapted organizational properties and increase or reduce the pace with which restructurings take place.

Our outline of a complex association theory should be regarded as a statement toward theory unification. Theories of interest group and business association behavior have reached a high level of maturity and are ripe for theory building. Their dispersion among various scientific disciplines, however, makes the endeavor more challenging as well as more appealing. We therefore have taken up the challenge posed by Knoke, Baumgartner, and Leech to synthesize the main strands of the existing theoretical landscape and have unified them under the umbrella of complexity and ecological theory. In this way we seek to bring theory development from 'simple' to 'complex'. We now provide a new variation in theory development, whose selection is dependent on its usefulness for explaining changes in systems of business association. Some hints at its usefulness will be given in the following chapters of this book.

Notes

1. However, critics may ask if system theory is not a relic of past and forgotten ages of theory development. Indeed, holistic political system theory in the tradition of Parsons, Easton, and Almond was successfully crowded out by structuralists during the 1970s, and by individualistic and institutionalist approaches during the 1980s and 1990s. On a global scale, the dominant theories in political sciences have in general become more conflict oriented and actor centered during the last decades, or taken a constructivist turn emphasizing the importance of discourse.

2. By material benefits Salisbury denotes concrete goods or services. Solidary benefits include socializing and the sense of group membership. Finally, purposive benefits 'consist of the realization of supra-personal goals, goals of the organization or group' (Salisbury, 1969: 16).
3. This strand of neocorporatism led to the development of the policy network (Kenis & Schneider, 1991; Börzel, 1998).
4. Note that liberal or societal corporatism very much emphasizes free associability; only state corporatism would give unilateral attention to top-down developments.
5. Woll (2005), for example, compares the involvement of US and European business in WTO negotiations regarding the liberalization of telecommunications and air transport, and concludes that US companies rely on independent lobbying activities, while European business is still coordinated by business associations.
6. This argument, of course, works only in so far as there are other business associations with similar domains and thus competition crowds out less effective and efficient associations.

3
Between Politics, Economy, and Technology: The Changing Environments of Business Associations

Achim Lang, Volker Schneider, and Raymund Werle

The central theme of this book is the adaptation of national systems of organized business interests to changing environments. In this chapter we take a more detailed look at the slices and layers of these political, economic, and technological 'exostructures' (Bunge, 1996). Our basic questions are: How do environmental changes affect business associations and how can they possibly trigger adaptation processes? As the overview of business association theories in Chapter 2 has shown, political factors have been given priority in explaining associational behavior and inter-associational structures, whereas economic and technological determinants still play a peripheral role. Nevertheless, it is commonly accepted that these factors have a strong impact on the membership base of business associations. Their neglect is important, because it is generally assumed that the expansion and contraction of membership may affect the entire interest group system. Furthermore, the ability of associational systems to include new and detach abandoned interests affects the legitimacy and effectiveness of public policy.

Two explanations account for this paucity. First, the relationships between techno-economic factors and business associations are mainly indirect. Business associations act in response to firms that either initiate technical innovations and expand their businesses, or accommodate changes in the market structure. These relationships are embedded in an institutional setting that generally changes at a slower rate than technological innovation. Secondly, interest group theories in the political sciences mainly deal with the effectiveness of interest groups in influencing public policy. Conditions and constraints of collective action are only addressed when group- or class-specific differences account for varying lobbying strategies and lobbying success. An extreme position is held by Marxism, which claims that capitalists have fairly homogeneous interests that facilitate collective action (Offe & Wiesenthal, 1980). In contrast, pluralists emphasize the role of individual interests as a main foundation on which the formation of interest groups rests. Pluralists are aware of changes at the membership level that may lead to the emergence of new interest groups and the abandoning of old ones. Their approaches, however, do not usually trace these changes back to economic or technological variables that may have affected the individual interest of firms. Political economists have proven group size to be a major variable of collective action, but do not account for anything more than size or density effects on the formation of interest groups (Olson, 1970 [1965]). State-centered theories such as (neo)corporatism focus on the characteristics of the state affecting the formation of associational hierarchies. Only a few strands of association theory – namely organizational ecology and parts of the corporatism literature – explicitly consider economic factors as important drivers of associational development. These theories focus primarily on the effects of economic variables on the composition of associational systems. Accordingly, market expansion and contraction are seen as the main drivers of associational foundation and disbandment as well as of changes in the strategy and behavior of business associations.

However, besides theoretical reasoning, the debate on associational development still lacks a summary of empirical findings on the whole spectrum of political, economic, and technological factors in the environment of business associations, and an assessment of the role these play in the processes of change and adaptation. The aim of this chapter is therefore to summarize and order the existing literature in which various environmental sectors are addressed. The chapter is divided into four sections. In the first we give an overview of various political environments at different levels of associational systems. The second section concentrates on economic environments and their impact on business associations. Since our book is among the first to put a strong emphasis on technological factors, in the third section we will consider some impact scenarios of technological changes and how these affect associational structures and behavior. Finally we compare the economic sectors of agriculture, chemicals, and information and communications in order to hypothesize likely adaptation processes of business associations operating in these sectors.

Political environments of associations and their adaptation strategies

The main external structure to which business associations have to adapt is the political environment. Even if business associations are highly service oriented with similarities to companies in the service industry, they are first and foremost political actors. Their principal function is to represent members' interests in the political sphere. Since 'political' has various meanings in English, we can distinguish between at least three dimensions or segments in the political environment: the polity environment, including the formal institutional arrangements in which national systems of business associations are embedded; the politics environment, including all structural factors and dynamics through which conflicts of interest are solved or intermediated; and finally the policy environment, including the spectrum of public policies and governmental programs by which the interests and resources of business associations are affected. In the age of internationalization and globalization, all these environments imply national, regional (i.e., European), and global levels. The – still rudimentary – global polity consists of the United Nations system and other intergovernmental organizations, and the increasingly powerful and differentiated institutional complex that has emerged at the EU level. Similar distinctions can be made with respect to politics and policy. Also in this respect, European and global processes and structural layers have emerged, by which the structural environment of business associations has become increasingly diversified and complex.

The way in which these slices and layers of 'the political' have affected the evolution of business associations at a general level was a core topic in Chapter 2. The structure and function of associational systems at the macro level are important in systems theory and neocorporatism. Different types of political systems imply different roles and functions for economic interest groups. Different forms of corporatism, such as voluntary organizations in societal corporatism and coercive forms of incorporation in traditional state corporatism, strongly affect the organizational landscape.

In the structural–functional perspective, political macro-structures such as the constitutional distribution of powers or the organization of the legislative, electoral, and party systems define various roles and micro-structures on which interest group behavior in the political process is based. For instance, American federalism and separation of powers create a different 'target structure' for interest groups than does the British Westminster democracy. In the US system, the decentralized party structure goes together with low party discipline and favors interest group penetration in legislation and regulatory rule making. In contrast, the centralized British system, with its disciplined party structure and strong cabinet government, protects the legislature from interest group influence and shifts influence targets to bureaucracy (Almond, 1958). The function of interest groups and the channels of interest intermediation are largely determined by the macro-structures of political systems, and changes in macro-structures breed particular forms of adaptation.

Changing polities, power shifts, and moving target structures

Because our study only covers the last two decades, and since we are dealing with consolidated democratic countries at an advanced stage of development, there have been only marginal changes at the polity level. This would have been different if transforming countries or even less developed areas had been included.

The main changes in national polities can be summarized as follows:

1. *The emergence of new independent administrative units within national political systems and the horizontal transfer of significant decision-making powers to these new autonomous governmental units.* Although this spread of 'non-majoritarian institutions' (Thatcher & Sweet, 2002) or 'agencification' (Pollitt & Talbot, 2004) is intensely discussed in Europe, this power shift started much earlier in the US and only diffused to other areas in the world during the 1980s and 1990s (Tenbücken & Schneider, 2004). Due to this unequal development, the political science debate on this 'fourth branch of government' and its relationship to business associations is more intense in the US than elsewhere, where regulatory agencies as lobbying targets of private interests form a established topic of research (Gais *et al.*, 1984; Furlong, 1997; Furlong & Kerwin 2005).

2. *The transfer of governmental decision-making power beyond the nation state and the emergence of the European Union as a supranational political system.* This development affects business associations in several ways. A transfer of competencies to international bodies first entails a loss of jurisdiction for national governments. Accordingly, national business associations may shift their lobbying to the supra-national level, or still use the national governmental channel to be indirectly represented in the supra-national arena. Since this topic has far-ranging implications many studies have been conducted during the last decade, but generalizations beyond policy cases and sectors are still lacking. Important rival hypotheses are that national channels

of interest intermediation are still important in comparison to the declining importance of the national level. An intermediate position emphasizes the combination of both developments in a multilevel framework (Lehmkuhl, 2000; Eising, 2007; Wonka in this volume).
3. Power shifts to the global level (Mathews, 1997) could also be seen as indicators of an *emergent global polity*. Since global transfers in functions and powers are much more restricted than power transfers at European Union level, these new institutional arrangements are more adequately described as international regimes, where the major action resources are still controlled by member states (Schneider & Werle, 1990). Despite such restraints, these new global institutions are not irrelevant for national associational systems and will be discussed in the following section.

Changes in politics alter the repositioning of organized interests

Globalization also alters politics. The first effect is that economic globalization enhances the size and power of multinational firms. Market expansion increasingly produces larger companies that are less and less dependent on national and international associations. The interest horizon of multinationals transcends traditional boundaries, and their immense resources enable them to represent this expanded spectrum of interests on their own by 'direct lobbying' (Schneider, 2006). In addition, multinational firms may also join international business associations. Both developments are likely to limit the capacity of national associations to incorporate multinational companies in collective commitments and discipline.

The direct pursuit of firms' interests leads to a further pluralization of political arenas. This increase in diversity seems to be a general trend. Political arenas in all countries and sectors tend to become more pluralized and fragmented. Besides traditional actors such as governments, administrations, parties, and business associations, novel players such as new social movements, public interest groups, and science in policy making grow in importance. Empirical studies on policy networks support such observations (Marin & Mayntz, 1991, Schneider *et al.*, 2008).

In trying to cope with these changes, national associations reorganize their strategic repertoire and develop new capacities. To compete with other forms of interest representation in domestic arenas, they improve service orientation and professionalism, and they learn to use the diversifying media environment (press, television, internet, and so on) in a more proactive and efficient manner (Kriesi *et al.*, 2007). Business associations develop lobbying strategies that do not only target specific political decisions, but try to shape and cultivate the overall political landscape. In subsequent chapters we called this 'political gardening' or 'societal lobbying'.

Adaptation with respect to international developments also entails the organization of regional and international federations of interest associations. In some international policy arenas, however, this type of multilevel interest representation may not suffice. A further option is to move to international or supranational terrain and establish national offices near the headquarters of international organizations (Schneider & Grote, 2006).

A final change in the politics environment is related to the cognitive level of politics: to shifts in political culture, dominant ideologies, and belief systems. A remarkable change during the last 20 years has been the shift toward the ideology of neoliberalism, which pushed for market expansion and a cutback of state intervention. As a number of studies demonstrate, this transformation was largely based on a diffusion process that started in the US and was amplified in Europe by particular structures of the European Union. The cognitive predisposition of the European Commission and the European Court of Justice for neoliberal policy models, for instance, is an important explanatory factor for liberalization and privatization policies in Europe during the last two decades (Schneider & Häge, 2008). Cultural changes also affect the position of business associations. In contrast to the era of Keynesianism, where macro-economic concertation of economic policies (Lehmbruch, 1984) favored political incorporation of encompassing business associations, within the last decade the same collaborative forms have been criticized as corporatist closure preventing innovation and industrial restructuring. On the other side, however, there are also countries in which corporatist social pacts were reinvented to moderate economic adaptation (Schmitter & Grote, 1997) and even to encourage structural change for innovation in high-tech development (O'Riain, 2004).

Policy changes and organized interests

Further changes in the political environment of interest associations, often described as changes in statehood, also result from changes in the nation state itself. Economic internationalization was, among other things, accelerated by the fact that markets were opened and previous state monopolies were privatized. In many areas, the nation state withdrew from public infrastructures and attempted to secure long-term control over private provisions by means of regulation instead (Schneider *et al.*, 2005). This makes traditional forms of associational self-regulation largely redundant and associations functionally less relevant. Indirectly, this may also lead to an erosion of the traditional support of associations by the state.

Parallel to this stepwise retreat of the state and the expansion of private markets, the role of regulatory policy increased, securing the remaining public purposes by means of regulation. This new policy environment is now populated to an overwhelming degree by the new administrative institutions described above, which are considered as constitutive elements of the new European regulatory state (Majone, 1997). Yet this institutional element was adapted from the other side of the Atlantic, and it is in the US where the long-term effects of regulatory policy making on the collective organization of business interests have been studied in detail (Staber & Aldrich, 1986). We expect that the expansion of regulatory policy in Europe will also have medium- and long-term effects on the development of business associations.

Another new policy environment for business associations is the emergence of global governance, the proliferation of regulatory regimes, and global policy networks. Within the spectrum of global regulation there are not only inter-governmental policy agreements such as the Kyoto protocol, but also a number of rules and norms that are based on pure self-regulation. In the area of business such forms may be administered through international associations, by global alliances, or through corporate self-regulation (Ronit & Schneider, 1999; Knill & Lehmkuhl, 2002).

Most of these changes trigger local and global adaptations; some can be discovered across all national and sectoral business interests, others are very much dependent on their national and sectoral context. Once again, in this area there are national and situational institutional legacies and path dependencies that are important topics in the discussion of historical institutionalism and the varieties of capitalism.

Changing economic environments and the adaptation of associational strategies and structures

While business associations are not firms whose survival is entirely determined by market success, they are not immune to economic turbulence. Although it is agreed that the establishment of business associations involves virtually no sunk costs and that their daily operations function at low overhead expenses (Aldrich *et al.*, 1994), they are nevertheless vulnerable to changes in their economic environment. Perturbations and shifts in market structure affect the membership base of business associations either by reducing or increasing the membership, or by partitioning it with respect to within-industry competition. The exposure of associations to the composition and demands of their member firms is due to the lack of genuinely independent goods and services that associations may offer on the market. The typical business association is therefore dependent on membership fees as its principal resource, which in turn allows only for small leeway regarding membership demands (Bennett, 1998, 2000).

Economic factors have few direct effects on business associations; it is indirect effects that are brought to bear by changes in the composition and structure of the economic sectors that the association represents (Aldrich et al., 1994; Schmitter & Streeck, 1999 [1981]). Distinguishing two types of economic factors according to the influence they exert on the membership base of national business associations is useful: economic factors that shape the competitive structure and composition of individual sectors directly at the national level, and factors that affect member firms and business associations more indirectly by change at the level of international economic development.

Domestic economic factors

National business associations draw their company members (almost) exclusively from their domestic markets, thereby leaving them particularly exposed to changes in the domestic market structure that, in the long run, will be reflected in the composition and structure of the associational system. National economic factors that affect the market structure and are frequently referred to are market growth, the composition according to different types of firms, the intensity of competition, and the level of cooperation among market participants (Kennelly & Murrell, 1991; Aldrich et al., 1994; Gray & Lowery, 2000).

Growing or shrinking markets increase or reduce the profitability of a particular sector. Its market volume usually affects the number of firms operating in the sector. This has serious consequences for business associations. An increase in the number of firms enlarges the resource base that can be exploited by existing or new associations. In particular, when relatively new branches of the sector contribute to an increase in the market volume, new niches emerge in which novel associations can be established without fearing rivalry of existing interest groups. In contrast, a shrinking of market volume and number of firms leads to an abandonment of existing niches and thus to a disbandment of business associations. This theoretical proposition concerning changes in the composition of associational systems has been frequently examined in population ecology studies. Aldrich *et al.* (1994) find that in the US, GDP growth had a significant effect on the establishment of associations and subsequent waves of association foundations. In general, processes of industrialization and market expansion increase the division of labor in the production of goods and services within an industry and lead to a greater differentiation of firms occupying different economic positions. Potentially conflicting economic interests then arise, which in turn increases the likelihood of collective action. Similarly, Gray and Lowery (2000) point to the significant effect of economic growth on the density of state-level associational systems in the US. Although confirming the results found by Aldrich *et al.* (1994), they identify certain capacity limits, as the number of associations does not rise to infinity but follows a curvilinear trajectory. They also identify a lower bound of associational density, particularly in small states, that seems to be independent of economic variables, due to the fact that government regulation forces firms to take collective action independent of the group size. Interestingly, their results indicate similar adaptation processes in quite different sectors, ranging from agriculture and manufacturing to environmental and welfare interests.

The size of firms in a given market is another economic variable that affects the composition and structuring of business association systems. Sectors with an unequal distribution of firm size organize themselves such that the big player(s) work alone and lobby on their own account, while the smaller firms join and set up their own interest groups (Schmitter & Streeck, 1999 [1981]; Boléat, 2002; Grote *et al.*, 2007). The concentration of an industry and thus the number of firms are subject to debate in the study of collective action. Olson's assumption that smaller groups face fewer free-riding problems and hence are more likely to act collectively (Olson, 1970 [1965]) is rejected by most empirical studies on business associations. According to Kennelly and Murrell (1991), highly concentrated industries are less likely to set up interest groups than are industries with a large population of firms.

The intensity of competition and cooperation also determines the organization of business associations. Firms in highly competitive industries can expect rewards from joint efforts in coordinating prizes and product standards, which decrease competitive pressure and lower the uncertainty regarding future developments (Schmitter & Streeck, 1999 [1981]). Transaction cost theory and its application in association research focuses on the associational capacities to regulate intra-industry relations and to coordinate the relations between industry members and their customers and suppliers. The lowering of competitive pressure provides an incentive for collective action, but it is an additional stimulus rather than the sole reason for establishing business associations. More important is an industry's representation by an association vis-à-vis government and its regulatory interventions into the economy (Schneiberg & Hollingsworth, 1998).

Intra-industry heterogeneity and interdependence are supposed to have seemingly contradictory effects on firms and business associations (Schmitter & Streeck, 1999 [1981]). Product heterogeneity in general leads to highly specialized markets, with firms occupying their own profitable product niches. Business associations in such industries face difficulties in recruiting members due to interest diversity. However, such industries often show a high degree of interdependence, meaning that firms are sellers and customers to each other at the same time. The lack of competition between firms and inter-firm dependencies are supposed to have the contradictory effect that the inter-associational relationships between business associations representing such industries are said to be competitive for their lobbying in support of favorable customer relationships. However, we still lack empirical evidence in support of this hypothesis.

International factors

International economic factors that influence the activities and structures of associational systems are largely unexplored. Few studies consider the development of imports, exports, and international mergers and acquisitions – to mention some international factors – as drivers of associational change.

Imports and exports are indicators of competitive pressure within economic sectors. Schmitter and Streeck (1999 [1981]) stress that competition with firms outside a particular industrial group tends to generate associative action against this external group of firms. Thus an increase in imports diminishes the threshold of collective action within the affected industries. Kennelly and Murrell (1991) show that as imports increase the competitive pressure on domestic firms, they set up business associations to lobby for protective measures against foreign suppliers. Increasing exports, in contrast, have no effects on collective action as long as the importing countries do not apply protective measures. In a similar vain, Grier *et al.* (1994) found that corporate contributions to political action committees in the US are highly affected by the share of imports an industry is facing. The higher the share of imports, the more resources firms invest in influencing policy makers to relieve them from competitive pressure.

The impact of foreign capital investments seems rather diffuse and has not attracted many scientific studies until now. An exception is Traxler's (2006) analysis of the impact of foreign direct investments on national employer associations. Another is Boléat's (2002) study of the effects on trade associations of foreign mergers and acquisitions by multinational companies. An important finding was that these processes inevitably lead to higher market concentration not only in the domestic market, but also in other countries where both firms had subsidiaries that were also taken over or had to merge. When a large part of the national market is controlled by international companies, the management of associations becomes more difficult, because foreign-owned members are primarily committed to their head office. The impact of international mergers and acquisitions is dependent on the status of the domestic subsidiary. In the case of a rather autonomous business unit, the impact on domestic interest groups is small, whereas a tight coupling of the domestic business unit to its mother company leads either to a synchronization of interest politics within business associations or to the termination of membership within the domestic association.

Technological innovations as drivers of associational change

Technology coevolves and interacts with political and economic institutions (Nelson, 1994). This process is driven by internal dynamics and is, at the same time, shaped by the interaction of technological and institutional factors. The interaction is indirect. It is mediated by actors who are positively or negatively affected by institutional and technological changes and who try to advance their interests and minimize their disadvantages through gaining control over these processes. In the context of this interaction-oriented approach, it is possible to assess how single business associations and the system of organized business interests are affected by technological changes. Usually firms whose interests are to be aggregated, represented, and brought to bear by business associations have a closer relationship to technology than do the associations. The literature on technical innovation stresses the significance of firms in the process of developing, producing, and utilizing new technology, whereas business associations are regarded as part of the organizational and institutional context within which the firms act (Steil *et al.*, 2002). However, the indirect link between technology and associations easily leads to underestimations of the importance of this relationship. Associations as corporate actors react to the challenges of technological changes and try to influence them in their own interest. First and foremost, these changes affect the membership side, i.e. the structure and the size of the associations' membership base. However, they also have an effect on the influence side, i.e. the associations' resources and the legitimacy of their goals and strategies.

For many firms it has become a matter of organizational routine to explore technological opportunities, improve search procedures, and refine their skills in developing and manufacturing new products (Dosi, 1988). Large firms with specialized R&D labs and as small firms with R&D facilities integrated into production are equally important in the process of technical advance (Nelson & Rosenberg, 1993). Moving the firms into the center of analysis of economic performance and technical innovativeness (Hall & Soskice, 2001b) does not imply that firms are innovative or that all firms are equally innovative. Nor does it imply that the firms, as single powerful units or as coordinated collective actors, control the course or the success of innovation processes. Some firms may enjoy a first-mover advantage that guarantees profits from a technical innovation, while others are often forced to adapt to the technology developed by more innovative competitors in order to survive in a market environment. Thus one does not have to assume a technologically determinist position to come to the conclusion that in a competitive environment, innovation frequently is a self-nourishing process in which 'innovation breeds innovation' (Baumol, 2002). It is the competitive pressure that drives the firms' search for innovation. This does not, however, rule out the possibility that the course of innovation is path dependent or remains in a narrow technological corridor shaped by internal dynamics.

Types of innovations

Many innovations remain within an existing 'technological paradigm' and develop along a given 'technological trajectory' (Dosi, 1982). They are incremental in nature and occur more or less continuously. Although these innovations are important because they help improve productivity and product quality, no single incremental innovation has dramatic effects (Freeman & Perez, 1988). Smooth adoption of incremental innovations may result in the competitive advantage of a firm, but the structure of an industry is rarely significantly affected by this type of innovation (Dolata & Werle, 2007).

Periods of incremental technological change may be interrupted by subsequent technological breakthroughs in which radical innovations evolve. In the first step they create 'technological discontinuity', which has been described as a process in which new firms and other actors such as professional associations and trade and business associations are set up. They frequently compete with established organizations and technologies (Rosenkopf & Tushman, 1994). Here, technologies and organizations coevolve, shaping and reconfiguring a 'technological community'. Generally only radical innovations have the potential to induce far-reaching changes at the level of firms as well as business associations.

Radical innovations render conventional technological knowledge obsolete and, in this sense, destroy competencies (Anderson & Tushman, 1990). They are based on different scientific and engineering principles and have the potential not only to replace specific components of technical systems, but also to significantly redesign products and reconfigure the architecture of production processes (Henderson & Clark, 1990). Two prominent areas of radical innovation are biotechnology and information and communication technology. Many observers consider the term 'revolution' to be most adequate to designate developments in both areas. Pharmaceutical and agricultural biotechnology is regarded as a technology that cross-cuts and overlays pharmaceutical, biological, and chemical knowledge. It has also fundamentally changed the methods of R&D in these areas (Evenson, 2002; Pisano, 2002). In the information and communication sector it was technical advances in the area of information technology that first drove the overall development. Digitization and the development of integrated circuits (microprocessors) have paved the way for the evolution of information technology as a general-purpose technology (Langlois, 2002).

Radical innovations, firms, and the strategies of business associations

Radical innovations threaten to erode the market position of established firms, because these firms are committed to successful incumbent technologies and often have difficulty in integrating radical innovations into production processes or into the products and services they offer on the market. Radical innovations provide the basis for the emergence of new firms and their successful market entry. New firms may outcompete previously dominant incumbents or even set up a new industry in the long run. But there is also competition between new firms. Several incompatible versions of a radically new technology may evolve and firms struggle to push through their respective variant. The new firms can be venture capital financed start-ups, but they can also be subsidiaries and spin-offs of established corporations and dependent on them in one way or another (Waesche, 2003). Market success of the new firms is contingent on the resources they have at their disposal and, even more, on their technical and scientific capabilities. Institutional factors and the strategy of business associations can also support or impede their entry into a new market and their market success. Associations are particularly important in periods of substantial technological, commercial, and regulatory uncertainty. Along with financial resources, information and consultation are urgently needed by firms established in an area of radical innovation. If and when a group of new firms evolves, they usually lack a developed structure of intermediaries such as business associations that meet their needs for organizational support, information exchange, or political leverage. Network relations among firms and links to some government agencies may serve as substitutes for business associations or for a few of their functions for some time. But it is likely that in institutional settings such as coordinated market economies in which business associations generally play an important role, associations will react to the emergence of new firms. Therefore, the landscape of associations will not remain unaffected by radical innovations, even if a group of new firms does not have the potential to establish a new industry and its intermediary structure.

Similarly to environmental effects on firms, radical technological innovations also create risks and opportunities for associations. Given that groups of new firms or new industries usually have some features in common with old industries and partly intersect or overlap with them, it appears likely that established associations in the respective old industries will try to extend their jurisdiction into the new domains. Otherwise they would not only miss the opportunity to gain new members, but also run the risk of losing those members who shift their core business from legacy to radically innovative technology.

Three complementary strategic options are available to established associations in order to attract new firms and new interests:

1. The first is *integration through internal differentiation*. Associations set up working groups that focus on the new technology and address the needs of firms that are active in this sector. Associations are very likely to choose this strategy if a number of their member firms have diversified into the new sector.
2. The second option is *establishing collaborative links with* neighboring *incumbent associations* if their jurisdictions reach into the new sector. They may jointly set up a new organizational unit as a *partly independent sector association* that focuses on the new technology. This strategy is attractive if two or more associations have member firms

that have diversified into the new sector. Such a sector association may *branch off* and develop into an independent organization if the new sector grows and is increasingly populated by new firms, but the association will maintain strong links to its 'parents'.
3. An established association can also *collaborate with emerging new associations* if new firms prefer to be represented by new associations that exclusively focus on the new technology. Collaboration with other associations in a new sector helps to avoid losing members that have diversified into the new sector and are looking for an association that addresses their interests and needs.

The relationship between established and new associations is not always collaborative and peaceful. Associations compete for members, and the competition is more intense the less a new sector differs from an established industry regarding the technological basis and the type of products and services offered by incumbent and new firms. This means, on the other hand, that competition is low or absent between associations in old industries and a new business association that has coevolved with a radical technical innovation and its industry.

Whether investors in new technologies prefer new business associations or are satisfied with the established ones is influenced by the characteristics of the technology. Generally again, radical innovations are likely to promote new associations because more often than not there will be a mismatch between what the established associations offer and what the firms in the new technological sector need. Whenever new technologies differ radically from established ones, the uncertainty with which firms have to cope if they invest in these technologies can be enormous. In this situation the firms will be interested in information and consultation services, professional conferences and training, opportunities to exchange information, and also standard setting. New associations specializing in the new technological sector often concentrate on providing these 'internal' services while their 'external' political leverage is low. But these internal services make them attractive to new firms in the early years of the development of a new sector. In a later stage when a sector is consolidating, the significance of political interest representation increases. This may prompt or strengthen collaboration between new associations and established ones.

Radical technological innovations tend to trigger the evolution of new sectors or industries and they change the structure of existing industries. All innovations do not have similar effects. Biotechnology, for example, is an innovation that cross-cuts, overlays, and augments pharmaceutical, biological, and chemical knowledge and supposedly does not trigger the evolution of a new industry. It may rather lead to a concentration of firms on their core competencies in the respective technological areas (e.g., pharmaceuticals, agrochemicals) and trigger a concomitant specialization of the incumbent business associations. This tendency will be reinforced by the divergent regulatory regimes governing the different sectors of this industry.

Information technology, however, is characterized by a general-purpose technology that can be employed in many industries. Apart from its universal applicability, information technology has the potential to create a new process-oriented industry or – more likely – to trigger the convergence of existing industries toward such an industry. Convergence candidates, aside from the traditional information technology industry (hardware and software vendors), are the telecommunications industry, the electronic media, and the internet sector, which to some observers already indicate the direction of convergence. Such a process does not only affect firms, but also business associations and the institutional and regulatory setting in which the industries are embedded. This technologically converging area is institutionally extremely heterogeneous in many countries (Müller & Werle, 2000). Technological change has induced institutional change, but processes of institutional reform have also been driven by economic and political-ideological factors that have no relation to technology (Schneider & Werle, 2007; Schneider & Haege, 2008). The tensions and dynamics resulting from parallel processes of change at the technological, institutional, and organizational (firms, business associations) level are illustrated in the next section.

The chemical industry, the dairy industry, and the information and communications industries compared

In this section we explore the economic and technological environments of business associations that operate in the dairy, chemical, and information and communications sectors in the UK, Germany, and the US. Obviously, these economic sectors are poles apart in their composition and economic performance. They originated in different centuries and thus represent different types of industry.

Agriculture is one of the oldest economic sectors in the history of humankind. The dairy industry as an agricultural subsector also evolved only slowly toward industrialization within the last 100 years. Today, the dairy industry still consists of small and medium-sized enterprises and is rather homogeneous due to low innovation rates.

The *chemical industry* originated in the eighteenth century with the advent of large-scale manufacturing of chemical products such as sulfuric acid. During the nineteenth and twentieth centuries it became one of the largest and probably most important economic sectors in terms of contribution to GDP and innovation rates. Additionally, the chemical industry is tied to almost all other economic sectors through sales and purchases, thereby enhancing its overall economic importance by means of linkage effects. In the last decades major innovations have taken place in the field of the life sciences, which have heavily affected the organization of the pharmaceutical and healthcare industries, although not the chemical sector in its entirety.

The *information and communications sector* is the most recent and one of the most innovative and rapidly changing sectors. Its foundations date back to the end of the 1970s when the introduction of integrated circuits led to a steady size and cost reduction in electronic devices. Together with digitization, it permitted computers to exchange data directly through the telephone network. On this basis diverse technologies converged, integrating telecommunications, the internet, but also broadcasting and new electronic media, leading to a multitude of innovations in the services and hardware market (Sandholtz, 1993; Latzer, 1997).

Recent economic developments in agriculture, chemicals, and information and communications are depicted in Figure 3.1. Similarly to technological innovation cycles, the economic potential varies considerably between these industries. Agriculture in Britain and Germany stagnated during the period 1992–2002, with low market growth and decreasing foreign trade. The chemicals sector, in contrast, shows rather high growth rates, in particular in the US, which clearly outstrips British and German market growth. Equally, foreign trade doubled in Germany and Britain but quadrupled in the US. The information and communications sector has not only undergone fundamental technological changes but has also seen extraordinary growth rates that far exceed other economic sectors. In all countries under study, the growth rates of market volume and foreign trade more than doubled. German market development is the only exception.

In sum, the dairy, chemical, and information and communications industries provide examples of industries at different stages of their economic and technological life cycles. The industries also reveal country differences that, as we hypothesize, should lead to different adaptation processes and strategies.

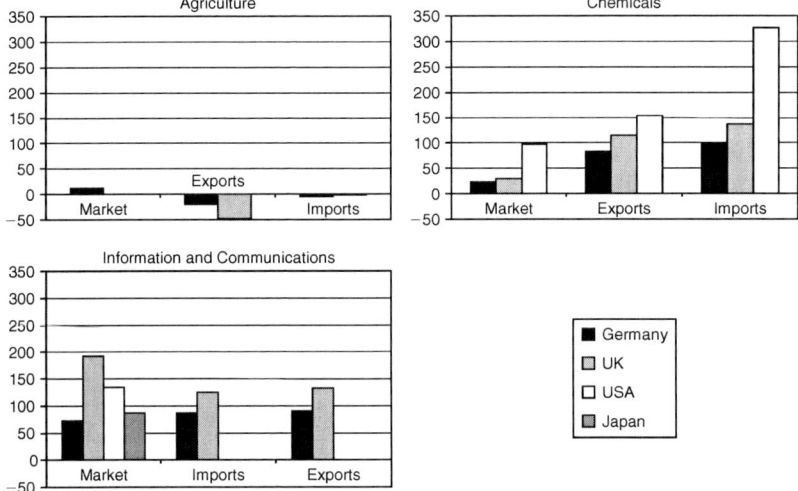

Figure 3.1 Changes in market volume and foreign trade from 1992 to 2002 (in percent)
Sources: EITO, 1994, 1999, 2004; OECD Stan Database, 2002; CEFIC, 2006.

Adaptation in different political, economic, and technological settings: Conclusions

In the previous sections we have outlined how political, economic, and technological environments affect business associations and associational systems. Our main argument is that economic and technological variables exert indirect pressures on business associations that are triggered by changes at the membership level, while political factors have a direct impact on associational interest representation. Of course, there exist several other causal chains by which economic and technological factors may influence business associations. However, these causal mechanisms are more remote and their effects are less obvious and more disturbed than the effects via the member firms of business associations (see Figure 3.2). We will thus concentrate on analyzing plausible and likely effects of this causal chain in the three sectors.

Political factors exert a direct influence on the structuring and behavior of business associations and associational landscapes. In the previous sections we have distinguished between various theoretical approaches that deal with adaptation of interest groups and organized business, and we separated the causal mechanisms according to the triad polity, politics,

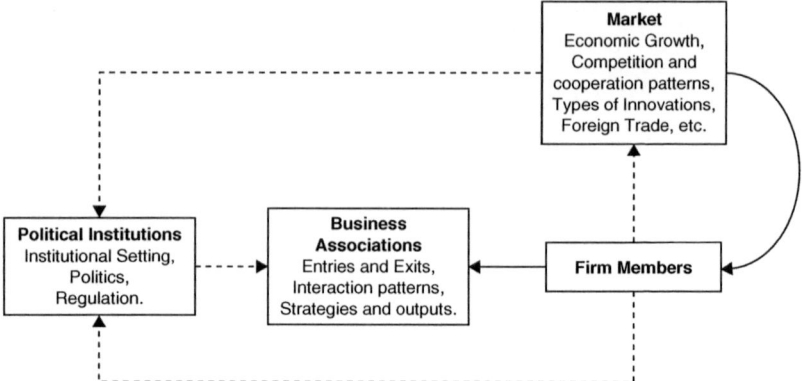

Figure 3.2 Economic and technological changes affecting systems of business associations

Note: Bold lines indicate a direct impact, dotted lines specify indirect causal chains.

and policy. Our main countries under examination – Germany, the UK and the US – have been affected by some of these political variables; however, not by all of them and not to the same extent.

Europeanization, conceptualized as effects of European integration within EU member states, is one of our analytical points of reference and an example of differential affectedness. We assume the effect of Europeanization to be restricted to EU member states. Likely consequences are the shifting of lobbying activities to the supra-national level, while domestic lobbying is reduced or held constant. Sector differences appear to be rather small. However, EU activities regulating the chemical industry started earlier than in the information and communications sector, which should make chemical industry associations more experienced at accessing EU institutions.

Another important issue, which was discussed in the previous sections, is the diversification and fragmentation of political arenas across countries and sectors, which includes the growing importance of novel players such as regulatory agencies. The transfer of decision-making powers to these independent and autonomous governmental units has changed the make-up of political systems, particularly in the information and communications sector. Yet the establishment of independent regulatory agencies started in the US in the 1970s and subsequently diffused to other areas in the world. As a result, regulatory agencies have increasingly become lobbying targets of organized business interests.

Table 3.1 Industry characteristics

	I&C	Chemicals	Dairy
Innovation rate	High	Medium	Low
Market growth	High	Medium	Low
Imports	High	Medium (growth rates)/ High (volume)	Low
Exports	High	Medium (growth rates)/ High (volume)	Low

In contrast to political variables that have a direct impact on business associations, the effects of economic and technological factors are mediated by the level of affectedness of the association's company members.

As has been shown above, the chemical, dairy, and information and communications sectors represent distant poles in terms of economic and technological development, which are likely to lead their associational systems to evolve in different directions.

The dairy industry represents a pre-industrialized sector that is characterized by saturated markets, low internationalization, and slow innovation. The chemical industry, in contrast, is globalized and exhibits medium market growth and innovation rates. However, some branches clearly stand out within the chemical industry. In particular, biotechnology is highly dynamic and has changed the make-up of the industry by blurring boundaries between sub-branches such as pharmaceuticals and agrochemicals. The information and communications sector currently marks the cutting edge in economic performance and dynamics, since it is highly productive and continually innovating (see Table 3.1). We hypothesize that these differences in industry characteristics lead to different trajectories of associational development across sectors as well as across countries. According to pluralist and population ecology accounts, associational systems mirror their surrounding environments. Economic and technological factors therefore change the composition and structures of branches and markets and then exert indirect effects on business associations via their members.

The dairy industry shows slow and marginal changes in technology, market composition, and foreign trade. Variance across countries is very low and insignificant. Based on these findings we do not expect major restructurings within the system of sectoral business associations that are affected by economic or technological factors.

The chemical industry has faced some changes in market structure, particularly in branches that have been affected by the biotech 'revolution'. Imports and exports have grown considerably. However, there exist major differences between countries. In Great Britain and Germany growth rates in import and export are fairly matched, while the US has seen import rates that clearly outnumber exports. Furthermore, market dynamics are significantly higher in the US than in the UK and Germany. We generally expect new business associations to be established in the realm of biotech and adjacent branches. But as the biotech 'revolution' cross-cuts existing branches rather than creates a new industry, incumbent associations are likely to expand their domains in order to include biotech or merge with other associations for the same purpose. Furthermore, given the differences between the US on the one side and Germany and Great Britain on the other, there will be major differences between countries concerning the structuring and behavior of associations. The US system should be more fluid than the two European countries regarding the creation and dissolution of associations.

The information and communications sector has undergone major changes in sector composition. In contrast to the chemicals industry with its cross-cutting biotech innovation, the information and communications industry has experienced a profound evolution toward an entirely new industry. The convergence – on the basis of a multipurpose technology with strong network effects – of formerly distinct branches toward a new process-oriented industry poses severe adaptation pressures on the existing systems of business associations. We expect higher associational dynamics, for example more foundations, 'acquisitions', and mergers in the information and communications sector than in the dairy or chemicals domain. Due to potentially overlapping interests, information and communications associational systems should display higher competition densities contrasted to the more settled organized interests in the other sectors. In addition, the continually changing nature of the information and communications industry is less likely to yield hierarchical associational structures than are less fluid sectors.

In conclusion, this chapter has provided a sketch of 'external' environmental factors that exert adaptation pressures on systems of business associations and has hypothesized likely outcomes for the dairy, chemical, and information and communications sectors. The following chapters will seek evidence of whether adaptation is indeed a reaction to the environmental changes mentioned above, or is rather driven by 'internal' factors such as the level of interconnectedness between business associations within each associational system.

Part II
Business Associations at the National Level

4
Persistent Divergence? Chemical Business Associations in Britain and Germany

Jürgen R. Grote

In many comparative accounts of industrial sectors, Britain and Germany have been taken to highlight the features of two distinct ways of (regulatory) policy making and of managing state–society relations. Policy making in the UK has been described as informal, confidential, and based on close relationships between public authorities and firms, while regulation is 'reasonable, practical, and flexible' (Brickman *et al.*, 1985: 225). At the same time, interest systems tend to be comparatively fragmented and state–society relations typically exhibit pluralist patterns (for many other characteristics, see Schmidt, 2006). In Germany, sectoral governance has been by self-regulation and policy making is significantly more formal and structured than in the British case. Both producer groups and public authorities prefer 'statutory precision' and a 'faithful execution of regulatory requirements' (Brickman *et al.*, 1985: 231). Germany's interest system, in turn, has been said to be relatively compact with state–society relations well ordered, highly formalized, and of an essentially corporatist nature. If this has been the case for many of the more traditional sectors, it has been even more pronounced in the chemical industry (see Grant *et al.*, 1988).

Meanwhile, as shall be argued in this chapter, the British associational system, after initial moves in the opposite direction, has become somewhat more structured while there are signs of disintegration at least at the margins of the German system. Although no profound changes have occurred over the past 30 years or so, divergence may be less persistent today. The path dependency still characterizing the core of interest intermediation in both countries is now eased by partial convergence in parts of the systems triggered by path-creating efforts of political entrepreneurs within the respective business communities, or by the laws of motion of globalization and Europeanization. This is the most one can say when considering institutional developments for which a couple of decades is anything but just an instant within longer trajectories that often reach back far into the eighteenth century and beyond – at least in the absence of path-breaking turmoil.

Globalization and Europeanization as new challenges to British and German chemical industry associations

Business associations need to respond not only to membership demands and expectations, but also to the interests and demands of public authorities. In their seminal treatise on the different logics to which business associations have to respond, Schmitter and Streeck (1999 [1981]) coined the notion of 'logic of membership' for exchange relations between business associations and their member firms. Exchange in this logic basically includes resource procurement and service provision. The 'logic of influence', on the other hand, denotes all associational activities related to interest representation and to strategies aimed at accessing public authorities (Bouwen, 2004).

Globalization and Europeanization in the world of chemicals production have had a lasting impact on the structure of markets and of political systems in the last few decades, thus affecting either the logic of membership or the logic of influence of chemical business associations.

Economic and technological challenges

The chemical industry occupies a leading position in terms of economic development and technological innovations among industrial and service sectors in developed countries. British and German companies are among the world's leaders in the chemical sector. From a global perspective, Germany is in third place behind the US and Japan while holding first place in Europe ahead of France, the UK, and Italy. Together, these four countries produce about 65 percent of chemical output in Europe. Export, import, production, gross fixed capital formation, and value added continuously increased between 1980 and 2000, in part doubling and tripling the earlier figures (Young and Partners, 2003a, 2003b, 2003c). These developments are both a result of and a condition for the sector's outstanding performance, which did not witness any dramatic downturn or loss in market share. Figures for most indices for Germany are roughly twice those of Britain.

The chemical industry is made up of seven branches. These are basic chemicals; agrochemicals; paints, varnishes, and inks; manmade fibers; soaps, toiletry, and cosmetics; other specialties; and pharmaceuticals. The great significance of the biotech revolution has slowly started to affect the sector as a whole. From the governance perspective at the population level of organized interests, the branch is increasingly difficult to keep within the boundaries of what the chemical industry has been throughout its postwar history. The interest domain is in a state of flux. If, as suggested by our interviews and by the data on traditional chemicals and on pharmaceuticals, sector identity is generally in decline, this is particularly pronounced among the young and dynamic entrepreneurs of the hundreds of research labs active in both countries.

Over the past two decades, the share of basic chemicals in Germany (industrial gases, dyes and pigments, basic organics and inorganics, fertilizers, plastic and synthetic rubber, and so on) has remained almost unaltered. It was at about 51 percent in 1979 and still is at 50 percent today. Pharmaceuticals grew from 14 percent in 1979 to almost 19 percent in 1999 (VCI, 2000), mostly at the expense of the remaining branches. In the UK, basic chemicals declined to 31 percent of the sector's turnover, while pharmaceutical products improved their position significantly, accounting for almost 32 percent in 1998 (Chemical Industries Association, 2000). Due to restructuring, UK pharmaceuticals are today stronger than basic chemicals.

While hardly anything of the above is particularly challenging to the industry, it is the side effects of internationalization that really matter. The current recomposition of the sector, it seems, mainly results from mergers and acquisitions. The increasing sector concentration resulting from this trend puts additional strain on associations, particularly with respect to the internal divide between the interests of larger and smaller companies.[1]

Political challenges

The presence of the EU is very pronounced in the chemical sector, where supra-national competencies are comprehensive and possess a long-established tradition. Within the first wave of chemicals regulation during the late 1970s, international activities by the OECD strongly interacted with legislation at the European and national level (Brickman et al., 1985; Schneider, 1988). Domestic politics and regulations are likely to remain of crucial importance to national business associations, which, of course, have also to react to international and European challenges, since these are steadily increasing in relevance (Ronit & Schneider, 2000).

The most important policy domain for chemical associations is environmental politics. In this area a continual growth in regulatory activity has taken place over the past two decades. Between 1980 and 1996, 31 Regulations, Recommendations, Decisions, or Directives were passed by both the Council of Europe and the European Commission. In addition, there have been 23 changes to Directives directly affecting the industry. Regulatory density has greatly increased, with 12 Decisions of the Commission within the timeframe 1991–6 (Munz, 2001: 44–8). Meanwhile a new wave of regulation resulted in a major initiative involving a large amount of organizational resources of domestic and EU-level chemical associations. This is the Commission's *White Paper on the Strategy for a Future Chemicals Policy* (EU Commission, 2001b). The document provides that 2700 new and around 100,000 old substances, previously examined according to different standards, be subject to a comparable control procedure within the framework of a unified system (REACH, i.e., Registration, Evaluation, and Authorization of Chemicals) by 2012. The White Paper has been a major political challenge for the chemicals industry and its organizations, not least because the Directives and Regulations resulting from it gradually came into effect after June 2007 and became fully binding in June 2008 (see Chapter 9). The final REACH timetable now spans the period from 2008 until 2018 (the end of the 'phase-in' period).

The Europeanization of politics continues to be important for business associations. It does not only result from the sheer number of regulations produced at that level, but equally concerns the emergence and spread of entirely new organizational forms – that is, EU associations, individual firms, and alliances of firms – which actively influence public authorities and thereby alter traditional patterns of access. The growth of EU associations has received ample attention, although with decreasing enthusiasm in more recent years. Euro-associations do not seem to be major challenges to domestic groups and this also holds for CEFIC, the European chemical industry's peak association (see Chapter 9). Although German associations have more voice in CEFIC than any other national group, tasks are generally divided among domestic and supra-national associations and both seem to benefit from that practice. More risky for these associations is the institutionalization of practices at that level (direct lobbying, roundtables), which still is exceptional for more corporatist countries. In direct lobbying, firms and alliances of firms are the key players. Because of the dual character of firms to be potential competitors on political markets and, at the same time, the major resource base of business associations, these activities are risky since they may operate from both below and above the organizational hierarchy.

Perception of challenges

Environmental challenges become relevant for the behavior and structuring of British and German chemical associations only if they are perceived as challenges by representatives of these business associations.

Leading officials of the two countries' chemical associations have very similar perceptions of the political, technological, and economic challenges that their associations have to face. The overwhelming majority of representatives in both countries (more than 80 percent) state that political challenges have been at least important for their associations, while technological challenges have rarely been noticed (lower than 40 percent) as major drivers of associative behavior and change.[2] The opinions about economic factors differ widely between British and German respondents. Only 34 percent of German representatives view economic challenges as important or most important, while 77 percent of British representatives do.[3]

Highly significant are the judgments made in relation to the territorial level identified as the origin of challenges. Most respondents agree on that point. British and German associations believe the national, European, and global levels to be equally important in terms of economic challenges. The European level is said to be significant primarily with respect to politics (UK 83 percent, Germany 64 percent), while most technological challenges are believed to result from global developments (UK 83 percent, Germany 70 percent).

Changes in structure and composition of the British and German systems of chemical industry associations

In the previous sections we described the major driving forces of adaptation and change in chemical industry associations. It has become clear that there are few differences between British and German associations regarding their level of affectedness. We therefore assume that both associational systems have not undergone significant changes, with the noteworthy exception of pharmaceuticals as well as biotechnology and life sciences, which would be expected to have developed differently compared to the rest of the branches making up the sector.

The transformation of the associational landscape: Entries, mergers, and splits

Apart from a couple of renaming events, especially in Britain,[4] over the past 20 years only a few new groups have been added to the set of chemical industry associations in general. Among our focal associations in

Germany, these are the association for surface protection liquids in industrial applications (IHO, founded 1992), the association of research-intensive pharmaceutical manufacturers (VFA, founded 1994), and the sector group for biotechnology companies (DIB, founded 1998).

In contrast to Britain where pharmaceuticals have established themselves as a sector in its own right, in Germany they continue to be regarded as part of the chemical sector. Accordingly, despite being strong and powerful within the pharmaceutical industry, which now accounts for a major share of chemicals as a whole, the focal associations representing the interests of that branch in both countries (especially Britain's ABPI and Germany's VFA) occupy rather marginal positions in the overall sector's ecology (see below).

The German case is of particular interest here. In fact, the combined effects of technological innovation (the emergence of biotechnology), political legislation (various reforms of the system of healthcare costs and of the patterns of competition), and new ownership structures (the bulk of pharmaceuticals in Germany now being produced by subsidiaries of large multinationals) as the main forces able to trigger interest cleavages across types of firms have found responses within the overall sector's interest population that are anything but typical of an otherwise rather corporatist set-up. They are also indicative of what might happen to corporatist interest associations under conditions of internationalization.

One of the most influential and best-resourced branch associations of the VCI, the *Bundesverband der Pharmazeutischen Industrie* (BPI), has been the main victim of the first break-off within the population. In 1993 the BPI split into an association for research-based and mostly multinational companies, the *Verband Forschender Arzneimittelhersteller* (VFA), and one for smaller and medium-sized producers (under the old name of the BPI). Triggers for this split were strong disagreements about the registration of pharmaceuticals and political measures for cost control, which surfaced out of severe conflicts between small versus large enterprises and research-based companies versus producers of generic and over-the-counter medicines. Today, the VFA is Germany's most important pharmaceutical association.[5] Albeit forming part of the group of 21 branch associations of the VCI, the VFA maintains a rather independent position vis-à-vis its peak association and is quite autonomous with respect to lobbying. The latter also applies to other groups not affiliated to the VCI, namely the voices of producers of over-the-counter medicines, (BAH, *Bundesverband der Arzneimittelhersteller*) and of generic producers (VAP, *Verband aktiver Pharmaunternehmer*). While organizational splits so far have mainly resulted from innovation, legislation, and ownership structures, a further cleavage line accounting for organizational fragmentation has been size.[6] Generic producers are today represented by *Pro Generika* (founded in 2004), which brings together larger enterprises, and by the DGV (*Deutscher Generikaverband*), which mainly counts small and medium-sized companies among its members. The division into five major branch associations plus further three biotech associations besides the DIB led one executive of the Ministry of Health to say that 'in no other branch is it easier to neutralize the lobbying efforts of different interest associations' (*Die Welt*, 22 December 2007). The low political profile of the branch in the country's capital has now been recognized by most affected associations themselves. There have been initiatives toward setting up a new peak association of pharmaceutical producers; although, at the time of writing, no result has been achieved yet.

In the British system of chemical industry associations the overall number of focal associations has remained relatively stable over the last two decades, now amounting to 14. The first of the two newly founded associations was the *Specialised Organic Chemicals Sectors Association* (SOCSA), which was set up in 1993 and, albeit not wholeheartedly, joined the country's peak association, the CIA (*Chemicals Industry Association*), in the same year.[7] The second was BCF, the *British Coatings Federation*, also founded in 1993. One remarkable change, however, was the creation of AIA (1991), the *Alliance of Industry Associations*, which functions as if it were a proper organization in its own right. In reality it merely represents a forum and coordinating device for a number of smaller associations that have combined to pool resources and to increase their clout in lobbying against the dominating influence of Britain's number one association, the CIA. Most associations forming part of our focal association set in Britain are AIA affiliates.

Overall, apart from the German VFA, IHO, and DIB and the British SOCSA and BCF, no further organizations have been added to the two domestic interest populations identified by us as focal association sets.[8] Due to this inactivity in terms of new foundations, splits, and mergers, some of the following information may seem somewhat redundant. We nevertheless include Figure 4.1 for the purpose of comparison across sectors and countries.

Cooperation and competition within associational systems

In the 1980s, the German system of chemical interest associations was frequently characterized as a typical corporatist configuration centering on one single peak association (Grant *et al.*, 1988). Little seems to

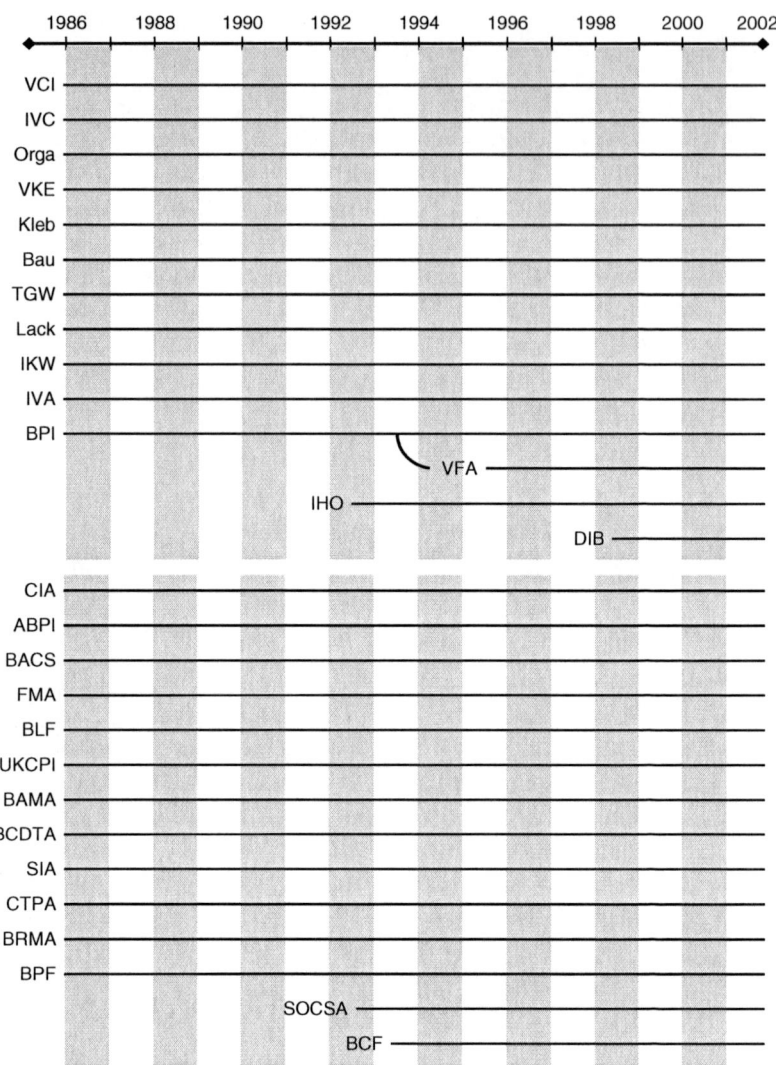

Figure 4.1 Entries, mergers, and splits in the German (above) and British (below) associational systems

have changed since then. Like 20 years ago, the associational system is dominated by one all-encompassing peak organization, the *Verband der Chemischen Industrie* (VCI). The VCI is internally divided among a total of 10 territorial associations, while its organizational core is its

21 branch associations (*Fachverbände*) and 10 sector groups (*Fachvereinigungen*). Most of these operate from the association's headquarters in Frankfurt, while the others run their offices close to the production sites of their major member companies. This structure has remained unaltered over the past two decades and has been in place since earlier studies on the sector (Grant, 1991a; Platzer, 1984). The same applies to the number of the more relevant of these associations. Grant reported that the number of important first-order associations was 'fifteen in chemicals' (Grant, 1991a: 48); that is, exactly half the overall number of VCI associates in Germany. Again, although Grant's focus was on a slightly different type of association (the peak association plus the most important branch associations of industrial chemicals outside the VCI), the result of our expert-panel-based boundary specification (see for this Laumann *et al.*, 1983) is almost the same, with today 14 focal associations forming the core of the organizational population.

To evaluate the degree of competition and cooperation, we asked CEOs of business associations first to name other trade associations with which they have frequent contacts, and second to indicate other business associations that are also active in the same branch. These relations were then combined in such a way that we are now able to identify symmetric as well as asymmetric patterns of competition and cooperation.

The German ecological network of chemical industry associations exhibits a perfect hierarchical structure with one central actor (VCI), with all other actors linked to it by way of cooperative – that is, mutualist – relations (see Figure 4.2). The links connecting VCI affiliates among each other are relatively sparse and predominantly indicate partial cooperation. Few competitive relations exist, for instance, between more recently established pharmaceutical, biotech, and life sciences associations. This may be taken as an indicator that pharmaceuticals is likely to establish itself as an autonomous sector in its own right in the near future.

In the early 1980s, the British *Chemicals Industry Association* (CIA) exhibited features similar to those of Germany's VCI. Albeit primarily organizing manufacturers of industrial chemicals, many of the smaller sector associations representing chemicals users and specialty producers (rubber, paints, coatings, toiletry, cosmetics, fertilizers, and so on) also originated from it or have in some way been affiliated. Until about that time, the CIA was a peak association for all sorts of subsectors and branches. Examples of this, in particular, are the older groups such as the *Fertilizers Manufacturing Association* (FMA) or the *British Chemical Distributors and Traders Association* (BCDTA), founded in 1923. Other more recently created groups such as the *British Aerosol Manufacturers*

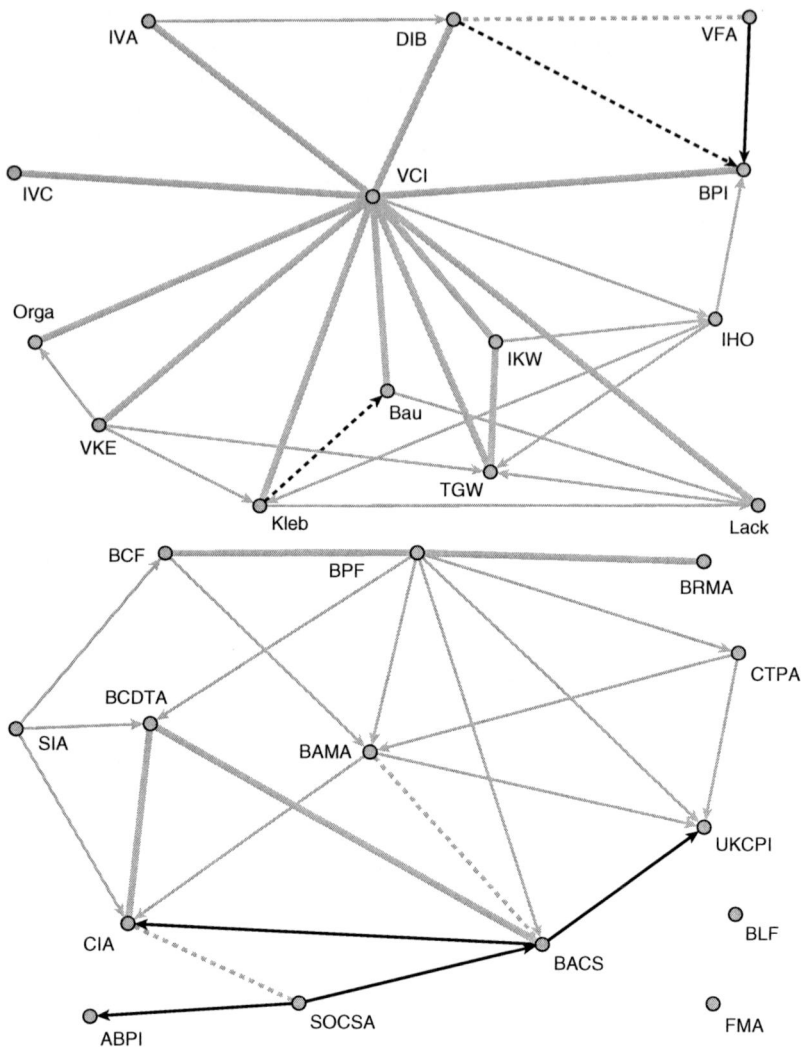

Figure 4.2 Ecological relations in the German (above) and British (below) associational networks

Notes

Relations (examples in parenthesis)
Gray, bold, continuous: Mutualism (e.g., BCDTA–BACS)
Gray, thin, continuous: Partial cooperation (Kleb–Lack, or SIA–BCF)
Gray, bold, dashed: Neutrality (BAMA–BACS)
Black, bold, continuous: Full competition (none)
Black, thin, continuous: Partial competition (e.g., VFA–BPI, or BACS–CIA)
Black, thin, dashed: 'Harmful' competition (e.g., DIB–BPI, or Kleb–Bau)

Association (BAMA), the *Crop Protection Association* (CPA), and the *British Association for Chemical Specialties* (BACS) also had strong links to the CIA or operated from its premises. Finally, another large and influential sector group – the *Association of the British Pharmaceutical Industry* (ABPI) – had always been one of CIA's affiliate members. By now almost outdoing its peak association both in terms of staff and financial resources, it continues to be so today.

Today, however, Britain's associational population of chemicals producers is far less centered on a single group. In particular, pharmaceuticals have emerged as the largest subsector, accounting for more than 30 percent of gross value added. Those branches characterized in terms of peripheral subsectors only a decade ago (Grant, 1991a: 50) have significantly increased their shares of the sector's turnover and output. Accordingly, the country's organized interest population is today divided up between three types of actors: the CIA, the ABPI, and the AIA.

The CIA still is the most important of these, not least because it is the only group trying to maintain organizational cohesion for the entire sector and to convince smaller associations to join. It has a staff of around 50 (CIA Annual Report, 2000), but probably employs close to 70 people including external collaborators and experts. The second association of relevance in the interest population is ABPI. It continues to be formally affiliated to the CIA but, essentially, is a properly autonomous association that operates in a field having little to do with chemicals in the traditional sense. Its staff numbers are almost the same as the CIA. Facing less membership diversity, it may well be more powerful than even its own peak association. Finally, the third central group is AIA,[9] an alliance of chemical specialty associations many of which were once formally affiliated to the CIA.[10]

One of the most important general features of the UK's associational landscape currently is the building of alliances among interest groups (see Boléat, 2000; Trade Association Forum, 2002). Chemical associations are affected by that as well. Diminishing resources as the result of members' exit and of company mergers have made the fragmented status quo less and less sustainable to smaller business associations. As mentioned by one of our interviewees, company mergers ultimately call for associational mergers (see also Brophy, 2000). Where this is not possible in the short term, other and less demanding organizational forms need to be considered.

AIA is the most articulate manifestation that these developments have taken in the chemical sector. It brings together almost all of the more relevant smaller associations outside the CIA and the ABPI. In our interviews, many of AIA's leaders underlined that they actually do not have feelings of belonging to what the chemical sector might have been in the past. Sector identity, instead, is based on product groups such as plastics, coatings, cosmetics, and so forth. AIA brings together downstream user associations operating in these branches. Its members meet several times a year to discuss matters of common concern and often take stances on regulatory matters that are sometimes in contradiction to the position of CIA. The Alliance is also trying to prevent what its members perceive to be a hostile takeover; that is, reintegration into the structure of CIA.[11] Although there are no permanent offices, AIA has a number of standing committees and ad hoc working groups on issues such as the EU's White Paper on a future chemicals policy. At the time of our fieldwork, meetings were at the premises of CTPA while the alliance was chaired by the director of BCF, an association that, in contrast to many other AIA members, has never been associated to the CIA. AIA meanwhile is so firmly consolidated that the prospects of the CIA reassuming its leadership role are quite low.

These changes in the membership base and attitudes have left their mark in the relational patterns of completion and cooperation between the UK's chemical industry associations (Figure 4.2). The ecological network is primarily made up of cooperative relations linking, in particular, AIA members, which have developed a dense network of cooperation that now dominates the entire structure. In contrast, the former peak association CIA is embedded in a network consisting of various relations such as mutualism (with BCDTA, which is an affiliate of both CIA and AIA), neutrality (with SOCSA), asymmetric cooperation (with BAMA and SIA), and asymmetric competition (with BACS). This illustrates that CIA has lost its once central position and is now surrounded by a multitude of smaller associations active in establishing a new point of gravity within the system around their point of reference, the AIA. Similar to the German ecological network, competitive relations are few and primarily center on the *Association for Chemical Specialties* (BACS).

Formal and informal hierarchies: Information exchange networks

Systems of business associations are not only integrated by networks of competition and cooperation, but may also operate according to forms of hierarchical or horizontal coordination. In order to grasp the extent to which chemical industry associations have established coordination capacities, we collected data on the sending and receiving of information and visualized them according to the centrality of business associations in the network. Central associations are located in the center of the graph, while less central actors are positioned at the periphery.

In the German case, the structure of information exchange[12] corroborates what has been argued above: The interest population exhibits features typical of corporatist associational systems (see Figure 4.3). The VCI dominates the entire flow of information and acts as information broker for most other sector associations. Only a few other associations maintain exchange relations among themselves. The VFA, as one of the VCI's most powerful members, turns out to be rather isolated. This results from the delivery of information not being reciprocated in that case. The few emerging clusters are due to product affinities (biotech and pharmaceuticals; textiles, soaps, and surface protection; construction, coatings, and adhesives). The overall result is an extremely pronounced hierarchy of relations with network density being comparatively low.

All this, of course, does not imply that individual sector associations do not communicate with each other at all. Most communication, however, is organized and mediated by the VCI's central infrastructure. Information relevant to the sector associations is collected and distributed within the VCI's committees and task forces, from where it can easily be retrieved. Individual members, hence, are to some extent relieved from approaching each other for important information. They thus acquire additional (relational) resources for pursuing contacts to other actors of their organizational ecology and are free to make investments in their wider contact portfolio (public authorities, international organizations, and so on) to an extent that would otherwise not be possible.

The British network of information exchange shows some similarities as well as some differences compared to the German system. A number of elements stand out. The CIA now occupies the central position in the network. At the same time, network density is considerably higher than in the German case. In other words, Britain's chemical interest population is far less dominated by any one of its most powerful organizations. A significant amount of time and other associational resources tends to be absorbed by activities of inter-organizational coordination spanning the entire space of the graph. Members of the AIA basically make up a network in their own right. If we were to remove the CIA from the center of the plot, the overall structure of exchange would not disintegrate thanks to the manifold direct links among the AIA's affiliates and other associations. Business associations more closely attached to the CIA, such as the FMA, have rather few ties to other associations. Others, such as the British Lubricants Federation (BLF) that are neither members of the AIA nor closely connected to the CIA, are less embedded in the information

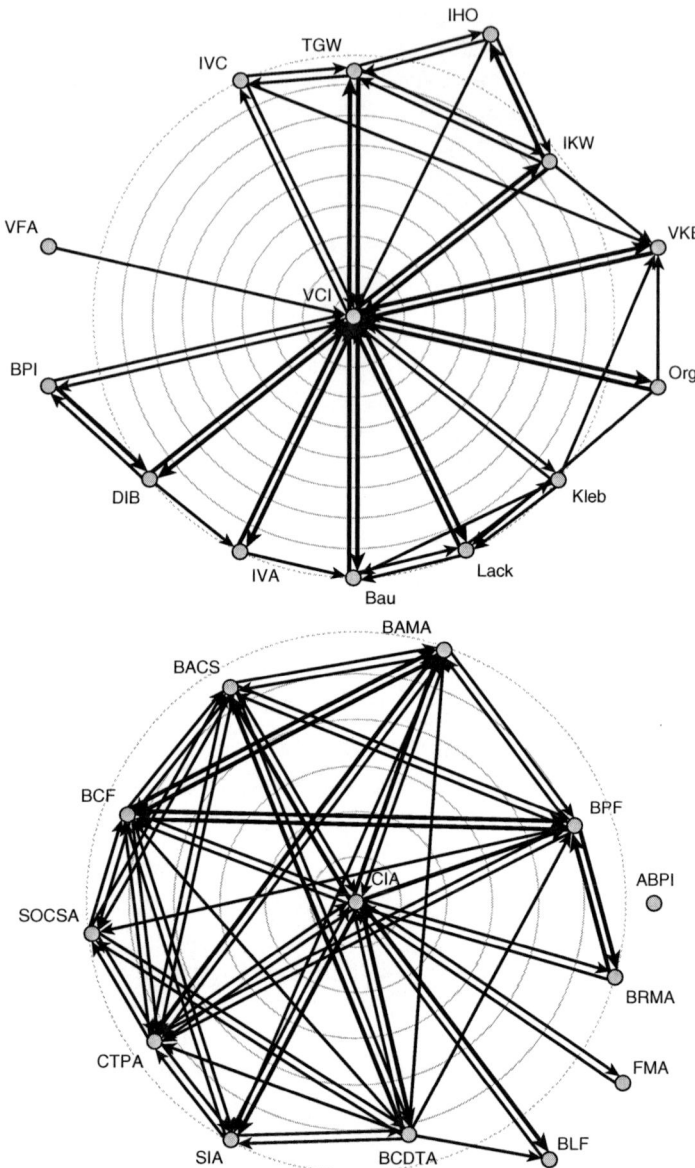

Figure 4.3 Information exchange in the German (above) and British (below) associational networks (betweenness centrality)
Notes
Relations:
Bold: frequent information exchange
Thin: occasional information exchange

exchange network. The British chemical interest population then turns out to be a 'network of organizations', while the German one more resembles a 'network organization'. Similar to Germany's VFA, but much more pronounced in this case, one important and powerful association (ABPI) remains isolated in terms of information exchange. Again, this is indicative of the autonomous position pharmaceuticals have obtained in both countries.

It is unlikely that the alliance network will transform into a properly merged structure in the foreseeable future. Considering the development over the past two decades, it is interesting to see how many of the groups today forming part of the AIA initially depended on the CIA. Although they have achieved more autonomy since the 1980s, they soon recognized the need for a more robust infrastructure to rely on and have, in their turn, decided to pool resources in the form of a less formalized alliance network. The picture emerging, therefore, is one of successive disintegration and reintegration. Integrative forces were particularly pronounced during the heyday of the CIA, up to about the early 1980s. Disintegration set in with the departure of smaller groups from the CIA and is most evident today in the increasingly autonomous position of the ABPI. Reintegration, finally, is now emerging around the AIA and yet other alliances of more peripheral actors not considered in this chapter. It is important to note that none of the ties represented in Figure 4.3 is redundant. The AIA's matrix structure in particular, on which most of its operations are based and according to which tasks are shared and responsibilities divided, makes these relations mandatory. Albeit weaker and less hierarchical than the ones connecting the German interest population, they absorb quite substantial resources precisely in a period where associations are facing increasing financial constraints and where different types of challenges are placing increasingly more requirements on domestic associations to extend the scope of their activities beyond the boundaries of their own population toward more encompassing organizational and policy communities.

The reorganization of associational tasks: Strategies of adaptation

Adaptation and change are not restricted to the population level alone but also cover the behavior and structure of business associations. In order to get an impression of how chemical industry associations invest their financial and personnel resources, we asked the respondents to allocate 100 points to nine different tasks, three of which concern lobbying

Table 4.1 Average resource allocation (in percent) and changes (frequency) of chemical business associations in Germany and Britain

Activities	Resource allocation				Changes			
	Mean		Standard deviation		Increase (frequency)		Decrease (frequency)	
	D	UK	D	UK	D	UK	D	UK
National lobbying	19.5	17.5	10.9	8.3	6	4	–	2
International/ European lobbying	11.0	10.2	5.0	5.3	6	10	–	–
Societal lobbying	13.4	6.3	7.4	5.3	1	2	2	1
Influence investments	**43.9**	**34.0**			**13**	**16**	**2**	**3**
Member consultation	13.4	15.8	5.6	7.6	–	–	3	1
Member information	13.3	18.8	6.0	7.8	4	2	–	–
Member conferences	17.8	12.9	11.5	6.7	3	1	–	1
Side benefits	2.5	4.8	3.7	11.1	1	1	4	3
Training	2.5	6.6	3.5	5.8	–	1	3	2
Membership investments	**49.5**	**58.9**			**8**	**5**	**7**	**7**
Other	6.6	6.8	7.8	11.7	–	1	–	1
Total	100	99.7			21	22	9	11

activities and five ways of directly servicing the needs of members. Table 4.1 presents the average resource allocation of British and German focal associations.[13] Even though they are remarkably similar, there are a few differences worth mentioning. There is a clear dominance of membership-related activities. Only about 40 percent of associational resources are spent on the provision of public goods such as lobbying at the domestic and supra-national levels. At the same time, both groups of associations invest around 55 percent of resources in servicing their members. Differences in resource allocation between populations can be attributed to the higher significance of societal lobbying (public relations, marketing, and 'sociopolitical gardening') for the German business associations. In contrast, British associations invest considerably more resources in membership activities.

In our questionnaire we also asked the representatives of chemical industry associations which of these activities had clearly lost or gained in importance over the last couple of years. The results were unequivocal. Most representatives reported an increase in lobbying activities on the national as well as on the European level, while only a few mentioned decreasing investments in, particularly, societal lobbying. With regard to membership activities, increases and decreases were balanced and evenly distributed across activities.

Descriptive statistics of resource allocation give a first impression of which types of activities are preferred by members of the two associational systems. However, it largely ignores within-system variation becoming manifest in form of differing degrees of specialization. Hierarchical cluster analysis is an appropriate tool for detecting profile homogeneity within associational systems. The results indicate that the British and German associational landscapes are internally diverse, but can be grouped into three relatively homogeneous clusters of business associations allocating resources in quite similar ways:

- In Cluster I, more than half of the chemical industry associations under study concentrate their resource allocation in membership-related activities (about 70 percent). Among these associations are the VCI, the more recently established associations IHO and DIB, and the British SOCSA.
- In Cluster II, one third of business associations split their resources equally between membership- and influence-related activities. The CIA and the ABPI are the most prominent associations included in this cluster, which is primarily made up of British associations.
- Cluster III contains three German associations. Their resource allocation concentrates on lobbying activities (about 65 percent) with a focus on domestic and societal lobbying (30 percent and 23 percent respectively). Among them are the research-based pharmaceutical industry association (VFA) and the agricultural and life science association (IVA). Both of these represent predominantly larger companies that are less dependent on associational services. The fact that both associations spend significantly more resources on societal lobbying than other associations is indicative of the high-risk products of their member companies and of ethical, health, and environmental issues of concern to a wider public.

Let us now look at the external contact portfolio of individual associations and at the importance attached by them to the actors forming their external environment; that is, their organizational or policy community. It was argued above that diverse network densities would allow for estimates of the span of the relations network to actors outside their population. Accordingly, the lower the density, the more the relational resources, or spare resources, that could be invested elsewhere. Vice versa, the higher the density, the fewer spare resources and the higher the likelihood that associational activity remains encapsulated within the boundaries of their own population. This expectation turns out to be largely exaggerated.

Both with respect to the relevance given to public authorities at the domestic and the European level and with respect to the intensity by which these authorities are approached from within the respective country's interest population, there are only a few differences. In the upper right part of the scattergrams we find domestic ministries and government agencies as the actors viewed as most important and approached with the highest frequency by associations of both countries.

These agencies are the Federal Ministries of Economics (BmWT), the Environment (BmUNR), Health (BmG), Consumer Protection, Food, and Agriculture (BmVEL) and the Environmental Protection Agency (UBA) in Germany; and the Departments of Trade and Industry (DTI), Environment, Food, and Rural Affairs (DEFRA), Transport and Local Government (DTLR), and the Environment Agency (E-DEFRA) in Britain. Something similar applies to at least two Directorates General of the EU Commission. DG Environment (EU-ED or DgUM) and DG Enterprises (EU-ENT or DgUN) occupy virtually identical positions in the two plot areas. The EU-level branch associations (Esec) of members of the two domestic interest populations rank equally highly in terms of information provision, although the British associations seem to attach comparatively less relevance to them. The opposite applies to the European sector association, CEFIC (European Chemical Industry Council): while an almost identical relevance is attached to it by members of both samples, CEFIC clearly is more frequently addressed by British as compared to German associations.

Two differences are worth mentioning. They concern, first, the pronounced position of the public institution most important to chemical associations in Britain. Although ranking similar to its German counterpart in terms of relevance, the DTI is more frequently approached by British associations, thus it occupies the top position. In contrast, DG Environment and DG Enterprises apart, all other directorates of the European Commission (Health and Consumer Protection, Economic and Financial Affairs, Agriculture, and Research) rank extremely low in terms of both relevance and lobbying. Secondly, turning to the German associations, the place occupied by the DTI in Britain is here taken by the VCI – an additional indicator of this association's outstanding role in terms of both relevance and the control of information.

Furthermore, chemical industry associations indirectly access the EU policy arena via European branch or umbrella associations: 80 percent

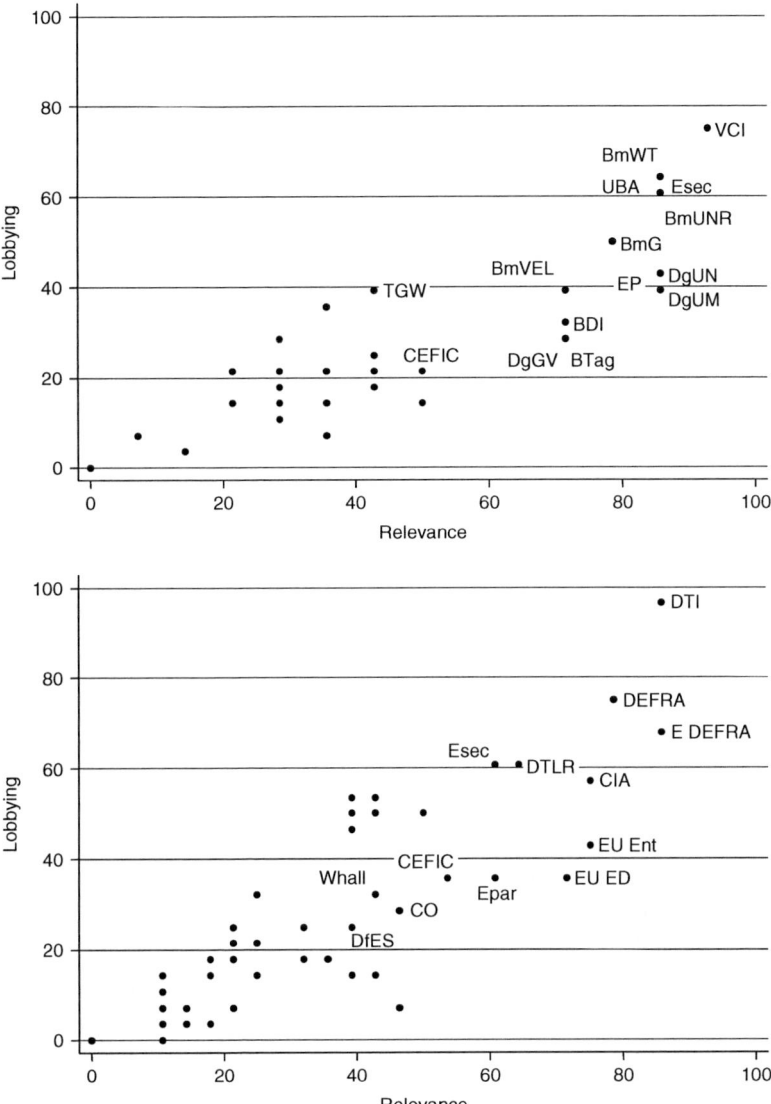

Figure 4.4 Lobbying targets and their relevance for German (above) and British (below) associations (in percent)

Note: The scattergrams combine two types of network data: (1) importance/relevance valuation of various organizations in the political (x-axis); (2) frequency of information provision, weighted by the intensity of information exchange (y-axis).

Table 4.2 Membership of domestic and international business associations

	European association	International association	Office in Brussels
Germany	VCI, IVA, Bau, IVC, IKW, VdL, BPI, TEGEWA, VFA, IVK, DIB	VCI, IVA, IKW, VKE, VdL, BPI, VFA, IHO	DIB, VCI, BPI (since 2008)
UK	CIA, BAMA, BACS, FMA, BCDTA, SIA, ABPI, BPF, BRMA, BCF, CTPA, UKCPI	CIA, FMA, BCDTA, ABPI, BPF, BRMA, BCF	–

of the entire sample under investigation is member of a European association, while almost half is affiliated to an international association (see Table 4.2). Although, as shown above, there are differences in terms of attitudes and behavior vis-à-vis these organizations, there are no country differences regarding formal membership of EU or international associations.

Only a few German associations have managed to establish a liaison office in Brussels. These are the two major associations representing pharmaceutical and biotechnology interests together with their peak association.

Conclusion

In this chapter use has been made of organizational ecology and complexity approaches that allow for decomposition of the analytical target into environmental conditions and two analytical levels, namely individual business associations and associational populations. It was asked whether the Europeanization of politics and the internationalization of markets have altered the associations' environments to any extent, triggering changes at either of these two levels.

In the interviews, it was found that processes of Europeanization and internationalization have been perceived and recognized by associations to be major challenges to which they had to respond. At the level of the *associational population* consisting of focal associations, only a few changes in the composition of networks could be detected. The structure of networks, however, changed in quite significant ways. In Germany, structural changes mainly occurred at the margins of the chemical industry's associational network, namely among those groups representing the interests of pharmaceutical companies. Some of these associations did not form part of the overall industry's focal organization set. However, it appeared that pluralistic fragmentation was not entirely impossible, even within an overall structure largely characterized by corporatist patterns of policy making and of the properties of interest systems. It was argued that this resulted from the combined effects of technological innovation, political legislation, company size, and economic developments such as changed ownership structures triggered by merger and acquisition activity. At least in pharmaceuticals, biotech, and life sciences, Germany's associations are similar to their presumably more pluralist British counterparts. Contrary to developments at the associational population's periphery, the core of the system of ecological relations and information exchange has remained unaltered over the past two decades and still exhibits the corporatist features detected by earlier research in the 1980s.

In the case of the UK a different picture emerges. The position of the sector's peak association (CIA) has weakened, so that the ordering of relations is today far less hierarchical than at the time of earlier studies. After an initial breakaway from the CIA, smaller associations of specialty products manufacturers now have an alternative structure (the AIA) that might become more compact over time, although it is still unlikely to become a proper association in its own right. A couple of pharmaceutical and biotech associations apart, hardly any new groupings have been added to the structure in either of the countries.

Pharmaceuticals associations (VFA and ABPI) that belong to the most powerful and relevant branch associations in both countries appear to be removed from information exchange networks. Change and adaptation at the population level are triggered predominantly by technological processes, namely the biotech and life science revolution that cross-cuts various sub-branches of the chemical industry (see Chapter 3). The overall message, then, is disintegration at the margins and reintegration in the core of the German and the British system respectively.

Developments at the *organization level* were triggered by processes of Europeanization; that is, the delegation of powers to the European level. The majority of our respondents underline the importance of the European level meanwhile having assumed a higher significance than national government for essential parts of chemical industry. This is a significant change compared to the early 1980s. However, lobbying efforts still concentrate on domestic institutions outcompeting international lobbying activities by a factor of two. Similarly, our respondents mentioned domestic institutions as their primary access channels, whereas EU institutions occupy third place even behind the national peak associations CIA and VCI respectively.

In summary, economic and technological factors led to changes in the composition of the associational landscapes in both countries. Innovations in biotech and life sciences triggered population dynamics that subsequently resulted in an increase in competitive relations and a decline in hierarchical coordination. Political factors, especially European integration, led to a broadening of lobbying activities, European as well as domestic. This clearly indicates the viability of the Europeanization debate (see Coen & Dannreuther, 2003; Grote & Lang, 2003; Eising 2004, 2007). What becomes clear is that economic and technological factors primarily affect the population level, while political factors most of all influence the behavior of individual business associations.

Notes

1. For more detailed information on economic, technological, political, and societal developments within the chemical industry and its associations, the reader might consult Grote and Lang (2003) or Grote and Schneider (2006).
2. Note that these figures only reflect the responses by the 28 members comprising the two focal association sets of both countries. In an earlier publication (see Grote & Schneider, 2006: 126), results obtained for a larger sample of 58 associations have been reported. They do not differ considerably from the ones mentioned here.
3. We also have measured the significance of societal challenges; that is, of threats originating from within social and environmental movements. For reasons of comparison across the chapters of this book, these figures are not reported here (but see Grote & Schneider, 2006: 124–6). Useful additional literature in that respect is Grant for the UK (Grant, 2000: 142–3 and 206) and Allen for Germany (Allen, 1989: 170–76).
4. Of our focal associations, BAMA turned into BRPPA (British Rubber and Polyurethane Products Association) in January 2006 and BCDTA changed its name to CBA (Chemical Business Association) in April of the same year.
5. For the most detailed analysis of that split, see Broscheid, 2002.
6. In another paper using the same data set, Grote and Lang (2006) have argued that size may represent a kind of third logic of collective action besides the class division and the division into producer and employer interests.
7. SOCSA itself mentions that, initially, there has been 'some trepidation about linking up with the CIA, often perceived as having a "big company mentality". However, while this may have been true in the past, the CIA is now anxious to emphasise its commitment to representing the interests of the broadest possible spectrum of the UK chemicals industry' (ICIS News, 10 January 1993).
8. For a more detailed account of organizational evolution within Britain's chemical interest system since the end of the eighteenth century, see Culpin (2000: 36–43).

9. AIA had eight business associations from our focal association set as members: British Aerosol Manufacturers' Association (BAMA), British Association for Chemical Specialities (BACS), British Coatings Federation (BCF), British Plastics Federation (BPF), British Rubber Manufacturers Association (BRMA; since 2006 renamed BRPPA), British Chemical Distributors & Trading Association (BCDTA; since 2006 renamed CBA), Cosmetic, Toiletry and Perfumery Association (CTPA), and UK Cleaning Products Industry Association (UKCPI). The remaining four affiliates not included in our sample are the British Adhesives and Sealants Association (BASA), the British Fragrance Association (BFA), and the British Colour Makers' Association (BCMA).
10. That this affiliation must have been a relatively loose connection becomes evident if the following is considered: at the time of the fieldwork, of our 14 focal associations 7 were listed on the CIA's webpage as affiliate members (ABPI, BAMA, BACS, BCDTA, BRMA, FMA, and SIA). According to information supplied by a more recent website from the CIA (2005), only one of these (FMA) had maintained an affiliation. In the association's last annual report available on the web, a special section for affiliate membership is entirely absent. The CIA has become a pure direct firm membership association and thus has lost all of the properties required by a proper peak association.
11. The CIA, in turn, aware both of its declining role in the sector and of what the association believes to be a wrong image of its policy, acknowledges that 'the perception of the CIA throughout the UK chemical industry does not reflect the reality of who we are, what we do and how we do it' (CIA Annual Review, 2004: 19). Accordingly, in order to change this it wishes 'to engage in discussions with other chemical trade associations about how we can develop more effective partnership relations' (*ibid*).
12. We asked the respondents to indicate from which business associations they receive information and to which they send information. The respondents could differentiate between frequent and infrequent exchange. In order to increase reliability, only confirmed relations were taken into account. Confirmed relations exist when association A indicates to send information to association B and B, in turn, confirms that it has received information from A. Thus a line between two associations indicates a confirmed but nevertheless directed information flow between both business associations.
13. Concerning the results of earlier publications based on a larger sample of associations, the caveat made in Footnote 2 applies.

5
Business Associability in the US Chemical Industry: Private Interest Governments in Pluralist Precincts?[1]

Hans-Jörg Schmedes

Unlike in any other country, the political system of the US has been analyzed with particular emphasis on the role of organized interest groups and the extent of their influence on public policy making, even going as far as perceiving the US as an 'interest group society' (Berry, 1984). Thus, a comparative volume on the conditions of business associability is almost bound to account for the American case and, in particular, for the case of the American chemical industry. The chemical industry as such, on the other hand, is an appropriate choice for analysis since it is one of the two sectors compared in this volume. Furthermore, the case of the US is not only significant for the American industry as a whole, but, more importantly, it holds the largest share of the world's chemical market (ACC, 2002: 11–12).

Chemical trade associations in the US: Environmental challenges and their organizational perception

Concentrating on a description of empirical change processes in the inter- and intra-organizational structures of trade associations in the US chemical industry in the period between 1980 and 2000, this chapter intends to trace these change processes back to their origin. Aside from the processes themselves, attention will be paid to the circumstances of business associability in the sector at the time the empirical investigation was carried out in September 2002. As with the investigation of the other associational populations in this volume, the following analysis is restricted to a particular set of 22 trade associations, the so-called focal associations, which are reputed to be especially influential. They have been selected according to the relevance attached to them by observers of the industry on the basis of a complete listing of all 161 sectoral trade associations with national scope that could be identified for the year 2000 through the handbook National Trade and Professional Associations of the United States (NTPA, 2001). These 22 associations belonging to the focal set were primarily investigated by means of a standardized questionnaire that was completed *in extenso* by 18 associations and to some extent by two associations in late 2002 and early 2003. In addition, face-to-face interviews following pre-formulated but open-ended questions were conducted with representatives of 18 of the 22 focal associations in September 2002. Further, information included in association handbooks (NTPA, 1981, 1986, 1991, 1996, 2001) and in publications of the associations under scrutiny was taken into consideration.

By conceptualizing trade associations as intermediate organizations between individual companies and the state (Schmitter & Streeck, 1999 [1981]), the aim of this chapter is to highlight two findings. First, the chapter will describe how the trade associations under investigation adjusted their organizational properties to their environment and which of the environmental factors were perceived to be most important in that regard. It will be demonstrated that associational activities in the sector under investigation underlie the prevailing logic of membership, which can be regarded as the *leitmotif* in analyzing trade associations in the American chemical industry. Secondly and more surprisingly, however, it will be shown that despite this rather pluralist logic, single activities by individual trade associations under scrutiny even qualify for the status of *private interest governments*; that is, 'regulated self-regulation' (Streeck & Schmitter, 1985b: 16), which has so far been regarded as the strongest instance of corporatism and could therefore assumed to be inconsistent with pluralist settings.

Changes in the environment of trade associations and their perception: Challenges of business associability in the US

Economic challenges: Growth and consolidation of the chemical industry

The chemical industry in the US plays a significant role both within the national economy and worldwide. As data compiled by the Organization for Economic Cooperation and Development (OECD)[2] reveals, the sector underwent an increase in production of more than 160 percent between 1980 and 2000. Internationally, since 1910 the US has maintained its position as the world's largest chemical producer (ACC, 2002; Arora & Rosenberg, 1998). Regarding America's exports and imports of chemical products, economic figures clearly show that international economic integration is not a new development for the chemical industry. Within the two decades analyzed herein, however, it has increased significantly: While exports grew by more than 230 percent, imports rose by more than 760 percent in the same period. Historically, foreign direct investments have played an important role in the history of the US chemical industry. With respect to the composition of the sector, Mowery (1999: 3) describes the chemical industry as 'highly concentrated, with a small number of global firms dominating capital investment and R&D [research and development] spending'.

Within the period under investigation, consolidation processes among chemical companies both on national and international levels have distinctively changed the internal structure of the industry.[3] This development coincides with pressure on chemical companies to return to their individual core competencies (ACC, 2002). While the general characteristics of the US chemical industry with regard to its position in the national economy as well as to its position among the chemical industries in the world remained largely constant, the internal structure of the industry changed significantly. Even though international economic integration is not a recent development for the chemical industry worldwide, its very nature has changed. This is indicated by the intensity of cross-border trade as well as by the rise of foreign direct investment both in the US and abroad, but particularly by national and international consolidation processes among the companies within the sector (Aftalion, 2001: 404).

Consolidation does not only reduce the number of companies that a trade association represents, but can influence associational resources directly. Insofar as the dues structure is capped – regardless of whether individual dues are based on production capacity or sales – trade associations can lose membership dues to a significant extent when two or more major companies that already pay the maximum amount of membership fees merge.

Political challenges: Environmental, health and safety regulations

The strength of interest groups depends on their resources, but also hinges on the characteristic features of other constituent units of the political system, particularly their strengths or weaknesses (Wilson, 1990: 40). The functions of government in the US are dispersed among its three branches; that is, Congress, the President, and the Supreme Court.

This fragmentation of power is amplified by the structure of the executive branch, which does not report to the President alone in his role as Chief Executive, but owes its loyalty to both the President and Congress (Grant, 1997). Interest groups command multiple access points to the different branches of government at the federal, state, and local levels. By making use of the leverage points in the individual branches of government at their disposal, interest groups arguably have a significant influence on decision-making processes in legislative and regulatory affairs, with different branches of government being 'sympathetic to different interests' (Wilson, 1990: 90; see also Grant, 1997: 204).

In general, the literature on pressure groups ascribes pluralistic features to the American system of interest intermediation and emphasizes its competitive character. The associational system of the US is reported to show a high degree of decentralization, fragmentation, and functional differentiation. Usually, interest groups do not have a representation monopoly at their disposal but compete with others for members. The literature suggests a low degree of integration between different interest organizations that pursue similar goals. Due to their fragmented, non-encompassing and competing character, interest groups can concentrate on pursuing specific rather than broad interests, which puts them in a favourable position toward the different branches of government (Wilson, 1990: 40, 73–6). In other words, while the fragmentation of governmental institutions reduces their capacity to withstand pressure from organized interest groups, the just as fragmented structure of these groups increases their ability to apply pressure more intensely for their specific interests.

Increasingly, state governments take on an active role with regard to environmental and safety issues (ACC, 2002). Furthermore, attempts to strengthen the role of the individual states under what became known as 'New Federalism' (Hesse & Benz, 1987; Conlan, 1988) intensified this development. However, while these attempts encouraged individual states to regulate more intensely, they did not permanently remove the focus of regulatory activities from the federal level (Conlan, 1988: 217–18). Federal agencies continue to play the most prominent role in the chemical sector, which is why a comprehensive account of the development of legislative and regulatory activities at the state level can be disregarded for the purposes of this study, since it concentrates on trade associations at the federal level.

The sector and related industries are federally regulated pursuant to several health, safety, and environmental laws (ACC, 2002). The Toxic Substances Control Act (TSCA), enacted in 1976, in particular had a significant impact on the chemical industry by 'convert[ing] the chemical sector as a whole into a regulated industry' (Schneider, 1985: 174). Essentially, TSCA gave the Environmental Protection Agency (EPA), established in 1970, comprehensive authority to regulate any chemical substance. Moreover, supplementary laws created or redefined additional regulatory competencies for numerous governmental agencies, such as the Occupational Safety and Health Administration (OSHA), the Chemical Safety and Hazard Investigation Board (CSB), the Food and Drug Administration (FDA), and others (Brickman et al., 1985), which have accordingly been nominated as highly relevant organizations by the associations under investigation herein (Schmedes, 2003). With regard to individual laws or amendments thereto, particularly the Clean Air Act (CAA), the Comprehensive Environmental Response, Compensation, and Liability Act (CERCLA, also known as Superfund), the Superfund Amendments and Reauthorization Act (SARA), the Resource Conservation and Recovery Act (RCRA), and the Food Quality Protection Act (FQPA) were stated as specific pieces of legislation with particular concern for the industry and, thereby, also for the associations under investigation (Schmedes, 2003: 67–8, ACC, 2002: 129–31).

With regard to legislative developments, the US has not experienced any delivery of sovereign national competencies to organizations at the international level. Even though Canada, Mexico, and the US have established the North American Free Trade Agreement (NAFTA), which came into force in 1994, NAFTA[4] constitutes – in contrast to the European Union (EU) – an exclusively economic undertaking of intergovernmental nature: 'NAFTA responds to the logic of markets, whereas the EU incorporates the logic of governments' (Clarkson, 1998). Due to the industry's international orientation, however, developments on the international level are of increasing importance[5] for the sector. Accordingly, many international organizations were stated as receiving significant associational attention, among them in particular the European Commission, the Organization for Economic Cooperation and Development (OECD), the United Nations (UN), the EU Council, the World Trade Organization (WTO), the World Health Organization (WHO), and the European Parliament (Schmedes, 2003: 68).

Technological challenges: Chemical innovations and ICT developments

Technological innovation within the chemical industry itself plays an important role for the sector (Landau, 1998). Landau and Arora attribute the high level of technological innovation in the chemical industry in the US to the level of competition among companies, which 'is just enough ... to spur the creation or improvement of products and processes and yet allow firms to make sufficient profits to provide the ability and incentives to invest in R&D' (Landau & Arora, 1999: 39–40). According to Aftalion (2001: 325), however, '[a]t the end of the 1990s the chemical industry in its main activities had reached a stage of maturation with respect to innovation'. This is evidenced by the fact that technological innovations did not fundamentally shape the form of the basic chemicals sector in the period under investigation. Instead, major changes in the life sciences and specialties segments occurred. This development can be ascribed particularly to the growing importance of biotechnology in both pharmaceuticals and agricultural products. Since the 1990s, biosciences have been the driving force behind technological innovation[6] in the chemical sector. Together with nanotechnology, they are expected to play an ever-increasing role over the next few decades (ACC, 2002: 158–62).

These technological developments are certainly reflected in the economic figures describing the composition of the chemical sector. Whereas the chemical output in basic chemicals grew by 8 percent between 1989 and 2000, production in specialties increased by approximately 73 percent and by more than 142 percent in life sciences.[7] Expenditure in R&D between 1991 and 2001 reveals similar results. Within that decade, R&D expenditure in basic chemicals rose by approximately 42 percent and by about 22 percent in the specialties segment. At the same time, however, R&D spending in life sciences increased by approximately 230 percent.[8]

Associational perception of environmental challenges

Just as in the case of the chemical associations in Germany and the UK (see Chapter 4 in this volume), the American associations under investigation perceive challenges in more than just one of their environments and from more than just one territorial level as being responsible for the necessity for organizational adaptation processes. As described above, the highest importance is attached to economic factors, followed by political factors and, to a much lesser extent, by technological factors. With respect to the relative weight accorded to each of the three territorial levels, domestic developments clearly dominate regional factors within the NAFTA countries and global influences.

Economic developments – particularly as expressed through national and international consolidation processes through mergers, acquisitions, and restructuring processes, which are considered by about 89 percent of the respondents as either most important or important for their association – have the highest significance for the associations under investigation. This could partially be traced back to the fact that a reduction of membership companies directly affects associational resources. In an associational setting in which the logic of membership is assumed to dominate, this development can involve far-reaching consequences. *Politically*, there has been no significant shift of competencies to international or supra-national institutions. Instead, major laws at the federal level have changed the nature of regulation over that industry sector. In addition, public interest groups have succeeded in gaining greater participation opportunities. Both factors may explain the high degree of importance attributed to political developments on the national level. In contrast, *technological* developments did not cause significant change processes; except for associations such as the *Biotechnology Industry Organization* (BIO) which represent segments of the industry that are permanently subject to major technological innovations.

The organizational population: Changes in structure and composition

When looking at the structural configuration of chemical trade associations in the US, one has to consider that there exists no comparative data from the 1980s or the 1990s that would allow for a comparison and description of information exchange networks or the degree of cooperation and competition among the associations under investigation over the past two decades. Nevertheless, the representation of the structural arrangement at the time the survey was conducted in September 2002 reveals important implications for the associational system. Particularly, the concepts of differentiation and integration – that is, the degree to which the associational system is composed of different organizational units and the degree to which these units are coordinated to achieve common goals – can be applied to answer the question of whether empirical evidence supports the notion of a rather pluralist system of interest intermediation in the US chemicals sector (Schmitter & Streeck, 1999 [1981]: 48–9). This would be true if there existed a multitude of interacting associations, none of which was in a position to exert hierarchical control over the others.

Before looking at the structural configuration more closely, however, the following section depicts the development of the associational system in the US chemical sector between 1980 and 2000, followed by a description of cooperation and competition as well as an illustration of information exchange networks among the focal associations under investigation.

Evolution of the associational landscape

With regard to the quantitative development of the associational system as a whole, the last few years have witnessed a decline of associations in the chemical sector. Whereas the number of trade associations in the chemical industry increased from 136 in 1980 to a peak of 177 in 1995, the number diminished to 162 associations in 2000 (NTPA, 1981, 1986, 2001). Six of the focal associations under close investigation experienced mergers or alliances within the period under scrutiny, whereas organizational division took place in only one of the associations under investigation since the 1980s, as can be seen in Figure 5.1.

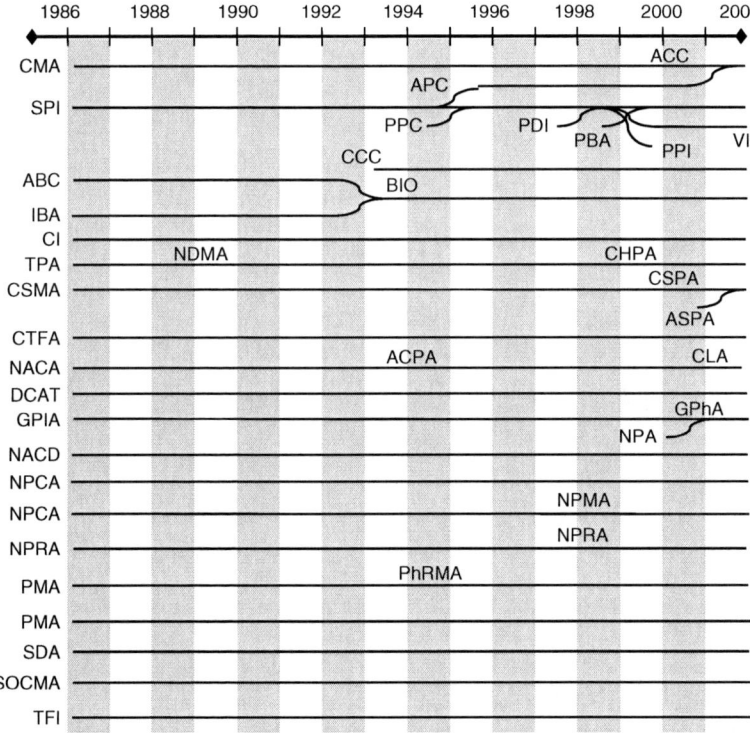

Figure 5.1 Entries, mergers, and splits in the associational system

Cooperation and competition among focal associations

In order to grasp the sector's inter-associational structure, Figure 5.2 displays the degree of cooperation and competition among the associations in the focal set. Accordingly, it includes information on existing relations as well as on their quality: The relationship between associations representing the same chemical subsector as well as maintaining relations is interpreted as cooperation, whereas associations representing identical subsectors without any kind of relation are seen as being in competition.

Keeping in mind that the associational system of the US in general is usually described as pluralist, characterized by a multitude of competing associations, the high degree of cooperation displayed in Figure 5.2 is surprising. While competitive relations exist only between a few associations, cooperative and neutral relationships clearly dominate. The

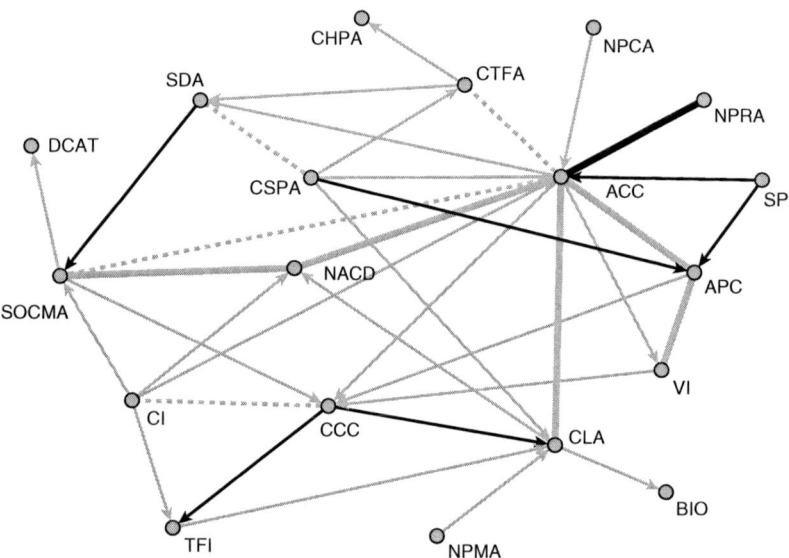

Figure 5.2 Ecological relations in the associational system
Notes
Relations (examples in parenthesis)
Gray, bold, continuous: Mutualism (ACC–CLA)
Gray, thin, continuous: Partial cooperation (SOCMA–DCAT)
Gray, bold, dashed: Neutrality (SDA–CSPA)
Black, bold, continuous: Full competition (ACC–NPRA)
Black, thin, continuous: Partial competition (CCC–TFI)
Black, thin, dashed: 'Harmful' competition (–)
Due to missing data, GPhA, PhRMA and PMA are not included.

American Chemistry Council (ACC) in particular maintains numerous cooperative relations. The discussion on associational outputs below may shed some light on the reason for the cooperative (rather than competitive) picture that emerges.

Information exchange networks

The quality of inter-associational relations represented in Figure 5.2 can also be found in the representation of information exchange networks among the focal association set; that is, the visualization of informal hierarchies. Figure 5.3 displays confirmed information flows between the associations in the focal set by employing the concept of

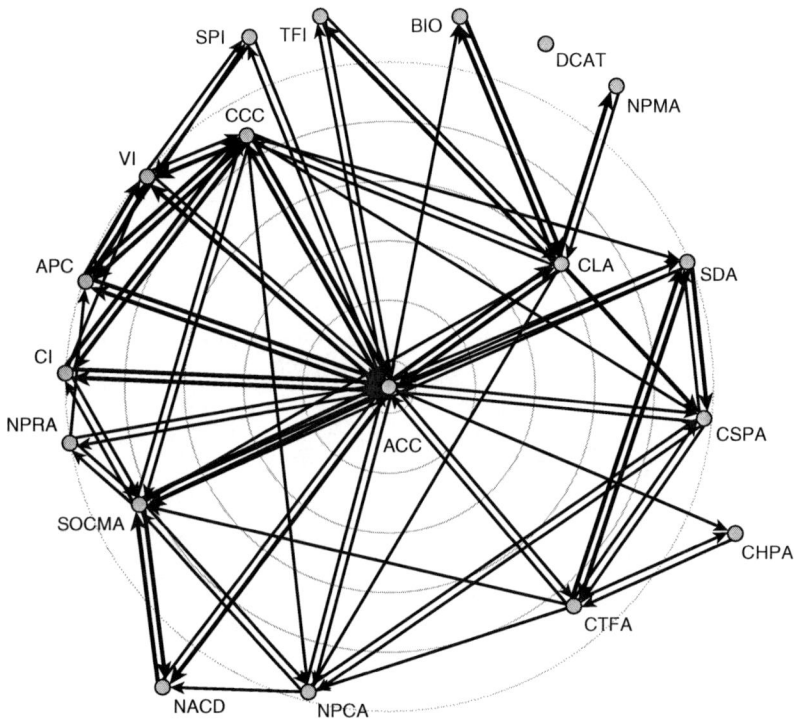

Figure 5.3 Information exchange among focal trade associations
Notes
Relations:
Bold: frequent information exchange
Thin: occasional information exchange
Due to missing data, GPhA, PhRMA and PMA are not included.

betweenness centrality, which measures 'the frequency with which a point falls between pairs of other points on the shortest or geodesic paths connecting them' (Freeman, 1979: 221), thereby indicating the individual association's 'potential for control' (*ibid.*). The circles correspond to certain levels of centrality, with the circle at the center of the graph representing the most central level (Brandes *et al.*, 1999).

Even though ACC holds a very central position, it does not dominate the associational network in a position of hierarchical control. Rather, the graph shows a densely connected web of organizations in which neither ACC nor any other association acts as an information broker that exclusively controls information exchange among less central associations that are unable to communicate directly. Instead, there exists a multitude of alternative paths bypassing ACC, through which the associations included in the focal set can interact with one another, providing empirical evidence for assuming a rather pluralist pattern of interest intermediation among chemical trade associations in the US. Altogether, the inter-organizational structure of the associational system as a whole can be characterized as a horizontally differentiated system with a medium extent of vertical integration. ACC is in no position to represent the American chemical industry in an exclusive, hierarchical way toward the government and other societal actors, nor does it have the capacity to control the activities of the remaining associations within the sector, yet it takes up a very central position among the focal associations, thereby contradicting purely pluralist assumptions that would deny the existence of such a comparatively central actor. This arrangement is the more surprising when acknowledging that ACC neither has an authoritative position granted by state institutions nor is a peak association in which the majority of other trade associations of the sector are members. However, ACC performs tasks on behalf of the chemical industry as a whole, as will be seen below. Second, ACC's comprehensive character leads to a concentration of its work on broader issues that apply to the industry as a whole, instead of its working on specific questions on behalf of individual subsections of the chemical industry. Still, in view of the pluralist anticipations, ACC's position is astonishing.

The organizational level: Change within business associations

After having obtained a horizontal overall view of the structural arrangement among the focal associations as well as its development in the previous section, the analysis now turns to a description of change

Table 5.1 Average associational resource allocation (in percent) and changes (frequency)

Activities	Resource allocation		Changes	
	Mean	Standard deviation	Increase (frequency)	Decrease (frequency)
National lobbying	18	16.1	3	1
International lobbying	7	8	7	0
Societal lobbying	13	9.4	6	0
Influence investments	**38**		**16**	**1**
Member consultation	12.7	10.5	2	0
Member information	14.7	17.4	2	2
Member conferences	20	19.3	1	0
Side benefits	1.6	3	0	0
Training	5.4	7	1	3
Membership investments	**54.4**		**6**	**5**
Other	7.6	15.9	2	0
Total	100		24	6

N = 19

processes over time in an aggregate, longitudinal perspective in order to provide an overview of changes within the trade associations under investigation. Organizational change in associations can be described along the dimensions of associational domains, structures, resources, and outputs, as Schmitter and Streeck (1999 [1981]: 45–94) have argued, with the description herein focusing on a portrayal of associational resource allocation and its development in Table 5.1. However, as an introduction, it is interesting to notice that with the exception of one, all of the 19 leading associational representatives that were interviewed perceive the necessity of organizational adaptation. The statement that 'Today, many associations require organizational restructuring to cope with the considerable need for adaptation and adjustment in organization and personnel' was agreed to by 18 of the 19 associational executives who returned the questionnaire. Accordingly, the question of whether there had been significant changes within their association occurring over the past 20 years was answered positively by 18 executives.

Although no great changes in the *domains* represented by the individual associations could be noticed, two-thirds of the associations under investigation indicated a widening of their interest portfolio, which includes, for example, the number of potential members and fields of interests.[9] Regarding *structural* change processes, one can state that besides the inter-organizational change processes shown above, intra-organizational reorganizations have explicitly occurred in the period under investigation. There is, however, no clear trend discernible in these efforts: Whereas the number of administrative units increased for seven out of the eighteen associations that responded (39 percent), it decreased for five associations (28 percent), with six associations (33 percent) indicating that the number of administrative units remained constant. In addition to restructuring processes, nine of the associations stated that they had been delegating tasks to external agents. Among them, five delegated tasks to their member companies, five to external agencies such as policy advisers and marketing firms, three to management or financial consultants, one to law firms, and another one to technical consultants and laboratories. In addition, ten associational representatives mentioned name changes since the foundation of their organization.

Resources, as the 'key determinants of the ability of associations to handle complexity' (Grant, 1991a: 47), consist of both financial and personal means. For a majority of 52 percent of the associations under investigation, overall income increased either moderately (16 percent) or steeply (36 percent), whereas 32 percent indicated a decline and 16 percent stated that the budget remained constant over the period under investigation. The largest share of the associational budget (66 percent) stemmed from membership dues, whose developments have balanced each other out. Only small shares are taken up by the sale of products and services for members (7 percent) and non-members (4 percent). In sum, the overall development of financial resources has clearly increased. Even though membership dues, as the largest share of the budget, have by and large remained constant, there are at least indicators of attempts to diversify associational income sources. This can be seen by the increase in associational proceeds from the sale of products and services for both members and non-members. Direct support by members for specific associational activities has also slightly increased.

Looking at associational *outputs* in more detail in Table 5.1, it can be seen that membership investments as selective goods that are only available for the members of the respective associations clearly dominate influence investments: Whereas these public pressure goods amount only to a little more than 38 percent of overall expenditure, almost 55 percent of the associational resources are spent on membership investments. It is, however, mainly influence investments that have undergone an increase in importance.

Table 5.1 reveals that the increase in membership investments – that is, selective goods offered by the associations under investigation to their members and/or sold to non-members – appears to be relatively small, although the provision of selective goods and services was named by a few associations as an important means of diversifying and stabilizing resource influx. These associations perceive themselves as in a constant struggle to find value-added services for their membership organizations, yet they regard this struggle as being necessary in order to keep up their members' interest in the association and to meet competition from other organizations such as lobbying firms, law firms, or consultancy firms that provide political advocacy as well. Influence investments, however, seem to have experienced a clear growth in importance, albeit the associations under investigation spent considerably fewer resources on public pressure goods such as the representation of the industry in the legislative and regulatory spheres as well as in the general public sphere. Nevertheless, political lobbying on the international level as well as societal lobbying on both the international and domestic levels have clearly gained in importance.

Looking at associational resource allocation in a comparative perspective by means of two hierarchical cluster analyses that focus on the associational lobbying level as being either national, international, and societal as well as on the associational lobbying profiles, both variation as well as homogeneity among individual trade associations become apparent. Following a hierarchical cluster analysis accounting for the associational lobbying focus, three clusters can be identified among the associations under investigation. Cluster I includes seven associations[10] that focus their lobbying efforts on the national level as well as, to a smaller extent, toward society, with activities directed at the international level only playing a minor role. In addition, they spend a considerable amount of their resources on membership services. The nine associations inside Cluster II[11] concentrate their resources even more on services for their members than on lobbying activities, although they engage in some lobbying activities toward society and, to a lesser extent, toward national political institutions. Cluster III consists of three associations[12] that mainly exhibit multilevel lobbying activities, investing the majority of their associational resources on societal, international, and national lobbying purposes. When comparing the associational lobbying profiles by means of hierarchical cluster analysis, four clusters can be identified as well as three associations outside of these clusters. While the eight associations inside Cluster I[13] maintain contacts to governmental organizations on the national level to a medium extent, they have virtually no relations to public interest groups or thinktanks and only a few relations to international actors. The two

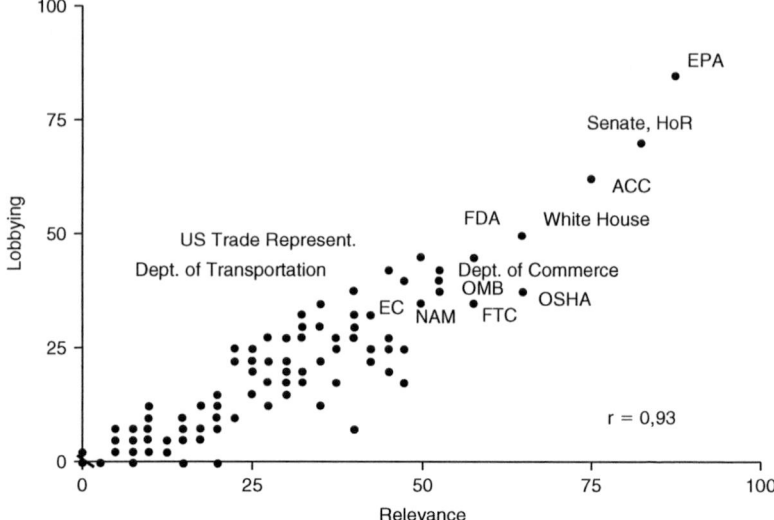

Figure 5.4 Associational lobbying targets and their relevance (in percent)

organisations in Cluster II[14] have frequent relations to trade unions or public interest groups as well as to thinktanks and, to a lower extent, to governmental institutions, and, even fewer, to international organizations. The four associations in Cluster III[15] have numerous contacts with governmental institutions, international organizations, and standardization bodies, but only infrequent contacts with public interest groups and trade unions. The two associations[16] in Cluster IV uphold frequent contacts with governmental organizations as well as with international organizations, yet only weak contacts with trade unions and public interest groups.

Focusing on associational lobbying targets and their relevance, the description in Figure 5.4 reveals a rather strong correlation between the relevance attached to individual organizations and the frequency with which they are contacted, which is expressed by a rather narrow distribution of organizations along an imaginary diagonal and a high correlation coefficient of 93 percent.

The Environmental Protection Agency (EPA) ranks highest in both categories, followed by the two chambers of the United States Congress (Senate and House of Representatives (HoR). ACC comes third, underlining the prominent, within a pluralist environment rather unexpected position that it holds. The White House takes up fourth position, followed by several governmental departments and agencies on the national level. This dominance of national organizations and institutions clearly demonstrates the importance attached to national agencies.

16 out of 19 interviewees stated that the extent to which their association cooperates with other associations increased in recent years. However, it is interesting to note that only the ACC is a member of higher-level national associations such as the *National Association of Manufacturers* (NAM), the *United States Chamber of Commerce*, and the *National Foreign Trade Council* (NFTC). Among the other associations, the *American Plastics Council* (APC) has reported being a component of ACC, whereas the *Vinyl Institute* (VI) has indicated its membership of APC and, thereby, also of ACC. In addition, the *Chlorine Chemistry Council* (CCC) is a business unit of ACC. Relating to the international level, ten associations declared themselves to be members in one or more international associations. Among them, two associations declared membership of an international association of global character – ACC represents the US chemical industry in the *International Council of Chemical Associations* (ICCA) and the *National Association of Chemical Distributors* (NACD) is a member of the *International Council of Chemical Trade Associations* (ICCTA) that represents chemical distributors worldwide – one named its membership in an European branch association (the *Federation of European Aerosols*, FEA), and seven declared themselves part of their respective international branch association such as the *World Chlorine Council* (WCC; two nominations), the *World Self-Medication Industry* (WSMI), the *International Generic Pharmaceutical Association* (IGPA), the *International Fertilizer Association* (IFA), the *International Paint and Printing Ink Council* (IPPIC), and the *Global Vinyl Council* (GVC).

Before concluding this section on associational outputs, light should be shed on another unexpected feature of the associations under investigation. Given the supposedly pluralist character of the US and its structure of interest intermediation, it seems unlikely that trade associations in America invest in monopoly goods, which can be characterized as associational participation in authoritative decisions of the state or the exclusive provision of crucial goods together with third parties such as the state or trade unions in exchange for associational information on members and their compliance with specific programs and regulations. According to Schmitter and Streeck (1999 [1981]: 90–94), monopoly rights can be vested in associations by state authorities, hinging significantly on the degree to which trade associations can exert compulsion over their membership. The degree to which associations can occupy such a privileged position, however, is usually viewed as being dependent on the extent to which the associational logic of influence prevails over the logic of membership (*ibid.*: 45–55).

Interestingly, in the early 1990s Jacek (1991) had already shown that, against all expectations, chemical trade associations in the US offered monopoly goods. Specifying the *Chemical Transportation Emergency Center* (CHEMTREC), which was launched by ACC's predecessor *Chemical Manufacturers Association* (CMA) as a 24-hour emergency phone line that provides information and technical assistance on any chemicals that are shipped by registered members; CMA's CHEMNET, a network of emergency response teams throughout the country; and CHLOREP, an emergency facility run by the *Chlorine Institute* (CI), Jacek (1991: 169) characterizes these 'seemingly technical programmes' as the provision of a 'rapidly growing instance of private interest government in the bosom of pluralist America', falling into the category of 'regulated self-regulation' that defines the concept of 'private interest government' (Streeck & Schmitter, 1985a). Furthermore, the independent *Cosmetic Ingredient Review* (CIR), which is run by the *Cosmetic, Toiletry and Fragrance Association* (CTFA) and had produced as well as published verifiable scientific data on the ingredients used in cosmetics since 1976, can be interpreted as another example of 'private interest government'.

In addition, the Responsible Care program is being claimed by the industry as a major self-regulation effort in order to improve its performance with regard to health, safety, and environmental quality, although it is not maintained under state license. Initially conceived in 1984 by the *Canadian Chemical Producers' Association* (CCPA), it comprises six codes of management practice that cover different areas. For ACC members, participation in Responsible Care is obligatory. Companies outside ACC's membership can participate through the Partnership Program that also extends to licensed partnership associations. Among the focal associations under investigation, these partner associations are CCC, CI, *CropLife America* (CLA), the *National Petrochemical and Refiners Association* (NPRA), the *Synthetic Organic Chemical Manufacturers Association* (SOCMA), and VI.[17] Critical observers of the industry, however, consider Responsible Care primarily as a public relations program and not a major self-regulation effort, in part basing their judgment on internal industry documents that were disclosed through litigation (PIRG, 1999; EWG, 2001).[18] In particular, the lack of verifiable, independently reviewed control of individual member companies' compliance with the program's standards, as well as the imbalance between the small amount of money spent on implementing the program's codes and the huge amount advertising the program, seem to contribute to this result.

In addition, the apparent lack of sanctions, as described by King and Lennox (2000), seems to make Responsible Care fall short of its own demands, although both authors acknowledge existing indications that attempts are underway toward a third-party verification system that would allow the effective use of sanctions (see *ibid.*: 714).

Conclusion

This chapter contains two important findings. First, an attempt was made to provide an empirical account of organizational change processes in business associations in the US chemical industry for about the last two decades and to describe to what extent these changes can be traced back to changes in the perceived associational environment. Since the member companies provide the associations almost exclusively with the resources necessary for their organizational survival, serving the interests of their members constitutes the center of associational activities in the sector under investigation. However, this prevailing logic of membership – *quasi* the *leitmotif* of the conducted analysis – makes the trade associations under investigation highly vulnerable to changes in the composition of their membership as well as to the altering needs and demands of their members. In order to reduce this dependence at least to a certain extent, the associations investigated apparently have recourse to strategies aimed at diversifying and stabilizing their respective resource base, for example by providing their members with selective incentives or by identifying additional income sources. Economic consolidation processes in particular have affected the number and the composition of members, forcing associations to broaden their interest portfolio and to explore additional financial resources besides the membership dues.

Secondly and more surprisingly, structural arrangements and associational programs were identified that do not correspond to the anticipation of a pluralist associational arrangement that would focus almost exclusively on the logic of membership. On the one hand, the empirical evidence suggests the existence of a multitude of trade associations with overlapping associational activities to a considerable extent. Moreover, none of the associations can act as information broker in an exclusive manner or is in any position to exert hierarchical control over other associations in the sector. On the other hand, the comparatively central position held by the ACC among the associations under investigation, as well as its role as advocate of a considerable part of the industry, is astonishing, as is the degree to which inter-associational cooperation by formal and informal arrangements takes place. Over and above that, however, the existence of associational programs that clearly correspond to the definition of private interest governments sharply contrasts with any theoretical assumptions about the associational system of the US and the prevailing logic of membership as empirically observed in this study. It remains the task of further research to analyze in more detail the conditions in which the existence of such far-reaching associational programs can be reconciled analytically with the dominance of pluralist patterns of interaction.

Notes

1. This analysis was conducted within a comparative research project at the University of Konstanz, Germany, and the European University Institute in Florence, Italy. I am thankful for the discussions with and the ongoing support from the members of the research project at both institutions. Particularly, I am grateful for the advice, encouragement, comments, and support of Volker Schneider, Jürgen R. Grote, Achim Lang, and Arndt Wonka. In addition, I would like to thank Achim Lang for providing helpful suggestions on the data analysis conducted herein as well as the participants of a workshop at the University of Konstanz in January 2004, who commented on an earlier version of the manuscript. Moreover, I am appreciative of the attention that leading associational representatives of 20 Washington-based trade associations in the US chemical industry paid to this study in sharing their insights and expertise with me.
2. The figures included in this paragraph represent my own calculations that were conducted on the basis of OECD data (OECD, div.-a, div.-b).
3. See the data by Young and Partners (2003a, 2003b, 2003c) for an overview of merger and acquisition activities in the chemical industry worldwide.
4. Consequently, it is not surprising that the associations under investigation ascribed the highest importance to economic factors in relation to the environmental challenges to which they are exposed: Almost 89 percent of associational representatives regarded economic factors as either 'most important' (66.7 percent) or 'important' (22.2 percent); only 11.1 percent of respondents viewed them as being 'less important'. According to these responses, almost 65 percent see economic processes as influenced by national developments and 35 percent by global developments.
5. Accordingly, political factors were attached the second highest importance as regards environmental challenges triggering organizational change processes in the associations under investigation. Almost 78 percent of respondents viewed political factors as either 'most important' (11.1 percent) or 'important' (66.7 percent), with 5.6 percent regarding them as 'less important' and 16.7 percent as 'least important'. Concerning their origin, 76.5 percent of respondents considered national developments as most relevant, 17.6 percent global developments, and 5.9 percent regional developments within the NAFTA countries.

6. Taken together, only less than one quarter of the respondents ascribed a high importance to technological factors in influencing organizational change processes in the associations under scrutiny herein. 11.1 percent of the respondents assessed them as being either 'most important' or 'important', but 50 percent assessed them as 'less important' and 27.8 percent as even 'least important'. 56.3 percent of respondents viewed technological developments of national provenance as most relevant, with 12.5 percent of respondents considering regional and 31.3 percent regarding global developments as more important.
7. These specifications are based on data made available by the *American Chemistry Council* (ACC) on personal inquiry. For the years 1991 to 2001, they are included in ACC's *Guide to the Business of Chemistry* (ACC, 2002: 14).
8. Again, this information is based on data made available by the ACC on personal inquiry. Partly, they are included in ACC's *Guide to the Business of Chemistry* (ACC, 2002: 93).
9. For a more detailed discussion of the observations described in this paragraph, see Schmedes (2003: 91–9).
10. ACC, BIO, CHPA, CSPA, GPhA, NPCA, and TFI.
11. APC, CIA, CTFA, DCAT, NACD, NPMA, NPRA, SOCMA, and SPI.
12. CCC, SDA, and VI.
13. CHPA, CI, DCAT, NACD, NPMA, NPRA, SPI, and TFI.
14. APC and VI.
15. CSPA, CTFA, NPCA, and SDA.
16. ACC and CCC.
17. The Responsible Care initiative is not restricted to the US or North America, but has spread to 46 countries under the management of the ICCA, covering 85 percent of the world's chemical production (ACC, 2001). In addition, there are several other associational initiatives in the US chemical industry that – directly or indirectly – supplement ACC's Responsible Care program, such as the Consumer Specialty Products Association's (CSPA) Product Care, NACD's Responsible Distribution Process, and the National Paint and Coatings Association's (NPCA) Coatings Care.
18. On a website called 'Chemical Industry Archives', the Environmental Working Group (EWG) made about 10,000 pages of internal documents from the chemical industry public in 2001. They can be accessed through the website's starting page at http://www.chemicalindustryarchives.org/ (accessed 1 July 2006).

6
Similar Responses to Similar Pressures? Adaptation Processes of British and German Business Associations in the Information and Communications Sector

Achim Lang

Business associations are an attribute of modern societies. In the nineteenth and twentieth centuries they emerged out of industrialization processes, which were characterized by societal and economic turmoil. During these turbulent times firm owners united for the first time in order to promote their interest collectively against state interventions, foreign competitors, and the growing workers' movement. The emergence of business associations indicates the transition to differentiated societies where business associations occupy an intermediary role between the economy and the state. The British and German systems of organized business interest both emerged in the middle of the nineteenth century and soon covered most economic areas (Ullmann, 1988).

Globalization and Europeanization as new challenges to British and German systems of organized business interests

Trade associations, as the major form of organized business interest, show a high level of adaptational flexibility (and therefore stability) as an organizational form. However, in the last few decades adaptability and flexibility have become increasingly precarious due to processes of Europeanization and globalization. In this respect, the information and communications sector (I&C) is an adequate representation of most economic and political processes triggered by internationalization (Latzer, 1997). High technological innovation rates and market liberalization have led to a steady increase in I&C market volume and production in both countries, while foreign trade has grown significantly and outnumbered production growth. Germany and Britain are similarly exposed to these economic processes and are part of the international division of labor within the I&C sector (EITO, div.).

The political dimension of associative action has also considerably changed since the late 1980s. European integration has modified the political landscape and has led to a new multilayered political regime that poses fresh challenges to trade associations and their lobbying strategies (Eising, 2004; Levi-Faur, 2004; Schneider & Tenbücken, 2004). The liberalization and harmonization processes in the telecommunications sector began with the publication of the 1987 Green Book of the European Commission, which served as an impulse for further community activities in the entire I&C sector. The further extension of liberalization competencies approved by the European Court of Justice brought about comprehensive EC parameters and climaxed in the liberalization Directive, setting the path for the introduction of unrestricted competition in the telecommunications market and the admission of alternative networks as of 1 January 1998 (Sandholz, 1998). The directive also included provisions on the creation of national regulatory authorities, whose arrangement remained at the discretion of the member states. In the audiovisual sector the Directive on 'television without borders' became the central norm for content transmission across borders. To date, it has primarily served to secure the provision of services beyond borders and the maintenance of program standards. In the content area there are no community regulations that go beyond the network infrastructure: these areas are still dominated by national provisions. However, despite growing globalization and Europeanization,[1] domestic patterns of interest intermediation and structures of organized business still build a baseline model for understanding the behavior of sectoral business associations. In this respect the British and German systems of business interest and of interest intermediation have different defining features: the British system comes close to US-style pluralism, whereas the German system features prominently among corporatist countries (Layard *et al.*, 1991; Siaroff, 1999).

The British system of trade associations is characterized by small and non-hierarchically integrated interest groups that try to extract their members from a small segment of the economy (Plöhn, 2001). Although the *Confederation of British Industry* is the peak association for British business, it does not occupy a particularly prominent position in British policy making. This tendency toward atomization and irrelevance of organized business was enforced by the Thatcher government, which replaced traditional conservative thinking by an atomistic neoliberalism that deteriorated the role pressure groups played in the policy process (Baggott, 1995). The situation has only slightly changed since New Labour came to power: pressure groups have been invited to participate in the formulation of policy, but the relationships are still asymmetric. Blair's much-quoted 'Third Way' still remains halfway to corporatism (Grant, 2000). The structure of the associational system was challenged by these changes in government attitudes. Major restructuring and rationalization led to a reduction in the number of trade associations from some 2500 in 1972 to 1300 in 1993. A decline in numbers was also the result of mergers, which eliminated many duplicates in the representation of sectors (May et al., 1998).

The German system of organized business has changed only incrementally and moderately compared to the British. The postwar period saw the reconstruction of the associational system following the path set by the structures and traditions of the German Empire (Ullmann, 1988). As early as autumn 1949, several representatives of industrial trade associations founded an industrial peak association, which was subsequently renamed *Bundesverband der Deutschen Industrie* or BDI (Federation of German Industry). Business interests in the third sector, however, did not develop a single hierarchical organization but founded several peak associations, which covered important subsectors of the German economy. At the same time, the employer peak association (*Bundesvereinigung Deutscher Arbeitgeberverbände*, BDA) was established and, in contrast to the BDI, covers all sectors of German economy. As a means of coordinating the often divergent interests of all peak associations, the *Gemeinschaftsausschuss der Deutschen Gewerblichen Wirtschaft* (Council of German Business) was established, in which the whole range of policy issues including labor relations is discussed (Reutter, 2001). During the past 30 years the number of trade associations has risen steadily in almost all sectors of the economy (Sebaldt, 1997), causing problems of integration within existing associational arrangements (Lang & Schneider, 2007). State–business relations have remained consensus oriented and all governments have kept to this practice without regard to their ideological orientation (Reutter, 2001).

The aim of this chapter is to analyze adaptational processes of influential and relevant[2] business associations operatjng in the British and German information and communications sector. The intention is to take the continually changing nature of this sector into account and to shed light on the mechanisms that triggered changes in organizational behaviors and structures between 1987 and 2002. As has been shown above, business associations in the information and communications sector have been exposed to fundamental changes in their environment, which are likely to set off similar processes of adaptation according to the theories of Europeanization and globalization. However, well-established state–business relations are likely to condition the behavior of systems of trade associations, which in turn should lead to different evolutionary paths. The following chapters will consider if the varieties of capitalism hypothesis still prevails or if global and European challenges lead to a greater homogeneity of sectoral systems of organized business interests.

Changes in structure and composition of the British and German systems of trade associations

The transformation of the associational landscape: Entries, mergers, and splits

The German associational landscape in the I&C sector has undergone fundamental changes since technological, economic, and political transformations took place in the 1980s. Until that point, the different subsectors were represented by a few sectoral peak associations that were members of either the national employer association, BDA, or the industrial peak association, BDI.[3] The former included the sectoral peaks in the publishing and printing sectors, while the latter contained business associations that covered telecommunications and electronic equipment and components manufacturers.

The picture has changed considerably since the 1990s. In particular, associations operating at the interfaces of different subsectors have established themselves. In 1990 the Association of Private Radio and Telecommunications (*Verband Privater Rundfunk und Telekommunikation* or VPRT) originated through the merger of previously independent associations. In 1995 the German Multimedia Association (*Deutscher Multimedia Verband*) was founded and included many subsectors of the field, while in 1998 two smaller associations merged into the Association of Distributors of Telecommunications Services and Value Added Services (*Verband der Anbieter von Telekommunikations- und Mehrwertdiensten* or VATM).

In 1999 a joint divisional association of the *Zentralverband Elektrotechnik und Elektroindustrie* (Central Association for Electric Technology and Electric Industries or ZVEI) and of the Association of German Mechanical and Plant Engineering (*Verband Deutscher Maschinen- und Anlagenbau* or VDMA) split from the VDMA and ZVEI. These divisional

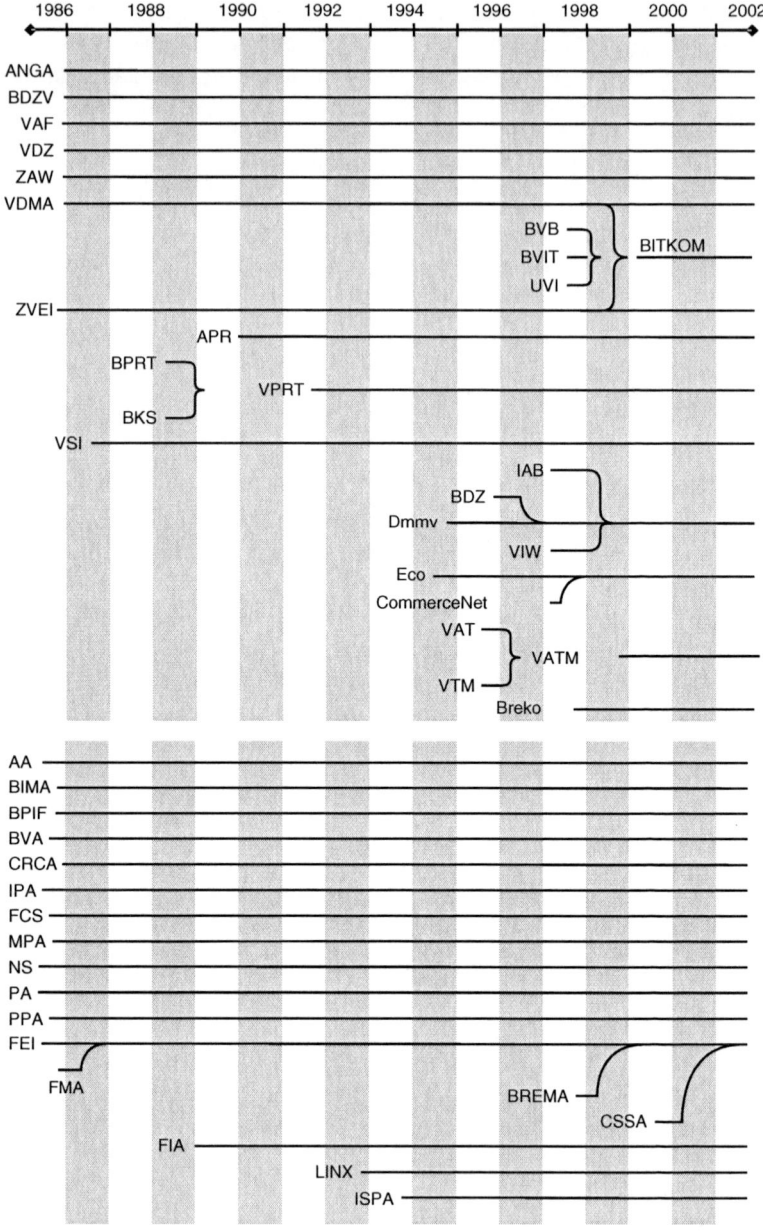

Figure 6.1 Entries, mergers, and splits in the German (above) and British (below) associational systems

associations subsequently merged with three other independent associations and became the largest I&C association known to date: BITKOM (*Bundesverband der Informationswirtschaft, Telekommunikation und Neue Medien*, or Federal Association of Information Economy, Telecommunications and New Media). It has taken on the task of putting an end to the dissipation of the associational landscape and of representing the entire I&C sector. For this purpose other associations have also joined BITKOM as members. Among them are the former parental associations VDMA, ZVEI, and VAF, which have all become closely aligned to BITKOM. In addition, several 'acquisitions' of formerly independent business associations increased the dynamics within the German population. The German Multimedia Association (DMMV) acquired three smaller business associations covering similar sectors between 1998 and 1999. The DMMV has become one of the largest associations within the new media sector due to its aggressive expansion strategy. The *Electronic Commerce Forum* (Eco) also enhanced its representativeness by including the members of the association *ComerceNet* into its membership base.

The British trade association system, on the other hand, has faced only moderate rearrangement since the 1980s. Almost half of the focal organizations were set up in or after 1980. Before that time trade associations representing the content industries dominated the associational landscape in the information and communications sector: these associations included the *Newspaper Society* (NS), the *Periodical Publishers Association* (PPA), the *Music Publishers Association* (MPA), the *British Printing Industries Federation* (BPIF), the *Advertising Association* (AA), and the *Institute of Practitioners in Advertising* (IPA). Before the 1980s only the *Federation of the Electronics Industry* (FEI) and the *Commercial Radio Companies Association* (CRCA) represented information industries based on electronic transmission.

Interest groups representing newly established content industries were the first to join the network of focal trade associations. Examples are the *British Video Association* (BVA), which was set up in 1980, followed by the *Federation of Communications Services* (FCS) just one year later. The *British Interactive Multimedia Association* (BIMA) was the last to be established in the 1980s, but the first to include new media and the internet in its domain. Technological changes and economic growth promoted the founding of additional organizations representing parts of the internet industries. The *Fibreoptic Industry Association* (FIA) was the first to respond to the needs of SMEs to advance coordination and mutual support in this newly established sector, and finally the *London Information*

Exchange (LINX) and the *Internet Service Providers Association* (ISPA) were the latest focal trade associations established in the 1990s. Both associations organize the interests of internet service providers, but ISPA also tries to cover neighboring industries.

In contrast to Germany, British associations have rarely taken an active part in these restructurings. Although Michael Heseltine, when President of the Board of Trade in the 1990s, encouraged the emergence of 'lead' associations to be responsible for the coordination and aggregation of interests within a sector, only few of these associations were formed (May et al., 1998). Among them is the *Federation of the Electronics Industry* (FEI), which incorporated several smaller business associations representing neighboring industrial branches. These so-called mergers were clearly dominated by the FEI. However, due to the increasing scope of interest domains, each acquisition was followed by a renaming.

Cooperation and competition within associational systems

The population dynamics of foundings, mergers and splits did not only affect the composition of the associational systems in both countries, but also had an effect on competitive and cooperative relations among the individual business associations. To evaluate the degree of competition and cooperation we asked representatives of business associations (1) to name other trade associations with which they have frequent contacts; and (2) to indicate other business associations that are also active in the same sector. These relations were combined so that we were able to identify symmetric as well as asymmetric patterns of competition and cooperation. For example, if associations represent identical sectors without having relations, it is interpreted as a sign of competition. If associations represent different sectors but have intense contacts, we interpret it as a cooperative relationship.

As previously mentioned, the German associational system has undergone fundamental changes since the 1980s. Trade associations that represented the I&C sector before the 1980s generally have cooperative relations with one another (see Figure 6.2). Associations representing traditional content industries such as publishing (BDZV, VDZ) and advertising (ZAW) are particularly known to cooperate with each other in matters such as the distribution of advertising revenues or the regulation of advertising conduct. In contrast, trade associations that organize interests in the telecommunications and electronic equipment industries, such as ANGA, VAF, ZVEI, and VDMA, typically developed competitive, yet asymmetric, relations to one another. However, relations between

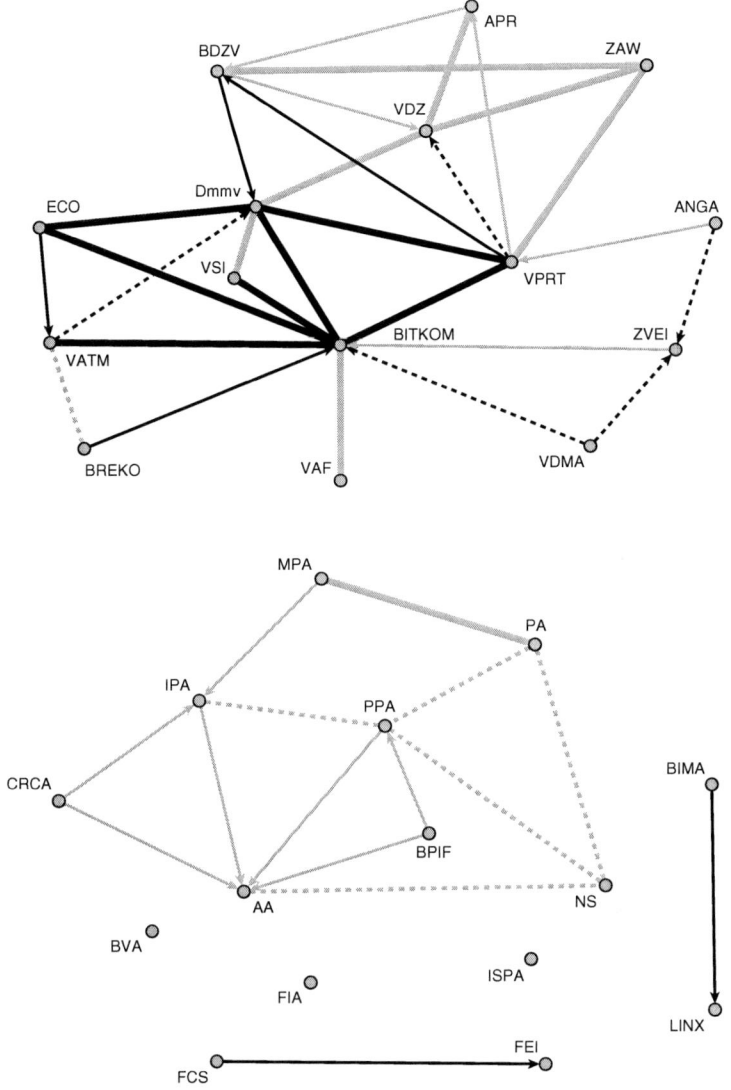

Figure 6.2 Ecological relations in the German (above) and British (below) associational networks

Notes
Relations: (examples in parenthesis)
Gray, bold, continuous: Mutualism (BITKOM–VAF)
Gray, thin, continuous: Partial cooperation (APR–BDZV)
Gray, bold, dashed: Neutrality (VATM–BREKO)
Black, bold, continuous: Full competition (VPRT–BITKOM)
Black, thin, continuous: Partial competition (BREKO–BITKOM)
Black, thin, dashed: 'Harmful' competition (VPRT–VDZ)

associations in the traditional communications sector are rare. Rather surprising is the fact that cooperation between BITKOM and its parental associations VDMA and ZVEI is not reciprocal and, in the case of the VDMA, that it exhibits competitive features.

Newly founded associations have positioned themselves at the intersection between different subsectors and have multiple domain overlaps to other associations. Relevant examples are the *Association of Private Radio and Telecommunications* (VPRT) and the *German Multimedia Association* (DMMV), which have competitive relations to several other media and telecommunications associations. The designated sectoral peak association BITKOM competes with no fewer than half of the focal associations. This is mainly due to the massive enforcement of an associational hierarchy in this sector by the national industrial peak association BDI, which aimed to incorporate this fast-growing sector under its umbrella. Negatively affected associations such as the DMMV, the VPRT, and the ECO reacted by increasing their domains and by 'acquiring' other (smaller) associations and business groups.

The structure of the British ecological network is comparatively sparse (see Figure 6.2). Domain overlaps exist mainly at the intersections between the established interest groups representing the content and printing branches. In contrast to the German structure, where no intermediating actor exists, the British structure provides such an organization. Tensions between most of these trade associations are mediated by the presence of an institutionalized communication structure offered by the *Advertising Association* (AA). The AA constitutes a federation that has the CRCA, the IPA, the NS, and the PPA as members. The AA stands for the mutual interests of its members and acts as a complement to them. It also provides a communication platform for resolving existing disagreements. The AA members have therefore primarily established neutral relations reflecting a division of domains and tasks. Furthermore, the establishment of the *UK Publishing Media Alliance* in 2001 provided a forum for conflict resolution and joint agreements.

There hardly exist any relations among trade associations that represent telecommunication and internet industries or electronic component manufacturers. Exceptions are competitive relations between BIMA and LINX as well as between FCS and FEI, which have been developed due to domain overlaps. However, since British telecommunication and internet industries associations tend to be rather small[4] with narrow domains, each of them acts in its own niche that is barely challenged by other associations.

Informal hierarchies: Information exchange networks

Population dynamics have also left their mark on the positioning of the associations in information exchange networks.[5] During the 1980s the German telecommunication interest system was dominated by two associations, the ZVEI and the VDMA. Within the system of organized business interests, they represented the private part of the sector that was not under the supervision of the present-day Telekom (at that time, the Federal Post Office). For the last half a century, the newspaper and periodical branch has been represented by the Association of German Periodical Publishers (*Verband Deutscher Zeitschriftenverleger* or VDZ) and the Association of German Newspapers Publishers (*Bundesverband der Deutschen Zeitungsverleger* or BDZV). At the beginning of the 1990s more and more actors entered this elite circle of business associations (in particular the VPRT), breaking their representational monopoly (Schneider & Werle, 1991). The population structure changed completely by 2002: ZVEI and VDMA were pushed out of the center of the I&C branch by associations founded a few years beforehand. The prominent actors in the information exchange network since the start of the new millennium are VPRT, Dmmv and BDZV (see Figure 6.3).

The BDZV is the only 'traditional' organization which was able to maintain its status as a prominent actor in the converging sector. VPRT, DMMV, and BDZV act as information brokers to important subgroups of the network. The VPRT links the associations of electronic equipment manufacturers (ZVEI and VDMA) of cable service providers (ANGA), of telecommunication tools (VAF), and the encompassing I&C branch association BITKOM to the other actors. The DMMV, on the other hand, connects the associations of software companies (VSI), telecommunication services providers (VATM and BREKO), and internet service providers (ECO) with the newspaper association BDZV and thereby with all the other associations representing new and old media. The BDZV, finally, is the actor that holds the whole network together through links to the DMMV and the VPRT, since these are not connected to each other.

The British information exchange network does not show a similar hierarchy in its relation structure: there are several isolated actors but no single dominant organization. The core of the network is comprised of business interest groups that were established before the 1980s. AA, CRCA, MPA, and PPA occupy a prominent position, but none of them is located in the center of all relations. The difference in the positioning of most trade associations is rather small compared to the German network.

The newcomer associations have difficulty acquiring a major role in the information exchange structure of the I&C network and are located

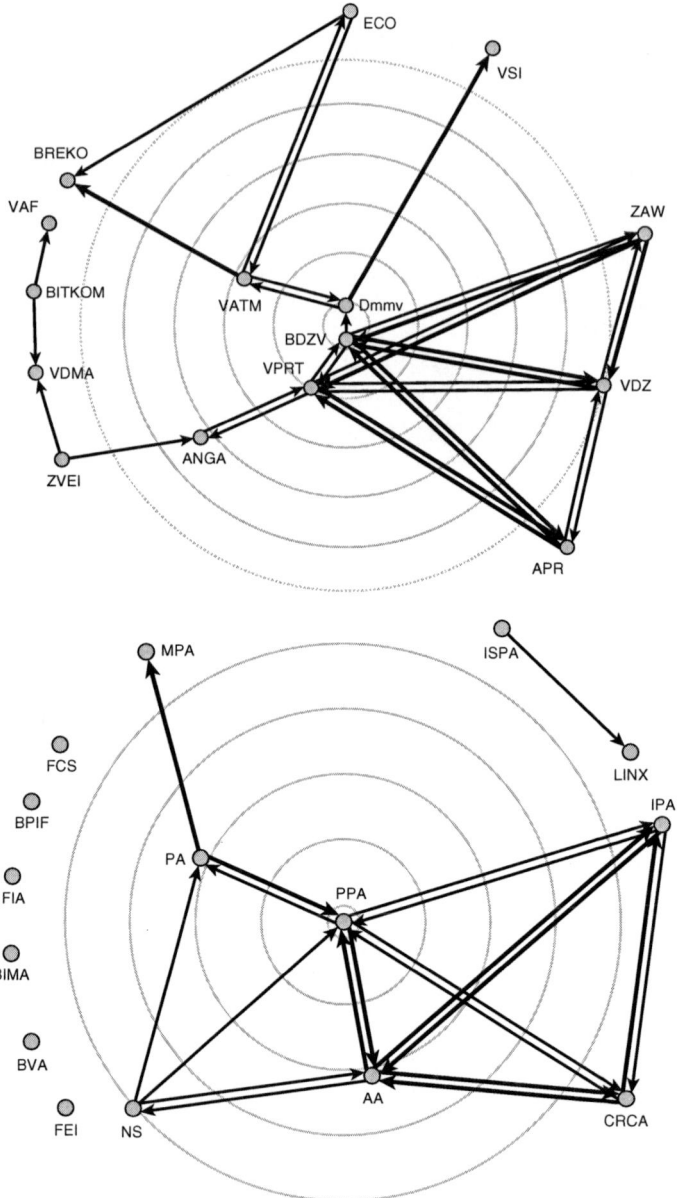

Figure 6.3 Information exchange in the German (above) and British (below) associational networks

Notes
Relations:
Bold: frequent information exchange
Thin: occasional information exchange

at a more peripheral position. The fact that these organizations have fewer contacts to other focal associations does not mean that they have fewer contacts in general. Due to the comparatively high number of trade associations (compared to Germany) representing the I&C sector, the British interest groups sustain more relations to associations outside this focal organizations set. This is true primarily for interest groups standing for the multimedia and internet branch.

In comparison to the German case, the British information exchange network has a relatively sparse structure. Six trade associations are isolated and do not exchange information with any of the focal organizations. Once again, media and advertising interests constitute the central part of the network. Only LINX and ISPA exchange information outside the main structures. Due to the limited information flow within the network, an information broker or 'gatekeeper' able to monopolize information exchange could not develop. Although the PPA and the AA occupy central positions, they control only a tiny fraction of information flows.

The reorganization of associational tasks: Strategies of adaptation

Apart from these population-level activities, trade associations also change their internal behavior and structure in order to cope with changes in their environment. Table 6.1 presents the average resource allocation of British and German trade associations. Even though they are remarkably similar, there are a few differences worth mentioning. British trade associations spent fewer resources on national as well as European lobbying than their German equivalents, which in turn provide fewer services to their members. The category 'others' was surprisingly often marked by British respondents: for example LINX dedicates 86 percent of its resources to peer-to-peer internet traffic or to joint stalls at a fair. BVA also represents an organization that assigns a great portion – a total of 30 percent – of its resources to 'other' activities, mainly in the provision of market analysis and benchmarking offered to members and non-members. In the German associational system one cannot find similar extreme cases. Only ANGA and Eco dedicate a significant share – 20 percent and 10 percent respectively – of their resources to 'other' activities. As can be seen from these examples, the category 'others' includes the greatest difference in the mean and the variance (or the standard deviation) of all categories between the two countries.

In contrast to the average resource allocation, the differences in the variances (or the standard deviations) are generally much more obvious.

Table 6.1 Average resource allocation (in percent) and changes (frequency) of British and German trade associations in the I&C sector

Activities	Resource allocation				Changes			
	Mean		Standard deviation		Increase (frequency)		Decrease (frequency)	
	D	UK	D	UK	D	UK	D	UK
National lobbying	25.6	19.6	12.3	13.9	5	5	1	0
European lobbying	11.7	6.5	8.1	8.8	6	4	0	1
Societal lobbying	8.2	5.6	8.9	9.3	0	1	1	0
Influence investments	**45.5**	**31.7**			**11**	**10**	**2**	**1**
Member consultation	12.1	13.3	8.8	14.1	3	2	1	0
Member information	11.7	14.1	7.0	7.2	1	1	0	0
Member conferences	15.5	13.3	13.8	11.4	2	2	0	2
Side benefits	7.1	9.0	9.4	12.9	2	3	1	0
Training	4.7	7.2	4.9	7.9	0	1	0	0
Membership investments	**51.1**	**56.9**			**8**	**9**	**4**	**2**
Other	3.4	11.4	5.7	23.7	1	0	2	0
Total	100	100			20	19	6	3

In almost every category the British associational system ranks higher than the German one, except for expenditure on conferences. The German ZVEI and the DMMV dedicate 50 percent and 40 percent respectively of their resources to the organization of member conferences, while other associations spend very little on this activity. Examples are the VDZ, the APR, and the BDZV with only 5 percent investment in conferences. In the British system the variance is less pronounced, but still ranges from 30 percent (AA, BIMA, FEI) to no expenditure (BVA, PPA, PA). The reason for the differences in organizing member conferences can be seen in the membership base of the various trade associations: associations representing a broad domain have considerably more problems organizing their heterogeneous membership than those embodying only a small subsector of the entire branch. More encompassing associations must therefore spend more resources on coordination activities like member conferences.

During the last 15 years some activities have clearly lost or gained in importance (see Table 6.1). In the British and German associational systems investments in lobbying activities increased considerably and surprisingly, both at the national and the European level. The other activities also gained in importance simultaneously, but not to the extent of the influence investments. Most of the respondents pointed to the fact that their associations had made great efforts in professionalizing their organizations, which subsequently led to a greater productivity in the whole associational system.

The analysis of each activity is suited to comparing the two associational systems. It serves to identify similarities and differences in resource allocation, but it largely ignores within-system variation that manifests itself in differing degrees of specialization. Hierarchical cluster analysis is an appropriate method to detect profile homogeneity within associational systems. Results indicate that the British and German associational landscapes are internally diverse, but can be grouped in four relatively homogeneous types of business associations that allocate their resources in similar ways:

- *Cluster I* contains three associations that invest their resources mainly in societal (28 percent) and national lobbying (22 percent). Other activities play a minor role. Examples are the *British Video Association* (BVA), which invests a great portion of its resources in public relations against copyright violations, and the German telecommunications association (VATM), which organizes campaigns against the former monopolistic carrier Telekom. This type of association may be labeled 'political gardeners'.
- *Cluster II* includes nine business associations that predominantly allocate their resources to membership activities. National (9 percent), European (5 percent), and societal lobbying (2 percent) does take place. These associations are clearly 'service providers'.
- *Cluster III* contains 14 associations that invest in lobbying activities at various levels. Investments in national lobbying (27 percent) rank highest and are followed by European lobbying (15 percent). These business associations can be labelled 'multilevel lobbyists'.
- Just two associations constitute *Cluster IV*. APR and FCS predominantly allocate their resources to domestic lobbying activities (55 percent) and can thus be labeled 'domestic lobbyists'.

British and German sectoral systems of business associations differ significantly with respect to the composition of associational types. In the British system 'service providers' clearly dominate. Half the associations belong to this category, while only four British associations have a 'multilevel lobbyist' profile. In contrast to their British equivalents, German business associations are mostly 'multilevel lobbyists'. Almost

75 percent of the German associations belong to this lobbying type. On the other hand, there are relatively few 'service providers': only the DMMV and the ZVEI belong to this category. However, both countries developed a small number of specialist associations that focus either on domestic or societal lobbying.

A comparison of lobbying targets and their perceived relevance in public policy making (Figure 6.4) reveals only slight differences in lobbying strategies between British and German business associations. In both countries the economic ministries are the most important lobbying targets, followed by the domestic lower houses of parliament, the Directorate General 'Information Society' of the European Commission, and the European Parliament. The results clearly indicate the multi-level aspect of lobbying in the information and communications sector. However, there has remained some divergence in lobbying activities. Above all, German associations have more frequent lobbying contacts with domestic and European institutions than do British associations. This finding clearly correlates with differences in resource expenditures. German associations devote more time and money to domestic and European lobbying than do British associations (for similar results see Eising, 2004). Another difference is marked by the higher relevance and more numerous lobbying contacts of the German regulatory agency for telecommunications (RegTP) compared to the British OFTEL. The reason for this difference lies in the fact that OFTEL was established much earlier than the RegTP and could therefore create and test adequate regulatory measures. Furthermore, OFTEL was independent from any government body (in particular from the DTI) from the beginning, and is only accountable to Parliament. In contrast, the German RegTP, which was initially set up as an independent regulatory agency, can be partially controlled by the BMWi because the latter remained responsible in some areas and is able to issue an instruction that overrules directives and decisions.

Similar to the resource allocation profiles that revealed high internal variance, a comparison of structural equivalences of lobbying activities illustrates that there are different lobbying patterns in Britain and Germany. The cluster analysis distinguishes three lobbying clusters that are highly similar to those found in the resource allocation profiles:

- *Cluster I* contains all business associations with frequent contacts to almost all relevant organizations at the national and European level. Among them are only German associations.

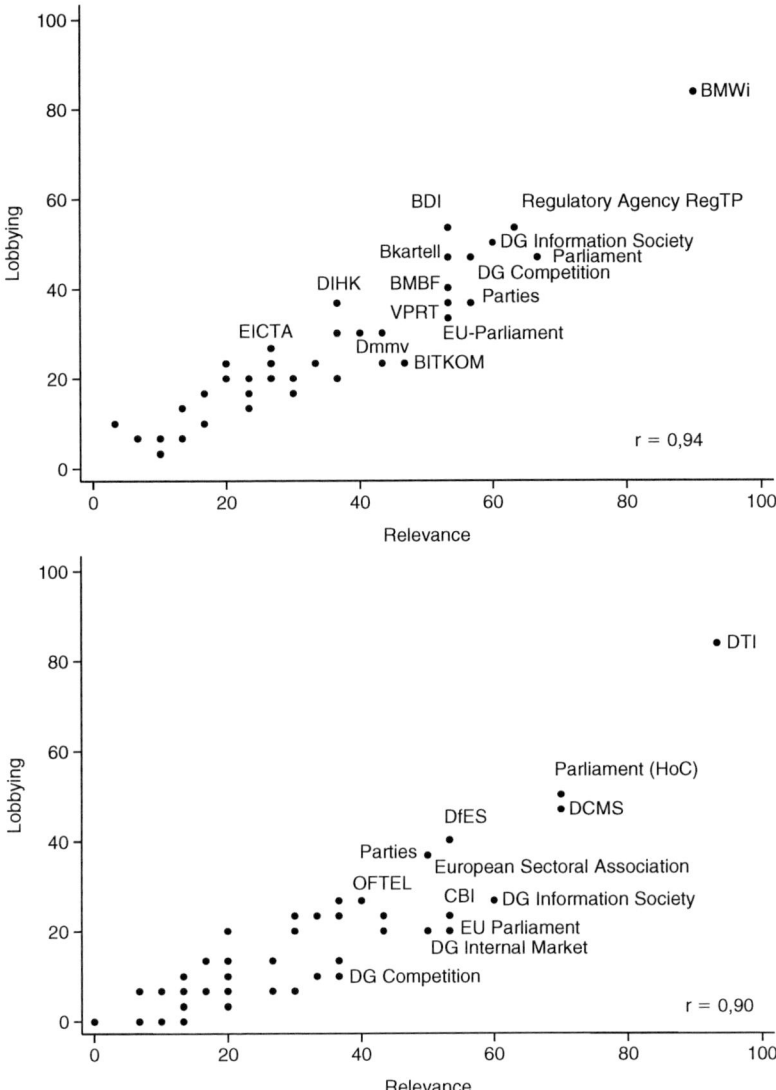

Figure 6.4 Lobbying targets and their relevance for German (above) and British (below) associations (in percent)

Note: The scattergrams combine two types of network data: (1) importance/relevance valuation of various organizations in the political (x-axis); (2) the frequency of information provision, weighted by the intensity of information exchange (y-axis).

Table 6.2 Membership of international trade associations and the maintenance of a liaison office in Brussels

	European association	International association	Office in Brussels
Germany	BDZV, BITKOM, DMMV, ECO, VAF, VDMA, VDZ, VPRT, ZAW, ZVEI	BDZV, BITKOM, VDMA, VDZ, ZVEI	VDMA, ZVEI, VPRT, VATM
UK	AA, BPIF, BVA, CRCA, FEI, IPA, ISPA, LINX, NS, PA, PPA	AA, BPIF, CRCA, FEI, MPA, NS, PA, PPA	ISPA

Note: The VDMA as a peak association is not a member of an international association, but some of its affiliated associations (*Fachverbände*) are.

- *Cluster II* consists of associations that have frequent contacts with the economic ministries (DTI or BMWi) but few contacts with other organizations.
- *Cluster III* associations have frequent contacts with national institutions BMWi/DTI, the lower house of parliament, political parties, the industrial peak associations BDI/CBI, and at the European level the DG 'Information Society'.

The growing importance of EU institutions in policy making has left its mark on the organization of associational access routes to these institutions. Apart from the infrequent direct contacts, the trade associations in both countries make use of the indirect access strategy via European branch associations. Two-thirds of the entire sample under investigation are members of a European branch association, while almost half are affiliated to an international association (see Table 6.2). Most of these organizations represent established sectors like the printing industry and are therefore capable of devoting time and staff to European and international activities. However, only a few associations managed to establish a liaison office in Brussels. German associations that operate in the telecommunications sector were especially eager to invest in their European lobbying activities.

Newly founded trade associations, however, are still consolidating their structures and routines and, as a result, operate mainly at the national level. Only those organizations that have been able to extract an extensive amount of members out of the represented sectors in the first years after their founding are capable of expanding their activities to both to the national and to the European arenas of interest representation.

Do domestic institutions have an effect on the adaptation process? Or do similar challenges lead to a similar evolutionary trajectory?

The information and communications sector has undergone fundamental changes since the 1980s. Technological revolutions have paved the way for the merger of formerly separated sectors and extraordinary economic growth rates have led to the emergence of new markets and industries. Although the excitement surrounding the 'new economy' has vanished, the I&C sector has outstripped other economic segments. It has become the dominant branch with regard to growth rates as well as innovation rates. At the same time, European institutions (with the European Commission 'leading the pack') emerged onto the political scene, acquiring an increasing number of competencies thought to be essentially national.

In the introductory chapter, the hypothesis was formulated that these fundamental changes become the dominant force, leading to similar adaptations within affected countries and associational systems. It should however be noted that every political system contains a specific set of organizing principles, which persist over time and can hardly be modified or even abandoned. The British and German ways of organizing business interest are deeply rooted in their particular traditions. Both are instances of typical arrangements and it can be said that they represent structural and behavioral counterparts: on the one hand the British system of small and particularistic associations that have only infrequent contacts with public authorities; and on the other hand the German system of encompassing trade associations that employ institutionalized channels to government.

The British and German systems of trade associations adapted differently to the external challenges. In both, new business associations were established due to the development of new sectors as well as high economic growth rates that led to the creation of new and larger resource pools. However, these developments are more pronounced in German associations than in British.

In the German associational system, newly founded associations represent innovative and converging sectors that cover different branches of the I&C sector. Their positioning within interest domains of established associations has led to an increase in competition, dividing the network into a cooperative network, which includes media and advertising associations, and a competitive network, containing telecommunications and electronic component associations. Another reason for the spread of competitive relations is the aggressive enforcement of a hierarchical associational structure by the leading industrial peak association, BDI, which evoked countermeasures such as mergers and acquisitions by some smaller associations. This in turn impeded the establishment of an encompassing sectoral peak association under the umbrella of BITKOM. The same holds for the German information exchange network, where some newly founded actors have reached central positions and have thereby replaced former sectoral peak associations ZVEI and VDMA. The designated peak association BITKOM was unable to position itself in the center due to the countermeasures of other associations that were enforced by the multiplication of competitive relations.

In the British case the transformation is less pronounced: the composition of the associational system only changed to a minor extent. Three associations have been founded since the mid-1980s but have not been able to play a dominant role comparable to that of their German counterparts. The British structure consists of a few neutral and cooperative relations that link established actors. On the one hand, the absence of competition is due to the inclusiveness of British trade associations that concentrate their interest domains on a small part of the total interest spectrum. This specialization results from the members' preference for undistorted interest representation, which necessarily implies a homogeneous membership base (Bennett, 1998, 2000). On the other hand, the low number of competitors in the British associational system is a consequence of the intermediary role that the Advertising Association plays within the different interests of the media and advertising industries. In contrast, business associations that represent telecommunications and electronics industries are disconnected from the core of the associational system. This also holds for the information exchange network, in which information flow is virtually restricted to media and advertising industry associations.

A closer look at the resource investments in associational activities reveals that there are only minor differences between the mean scores of each activity. Resource utilization follows a similar pattern in both systems: the largest share is spent on national lobbying activities, followed by investments in the coordination of member interests, such as member information and conferences. However, the internal variance of resource investments is significantly higher in the British system: it therefore appears that British associations have established different priorities regarding their activities. In contrast, differences between German associations are less pronounced. The cluster analysis reveals that British associations are more specialized in particular activities than their German equivalents. Furthermore, the British system contains a higher share of service providers, while in the German system multilevel lobbyists prevail. Similarly, German associations have more lobbying contacts to either domestic or European institutions, which (once again) illustrates that the share of multilevel lobbyists is considerably higher in the German associational system. In contrast, British associations are more often members of European and international branch associations than their German equivalents, which in turn are more likely to maintain a permanent office in Brussels. Direct lobbying strategies are therefore more frequent in the German associational system than in the British in which – in particular for European lobbying – indirect strategies via European branch associations prevail. Different priorities and internal variances of associational activities result either from the diversity of preferences of member firms or from differences in the embedding of associational structures. Diverse and dominant preferences of member firms are the overarching logic in the British associational system. British firms clearly prefer an undistorted interest representation and, more importantly, an adequate provision of services. Due to the relatively small interest domains and the resulting greater homogeneity of member preferences, British associations can narrow their range of activities and concentrate their resource expenditures on few activities. The German associations, in contrast, have to diversify their activities in order to satisfy their apparently more heterogeneous membership base. They also have to upgrade their lobbying strategies to a multilevel scale in order not to fall behind rival associations that have, at least in part, overlapping interest domains.

In conclusion, it is clear that exogenous factors have initiated similar adaptation processes in the British and German associational systems. High growth rates and technological innovations have led to an increase in the number of business associations in the information and communications sector, while Europeanization brought about more lobbying activities at the European level. Aside from these similarities, both associational systems adopted different evolutionary paths that have been paved by endogenous factors. The low integration of the British associational system in particular has led to the dominance of the logic of membership, in which the narrow preferences of the member firms prevail. These contain undistorted interest representation and service provision. British business associations hardly need to pay attention to rival associations that operate within their interest domain and therefore do not have to fear being overtaken in their lobbying activities (at least by potential domestic rivals). Most associations are able to find a stable and unchallenged niche where they can focus their activities on a small range of tasks. The German associational system, on the other hand, is highly integrated due to external enforcement of a hierarchical structure and counteractions by potential losers of a vertical integration. Consequently, the associational system is characterized by a high density of competitive relations, which, in turn, increases competitive pressure, leading to a convergence of associational activities, in particular lobbying activities. It is therefore apparent that multilevel lobbyists are more frequent in the German associational system than in other associational types.

Notes

1. British and German trade associations show a high degree of similarity in their perception of external challenges. Representatives of British and German trade associations were asked to state the importance of economic (e.g. recession, business cycles), technological (e.g. innovation, replacement processes), political (e.g. regulation, laws), and societal (e.g. environment awareness, consumer needs) challenges that account for the need for adaptation. A great majority of business association representatives regard economic (Germany 60 percent, UK 83 percent) as well as technological (Germany 66 percent, UK 92 percent) and political (Germany 93 percent, UK 58 percent) challenges as 'important' or 'most important' for their organization. While the activities of their British equivalents are predominantly driven by economic and technological factors, there are some differences in political challenges that are the main impetus for the behavior of German trade associations. The respondents in both countries locate the origin of the diverse challenges predominantly at the European or global level. More specifically, technological challenges act on a global scale, while political challenges are European in nature.
2. The selection of influential and relevant business associations was based on a 'realistic' sampling procedure (Laumann et al., 1983): After extensive internet and document searches, 86 British and 38 German business associations could be identified that operated at that time in the information and communications sector. Several experts were then asked to evaluate these associations according to their influence on sectoral policy making. These experts used a three-point scale to indicate the importance of individual associations. Business associations that received 25 percent or more of the accumulated influence score were selected for further research. Of these 20 British and 18 German associations, 15 responded in each case. However, both focal populations contain the ten highest-ranked associations.
3. The BDI only covers industrial and neighboring sectors.
4. An exception is of course the *Federation of the Electronics Industry* (FEI).

5. Respondents were asked to indicate from which business associations they receive information and to which associations they send information. The respondents could differentiate between frequent and infrequent exchanges. In order to increase reliability, only confirmed relations were taken into account. A confirmed relation exists when business association A indicates that it sends information to association B, and B confirms that it receives information from A. Thus a line between two associations indicates a confirmed directed information flow between both business associations.

7
Cooperation, Competition, and Mutualism in the US Information and Communications Sector[1]

Johannes M. Bauer and Volker Schneider

US information and communications (I&C) industries are a particularly interesting case for exploring the responses of associations to external change. They represent a large segment of the economy and have even higher indirect importance as critical material and immaterial infrastructures, closely intertwined with nearly all other social and economic activities. Firms need to survive in a turbulent technological and market environment, characterized by rapid change and particularly trying economic conditions. Many segments of the I&C industries exhibit very high fixed costs combined with relatively low incremental costs, a situation that is very different from the conditions of the industrial age. During the past three decades, these industries have been subject to significant policy transformations on a global scale toward private ownership, open market entry, and reduced regulation. New issues that have disrupted the historical relations between stakeholders include the technological blurring of traditional industry boundaries, which has created hitherto unknown forms of competitive rivalry; the migration to next-generation networks and services that pitches network operators against content providers; the global problem of piracy of intellectual property; and information security and privacy. All these forces constitute powerful challenges for the existing business associations and the political system.

The two predominant frameworks used to conceptualize the responses of political systems in general and associational systems in particular to environmental transformations, discussed in the introductory sections of this book, diagnose either a 'deep impact' or 'slow change'. Both approaches, however, assert that such change is relatively independent of the national context. We juxtapose these extreme positions with an intermediate, hybrid approach that recognizes that the unique political features of a nation, the particular historical evolution of institutional arrangements, and the particular organization of the associational space, all may lead to variations in adaptation. We examine the plausibility of these competing positions theoretically and empirically for the associational system of the US information and communications sector.

The US associational system is often characterized as a prototype of a pluralist model. A close examination promises insights into the adequacy of this description and the responses of an admittedly differentiated associational system to external challenges. We apply a new version of systems theory to the evolution of associational structures in I&C. Our approach goes beyond the traditional perspective, which typically assumes that there is a 'single logic' of interaction; that is, societal phenomena are explained by reducing them to only a few organizing principles. In contrast, complex systems approaches recognize that societies are multilayered and multisectional, involving a variety of components, levels, and multiplex relations (Bauer, 2004; Schneider & Bauer, 2007). As will be discussed in more detail, this approach has profound consequences for theorizing adaptation.

Technological and economic convergence has blurred the traditional boundaries of the I&C industries. Hence, for the purposes of our study, we adopted an inclusive definition encompassing newspaper publishing, computing, broadcasting, cable television, wireline and wireless communication services, information services, and equipment needed to operate and use communication services. In 2006, the I&C sector as delineated contributed more than 12 percent to US GDP. To assess our theoretical arguments, we gathered detailed data on a focal set of business associations. These associations were selected on the basis of political relevance as judged by a group of I&C scholars and experts. Representatives of the organizations were interviewed in 2001 and 2002 using standardized questionnaires. Furthermore, our chapter draws on findings by the other members of the research team studying other sectors in the US and in other countries (Grote & Lang, 2003; Grote & Schneider, 2006; Lang, 2006).

By way of providing some background, the following section describes the environmental challenges faced by the US I&C sector. The chapter then discusses the structure and composition of business associations in the US I&C sector. After that we explore in detail structural features of the associational space, such as the degree of cooperation and competition, formal and informal mechanisms of information exchange, adaptation measures, as well as association strategies and lobbying targets. Major empirical and theoretical conclusions are then summarized. Overall, we find that the US I&C associational system and its responses to change are much richer than is suggested by existing theoretical approaches. Integrating notions from complexity theory into traditional theoretical concepts allows this diversity to be captured in an overarching framework.

Environmental challenges for I&C associations

American I&C associations have to confront the effects of continuous economic, technological, and political changes on their members. As economic and technological factors are closely related, they will be dealt with jointly. Many political challenges are related to the continuing fragmentation of the legal and institutional framework in which I&C industries operate. Thus, the main aspects of this institutional context will also be touched on briefly.

Economic and technological challenges: Convergence and new forms of rivalry

Historically, the various segments of the I&C industries operated based on very different technological foundations. Each used a technology engineered to achieve a specific purpose efficiently. Telephony was very different from over-the-air broadcasting or cable television systems. This started to change, gradually at first but then at increasing speed, with the onset of the information and communication revolution during the 1970s. Rapid advances in the design of microelectronic components led to a steady reduction in their size and cost, lowering energy consumption while increasing information processing and storage capacity at the same time. Simultaneously, the process of digitization set in, allowing for the representation, processing, and transmission of information as binary code. This technology permitted computers to exchange data directly via digital networks without having first to convert the information into analog signals. This convergence between telecommunications and computers into a hybrid 'telematic' sector paved the way for a multitude of innovations in the hardware and services market, eventually culminating in the creation of the internet.

Until the late 1990s, the radio and print sectors were not affected directly by this first wave of convergence between telecommunications and computers (Sandholtz, 1993; Latzer, 1997). However, the logical architecture of the internet (the TCP/IP protocol), combined with digitization of all forms of information, allowed the integration of the existing different fixed and radio networks into one increasingly seamless general-purpose platform. The infrastructure for data transmission improved with the introduction of more powerful satellites, the diffusion of broadband coaxial and fiber networks, and the improved usage of radio frequencies. This facilitated the further technological fusion between telematics and media into a 'mediamatic' sector, which started slowly during the 1990s. Consequently, the boundaries between the segments of I&C became more fuzzy: with the entry of telephone companies into entertainment and of cable companies into telephony and internet access, the emergence of wireless broadband services, and the introduction of digital broadcasting, new competitive relationships and rivalries emerged.

For several reasons, convergence is a particular economic challenge to I&C industries. A first factor is the unique cost conditions of I&C industries: high up-front fixed costs combined with relatively low incremental costs. To earn a profit, firms facing such cost conditions have to mark up their prices significantly above costs, often by offering highly differentiated services or by attempting to become the dominant supplier in a niche or an entire market segment. The second strategy faces the risk of antitrust oversight or renewed regulatory intervention. Either strategy is, second, complicated by the new forms of rivalry enabled by convergence. Firms in different industry segments have unequal starting positions. Due to their strong market presence and general-purpose network infrastructure, network-based operators, in particular cable television and telephone companies, have advantages over broadcasting companies or the new players emerging from the internet, even if they are as large as Google. Third, given the relative ease with which applications and services in the information industries can be imitated, players increasingly work in a hypercompetitive market environment. Associations play an important role in helping defend market positions and boundaries and shaping a legal environment conducive to the interests of the particular industry segment. However, multiple rifts run across the information industries. For example, the conflicts about music and film piracy pitch the content industries against search engines and network service providers.

Political and institutional challenges

Key political challenges for the I&C industries emerge from an increasing belief in market forces and competition that sometimes conflicts with the fundamental economics of the industry; the fragmentation of the legal and regulatory framework as well as jurisdiction; the asymmetry of the legal and regulatory framework; and the ensuing stakeholder conflicts (see Brock, 1981, 1994, 2003 as well as Temin & Galambos, 1987 for a detailed discussion of the historical evolution of I&C industries). The different segments are regulated according to four major legal regimes for information flows (Noam, 2001: 211). Publishing is based on the constitutional (sometimes 'print') model, which gives the owners fundamental free speech rights and protects them from government regulation. Very limited exceptions exist only for obscene content, defamatory speech, or information that is deemed to jeopardize national security or public safety. Telecommunication service providers, defined by law roughly as service providers that transport information without modification, include fixed and mobile voice service providers and some basic data communication platforms. They are treated as common carriers, which have to make their services available on a non-discriminatory basis and at reasonable prices. Moreover, common carriers have no editorial control over the information transported on their networks.

Information service providers, more or less defined as service providers that modify the content transported, include internet service providers, online service providers, and other value-added service suppliers. They are essentially unregulated. Given digitization and convergence, this continuing differentiation raises complex classification issues. For example, the Federal Communications Commission (FCC) currently struggles with the issue of whether internet telephony should be treated as common carrier or as information service. Cable television and information services, recently also including broadband internet access, are treated as private contract carriers. The owners of such electronic conduits exercise commercial freedom and can, in general, freely contract with customers and business partners. Likewise, with very limited exceptions, they enjoy editorial control over the content transported over their networks. Over-the-air broadcasters are treated as trustees of the public interest, subject to only light regulation of content and ownership limits.

Jurisdiction over I&C is assigned in a fragmented and heterogeneous fashion to local, state, and federal levels. Large segments of the I&C industries are regulated by the FCC, an agency established in 1934. The Federal Trade Commission (FTC), with its jurisdiction over consumer protection and antitrust, as well as the Department of Justice (DoJ), which shares antitrust enforcement with the FTC, also are influential federal agencies. In addition, 50 state public utility commissions (PUCs) and more than 16,000 local authorities have some jurisdiction over parts of the sector. State agencies are, among other things, involved in setting policies for access to local telecommunication networks, universal service, and emergency calling. Municipalities, and in some cases state regulatory agencies, have jurisdiction over the franchising of cable television and video platforms and may be involved in the deployment of broadband access networks. In practice, no sector-specific policies and regulations exist for publishing and for information services, such as broadband internet access. However, they are subject to the general policies established by antitrust laws. Although the overall vision and specific measures of I&C policy have changed substantially since the 1930s, the organization of policy making toward I&C industries have remained largely unchanged.

The intensity of regulation differs widely between segments of the I&C industries. The most detailed regulations exist for common carriers. Within this group, the detail and intensity of regulation are highest for local and lowest for long-distance service providers, with mobile service providers in between. Local exchange carriers (LECs), which offered services at the time of passing the Telecommunications Act of 1996 ('incumbent LECs' or ILECs), are subject to more stringent provisions regarding interconnection, network unbundling, and resale than later entrants ('competitive LECs' or CLECs). While these asymmetries are justified with the specific technological and economic conditions of the industry, they often create conflicts over policy or regulatory issues with strong zero-sum aspects. For example, CLECs are interested in access to the networks of ILECs at conditions that favor their business model, including low prices for access, whereas ILECs often have diametrically opposed interests.

The proliferation of players and the multiplication of conflicts of interest have contributed to the growth of business associations and shaped their interaction and mission. Government agencies are regularly used by stakeholders to influence the competitive conditions in a market. Business associations often are the channels through which such influence is sought. However, several industry segments have also adopted forms of self-regulation and co-regulation, often intended to fend off more explicit government control. This provides an additional field of activity for trade associations.

Business associations in the US information and communications sector

From a systems perspective, trade associations are important elements of modern political and economic systems. In contrast to traditional systemic accounts, in which the contribution of associations to the US political system was reduced to 'interest articulation' (Almond & Powell, 1966), business associations fulfill a multiplicity of functions that go beyond mere lobbying and the exertion of influence. In modern societies business associations are also involved in many aspects of horizontal self-coordination, self-regulation, and even self-governance of industries (Streeck & Schmitter, 1985b; Schneiberg & Hollingsworth, 1998).

Organization and development

The emergence and growth of interest associations thus co-evolve with the general political and economic development of the political and economic systems in which they are embedded. During the past 150 years, the evolution of these organizational forms paralleled the general process of societal modernization and formal organizations (Coleman, 1974; Perrow, 2002). The very first associations emerged in the late nineteenth century: the predecessor of the *United States Telecom Association* (USTA) was founded as the *National Telephone Association* (later changed to *United States Independent Telephone Association*) in 1897 to organize the interests of the independent telephone companies against the dominant Bell System. After the break-up of the Bell System in 1982, the association opened membership to the 'Baby Bells', the spin-offs from the former monopoly, and dropped the label 'independent' from its name to become the United States Telephone Association. After the passage of the Telecommunications Act of 1996, the association once more changed its name to USTA to reflect the broader interests of its members as providers of telecommunication services other than voice telephony.

Strong growth in the number of associations in the I&C sector set in only after World War II and was particularly swift since the 1970s, coinciding with the beginning of the 'digital age'. In a long-term perspective the growth of associations in the I&C sector was influenced by political events such as wars and the creation of regulatory agencies (see the peak in the 1930s). It was also shaped by broad economic processes and events such as the world economic crisis, the boom after World War II, and especially by waves of technological innovation.

In addition, a look at this organizational population shows a broad spectrum of organizational forms that vary greatly in size, mission, geographic reach, and political influence. For instance, there are large key players with a broad mission like USTA or the *Telecommunications Industry Association* (TIA), but also smaller and more specialized groups like *Women in Cable and Telecommunications* or the *Pattern Recognition Society*. Besides trade associations in the narrow sense, there are a large number of professional and learned societies in the associational population of the I&C sector, for example the *Association for Computing and Machinery* (ACM) or the *Institute for Electrical and Electronics Engineers* (IEEE).

Given the vast number of associations in this sector, a complete analysis of associational change was impossible given the scope of this research project. Therefore, we focused our study on *focal trade associations*, whose selection was described above (see Table 7.1). Tracing the evolution of these associations between the 1980s and the late 1990s in terms of organizational stability and change leads to some astonishing results, summarized in Figure 7.1. In light of the 'deep impact' hypothesis mentioned above, it is surprising that there were rather few radical changes among the focal associations. Half of the associational population remained untouched, while the other half experienced a few mergers and a series of name changes. These observations corroborate the findings of the European country studies of our research group (see Lang in this book) which at least in the I&C sector reported changes of a similar magnitude.

Throughout the history of I&C, technological developments have led to the establishment of new associations or the modification of existing ones. For example, the emergence of mobile communications spawned the *Personal Communications Industry Association* (PCIA) to represent the interests of the new market entrants against the incumbent firms that were often affiliated with the providers of fixed telephone services. The gradual introduction of competition in local telephone markets, beginning in the 1980s, led to the establishment of the *Association for Local Telecommunications Service* (ALTS). More recently, the emergence of the internet contributed to a reorientation of major existing associations, often reflected in a change in their names without a change in their recognized acronyms. Like USTA, mentioned earlier, the *National Cable Television Association* (NCTA) reinvented itself as the *National Cable & Telecommunications Association* and the *Cellular Telephone Industry Association* (CTIA) morphed into the *Cellular Telecommunications and Internet Association*.

Responses to environmental upheavals and challenges

An analysis of political and organizational aspects of organized business interests also requires one to take into account the general political, economic, and technical constraints faced by business and the deep structural changes by which these contexts are transformed. The political environment of I&C business associations encompasses the governmental and 'non-governmental organizations and institutions

Table 7.1 US I&C associations in the focal set (as of 2001)

	Name	Abbreviation	Staff	Budget (in million $)
1	Association of American Publishers	AAP	30	5–10
2	Association for Computing Machinery	ACM	94	25–50
3	American Electronics Association	AEA	125	25–50
4	Association for Local Telecommunication Services	ALTS	10	1–5
5	The Association of Local Television Stations	ALTV	8	1–5
6	Computer & Communications Industry Association	CCIA	11	1–5
7	Consumer Electronics Association	CEA	110	25–50
8	Cellular Telecommunications & Internet Association	CTIA	110	10–25
9	Information Technology Association of America	ITAA	35	5–10
10	Motion Picture Association of America	MPAA	142	5–10
11	Newspaper Association of America	NAA	180	25–50
12	National Association of Broadcasters	NAB	175	25–50
13	National Cable & Telecommunications Association	NCTA	85	25–50
14	Organization for the Promotion & Advancement of Small Telecommunications Companies	OPASTCO	20	1–5
15	Personal Communications Industry Association	PCIA	95	5–10
16	Recording Industry Association of America	RIAA		
17	Satellite Broadcasting & Communications Association	SBCA	22	5–10
18	Software & Information Industry Association	SIIA	42	5–10
19	Telecommunications Industry Association	TIA	95	10–25
20	United States Telecom Association	USTA	73	10–25

Note: RIAA did not respond to our request for information.

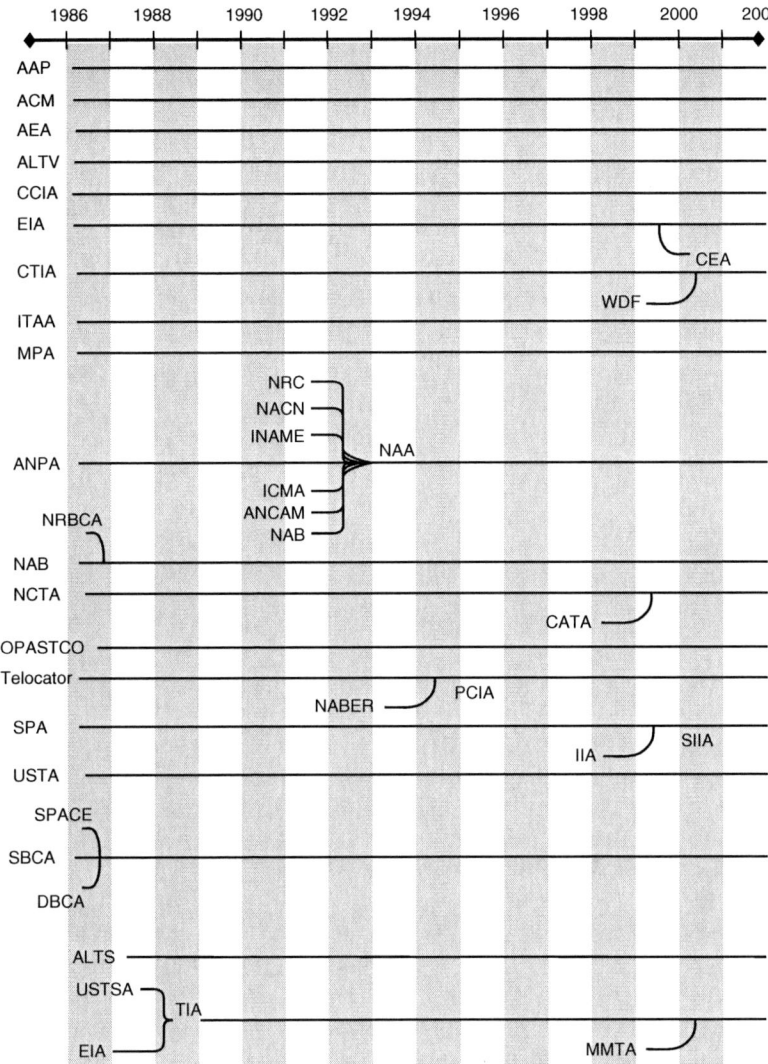

Figure 7.1 Entries, mergers, and splits in the US associational system

that set the 'rules of the game' in the I&C industries or influence the evolution of the I&C sector in other ways, for example through lobbying activities directed toward these organizations. The working conditions of American trade associations are shaped by the specific features of US government – such as strong presidentialism, federalism, and bicameralism – with its particular concentrations *and* separations of powers between the various branches of government. The particularities of the political-administrative system, mainly the degree to which executive departments and agencies are horizontally fragmented and autonomous, also influence the associational system. A particularly important role is played by independent regulatory agencies, which are hybrid constructs combining legislative, administrative, and executive functions and wield far-reaching powers. The overall system is characterized by a high dispersion and fragmentation of power, providing associations with multiple access points at the federal, state, and local levels.

During the past two decades, American trade associations in the I&C sectors were exposed to various challenges and diverse environmental changes. It is interesting how these challenges have been perceived by the major associations in the sector. The interview partners were asked to assess the importance of three types of external challenges. The data shows some clear differences in the rating of these challenges. The highest importance was attributed to economic factors, which 61 percent of the respondents considered as 'very important'. While technical and political challenges were only viewed by 33 and 39 percent of our respondents as 'most important', a majority assigned an 'important' ranking.

Another question asked about the level from which the transformative forces originate. The globalization hypothesis would imply that most of the challenges emanate from the global level. For the sample of associations in our study, this thesis is only partially supported by the data. The main message is that domestic factors dominate global and regional influences as a source of economic and political stress. Only in technology development (67 percent) is the global level seen as a major source of external challenges. With respect to economic pressures, 39 percent of the respondents perceived the global level as an important source of environmental changes. In all three categories, regional developments were attributed an almost negligible role.

When asked for specific types of challenges, such as interorganizational competition, mergers, industrial relocation, or, most general, the emergence of new tasks, highest importance was accorded to the last item, new tasks (79 percent). With respect to the globalization hypothesis it is interesting that only 42 percent of our respondents perceived industrial relocation and foreign investments as a 'most important' or 'important' type of external challenge. Another indication of a possible overstatement of globalization effects on associational behavior is that only slightly more than a third (37 percent) of our trade associations were members of an international association.

Nevertheless, 83 percent of the associations reported having experienced important structural changes during the last decades. Expansion and growth were mentioned by 64 percent, while 14 percent of the associations reported downsizing measures. The overwhelming majority of associations (88 percent) pointed out an extension of their interest portfolio. Only 6 percent indicated a trend toward increasing specialization. Membership growth was reported by 69 percent of the respondent organizations; only 8 percent indicated a decline in the membership base.

Besides these perceptions, an important question is how the American associational *system* with respect to its components and structures of interaction has changed during the last 20 years. Hence, we analyzed adaptation processes not only at the organizational but also at the system level; that is, related to changing positions and interactions with respect to all major associations operating in the US information and communication sector, documented in the following sections.

Cooperation and competition

In the long-term evolution of the associational system, various forms of change also affect the structure of competitive and cooperative relations. Structures of interaction, internal organization, and life cycles of I&C associations are shaped by growing differentiation and other strategies of adaptation. Organizations typically respond to environmental changes either by specialization or generalization strategies. Due to the pluralist structure and to overlapping missions, competition among business associations is an important element of the American system, but, as we will see, not the only one. To assess the extent of this competitive aspect in the associational population, we asked the respondents (1) to name other trade associations with which they have relations and to indicate the strength of that relation; and (2) to identify other national trade associations that are also active in the same sector. Both aspects are represented in Figure 7.2, which displays the degree of cooperation and competition among the associations in the focal set.

The combination of these relations allows us to generate information on various hybrid types in which cooperation and competition are combined. For example, if associations represent the same domain and report intense relations, it is interpreted as a sign of cooperation. If associations

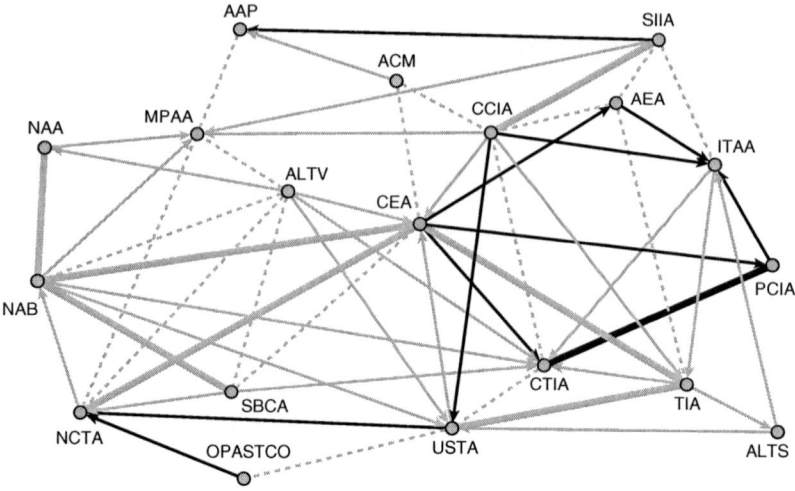

Figure 7.2 Ecological relations in the US associational system
Notes
Relations (examples in parenthesis)
Gray, bold, continuous: Mutualism (NAA–NAB)
Gray, thin, continuous: Partial cooperation (NAA–MPAA)
Gray, bold, dashed: Neutrality (CEA–SBCA)
Black, bold, continuous: Full competition (CTIA–PCIA)
Black, thin, continuous: Partial competition (OPASTCO–NCTA)

represent identical subsectors without having any kind of collaborative relation, we interpret it to imply a competitive relationship.

In the theory of neocorporatism the American system of organized interest – in contrast to the European system – is often characterized as pluralist with many associations that are involved in competitive relationships. Thus, the prevalence of cooperation displayed in Figure 7.2 is astonishing. Similar observations have been made by Schmedes for the US chemical sector (see Chapter 5 in this book). Surprisingly, in the I&C sector only a few associations relate to others via distinctively competitive relations.

Rather, cooperative and neutral relations dominate. Full and partial competition only exists between a few associations. Most intensive competitive relations seem to have evolved between CTIA and PCIA, both representing the fast growing sectors of internet and mobile communication. This observation supports our general skepticism against holistic theories and approaches that derive behavioral and structural patterns of whole societal domains from a single or at least from a few 'logics'. These approaches greatly overestimate the orderliness and structural homogeneity of the associational systems.

Nevertheless, the characterization of the American system of organized interests as pluralist is not completely erroneous. The sheer number of associations and the prevalence of membership in multiple associations provide evidence in support of a pluralist structure. Another aspect supporting pluralism is the fact that many large corporations organize their own lobbying activities and that business is also represented by specialized lobbying firms in the political arena. Individual captains of industry, large corporate firms, and specialized political action committees (PAC) also influence government and legislators through campaign contributions. Nor surprisingly, given the dynamics of the I&C industries and the high stakes that are involved in these industries, they are among the most important contributors to political campaigns.

To get a systematic idea of the importance of corporate lobbying, we asked the respondents how the association would deal with bypassing strategies of member firms. Interestingly, 40 percent indicated that they even encourage their members to act independently, and only 6 percent revealed that they would try to restrain such individualistic behavior. This contrasts sharply with the orientation of European trade associations, where more than 33 percent indicated reservations vis-à-vis corporate direct lobbying.

Another remarkable feature of the US associational systems is the lack of formal hierarchical integration. Whereas most European associations are members of sectoral or intersectoral peak organizations, in the US I&C sector almost 90 percent of the interviewees stated that their associations were not part of any such association. Some of our interview partners were not even familiar with the idea of an umbrella association, and had to be informed about this widespread phenomenon in Europe. However, as we shall see in the next section, many associations seek ad hoc coordination through alliances and other horizontal links and relations, and some associations informally play the role of peak associations.

Informal hierarchies and exchange networks

Inter-organizational networks in associational systems can be a functional equivalent to hierarchical integration by peak associations. To examine the role and extent of this mode of coordination in the US case, we collected data about information exchange between associations as

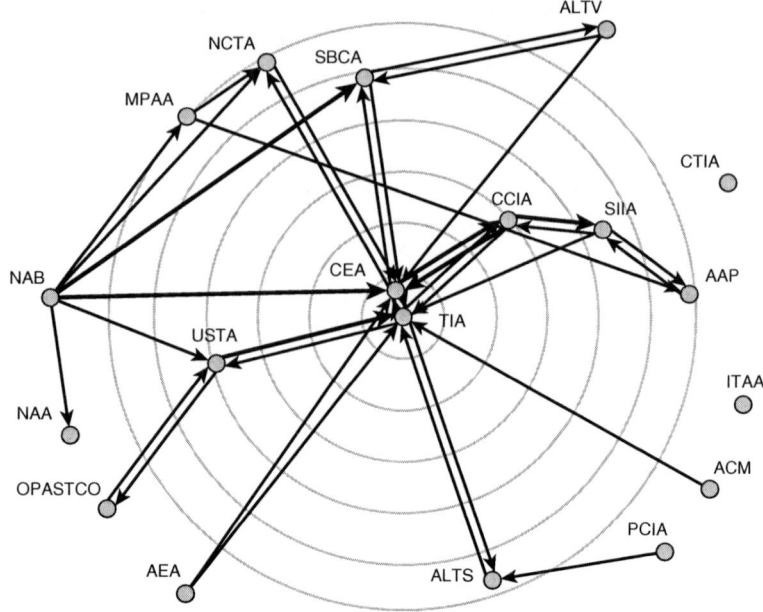

Figure 7.3 Information exchange in the US network (betweenness centrality)
Notes
Relations:
Bold: frequent information exchange
Thin: occasional information exchange

well as the specifics of any such sharing. We acquired information on the direction of exchange (passing on to another association or obtaining from another association) of information relevant for the political goals of the association. In their ratings the respondents could differentiate between occasional and frequent information exchange. To increase reliability, only confirmed relations were taken into account. These are relations where A indicated sending information to B, and B confirmed receiving information from A. Thus a line between two associations indicates a confirmed directed information flow between the two.

The result of this data collection and analysis is depicted in Figure 7.3. Associations represent nodes that are linked by flows of information exchange. The network diagram displays information flows among the 19 associations in our focal set of organizations. Varying thickness of the lines indicates differences in relational intensity, with thick lines representing frequent information exchange.

The overall configuration is displayed so that associations with important intermediary positions are located in the middle of the graph. Whether and to what degree an association is in an intermediary position is measured by centrality based on betweenness. This metric indicates the relative frequency with which an organization is located on geodesics between the various associations; that is, the shortest pathway that connects two associations in a network of information exchange. In this respect CEA and TIA, representing the electronics and the telecommunications industry, have the most central positions in this relational network. They indirectly link and intermediate between many associations of several subsectors, but also have intense information exchange among each other. The central positions of both associations reveal their informal coordination function between the various subsectors, a central role that might be played by peak organizations in other countries.

The whole network depicted in Figure 7.3 is less decentralized than a pluralist perspective would predict. Only a few associations are in the center of the graph and most other associations occupy peripheral positions. In a pluralist setting, in contrast, associations would be positioned more evenly across the entire space.

Associational tasks and strategies of adaptation

Apart from these population-level activities, trade associations can also change their internal structure and their strategies to cope with changes in their environment. We supposed that these strategies are reflected in the diverse ways in which the different associations allocate their resources toward various activity domains. We asked respondents to indicate how their association approximately allocates its total expenditures to activities ranging from lobbying and membership information to conference organization.

Table 7.2 summarizes the average resource allocation of the associations. It indicates that, while political lobbying is an important share, US trade associations invest – on average – an even greater proportion of resources in membership relations. The answers also indicate that the associations increased influence investments and decreased membership investments. Averages conceal, however, the great variation among associations' profiles of resource allocation. For instance, the lobbying investments vary between 5 percent for the CEA and 75 percent for the NCTA. This is reflected in the greater differences in the variances (or the standard deviations).

Table 7.2 Average resource allocation (in percent) and changes (frequency) of US business associations in the I&C sector

Activities	Resource allocation		Changes	
	Mean	Standard deviation	Increase (frequency)	Decrease (frequency)
National lobbying	29.8	19.6	10	–
European lobbying	5.5	7.0	3	2
Societal lobbying	7.4	7.5	2	–
Influence investments	**42.7**		**15**	**2**
Member consultation	12.2	10.5	1	1
Member information	10.3	8.0	–	–
Member conferences	17.2	14.0	2	5
Side benefits	3.5	7.2	1	3
Training	6.1	6.3	–	2
Membership investments	**3**		**4**	**11**
Other	8.0	15.9	3	–
Total	100		22	13

Expenditure on international lobbying is, on average, only a fifth of the national lobbying investments. However, there are a few associations that put a substantial share of their resources into international lobbying. The top position is held by MPAA, which spent more resources at the international level (20 percent) than in the domestic arena (15 percent). CCIA and TIA exhibit a comparable distribution of expenditure. All three represent highly internationalized segments of the I&C sector. However, their strong involvement in international affairs does not mean that it replaces domestic activities, as claimed by a popular globalization hypothesis. Our results indicate that internationalization does not undermine the national organization of interest, but rather expands the scope of associations' activities.

MPAA, which organizes Hollywood's movie industry – the big seven mega film producers: Walt Disney, Sony Pictures Entertainment, Metro-Goldwyn-Mayer, Paramount Pictures, Twentieth Century Fox, Universal Studios, and Warner Bros. – is a good example of this development. As digitization and the expansion of international trade increasingly undermined the protection of intellectual property rights (e.g., illegal copying of DVDs), MPAA put substantial resources into fighting piracy. It had considerable influence on the American Digital Millennium Copyright Act of 1998. It also participates actively in promoting the international expansion and enforcement of intellectual property rights through global and regional institutions, such as WIPO, the WTO, the OECD, and the European Union.

The analysis of each activity can be used to identify similarities and differences in resource allocation. However, it largely ignores within-system variation that manifests itself in differing degrees of specialization. Hierarchical cluster analysis is an appropriate method for finding these patterns of structural similarity and clustering. It identifies four groups of business associations that allocate their resources in similar ways:

- *Cluster I* – 'Service providers' are a relatively homogenous group of computer and communications associations (CEA, PCIA, ACM), but also the *Newspaper Association* (NAA).
- *Cluster II* – 'Domestic lobbyists' constitute mostly associations from the communications subsector, including ALTS, SBCA, NAB, USTA, and AAP.
- *Cluster III* – 'Pure (domestic) lobbyists' consist of only two organizations involved in the communications and broadcasting sector.
- *Cluster IV* – 'Multilevel lobbyists' are a very diverse group of computer associations (SIIA, CCIA, AEA, ITAA), two telecommunications associations (TIA and OPASTCO), and MPAA.

Articulation and representation of interests

A major – but not the only – function of trade associations is the articulation and representation of interest at the various political levels: domestically and internationally. In this respect, the US political system provides for a number of channels through which interest groups participate in public policy and regulation. Most important are hearings before Congress and regulatory agencies, but informal contacts with senators, members of the House of Representatives, and agencies also belong to the repertoire of lobbying.

We have measured these types of contact with network analytical methods, describing information exchange of associations and relevant actors in their political environment. The result of this analysis is summarized in Figure 7.4, in which two types of information are combined in a scatter plot: The horizontal axis represents the rating of political organizations as influence targets as seen by associational representatives (importance/relevance assigned to various organizations in the political arena). How often an organization was evaluated as a target for information provision, weighted by the intensity of information exchange, is represented on the vertical axis. For instance, Senate and House received

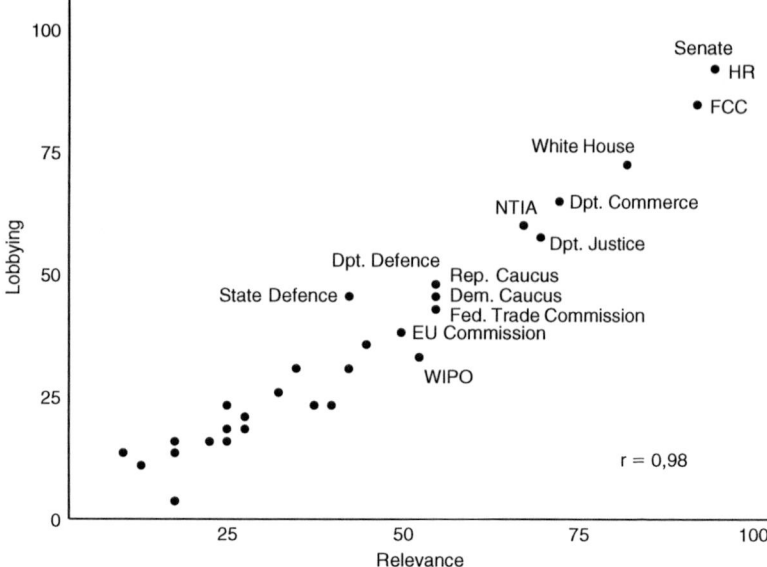

Figure 7.4 The targets of lobbying and information exchange

the sum of 37 points by the respondents (equaling 97 percent of the maximum number of points) with respect to their political importance and 36 points with respect to being targets for information provision. The fact that most of the observations are situated near the diagonal of this diagram reveals a very high correlation between these two variables of $r = 0.98$.

The most important influence targets were legislators (Senate and House) and the FCC as the most important regulator. The White House and the Department of Commerce ranked third and fourth. Very interestingly, international organizations such as the European Commission or WIPO ranked as influential organizations to which associations targeted information exchange.

The profiles of information exchange and influence targeting among the focal associations, however, vary greatly. As the subsectors of the I&C industry are organized and regulated in rather different ways, the mix of activities of an association differs accordingly. Computing, software, consumer electronics, and content providers are generally not subject to industry-specific regulation. The respective organizations therefore are more involved in influencing legislators and using the court system to pursue the interest of their members. For example, internet service providers (ISPs) and large content providers strongly shaped the Digital Millennium Copyright Act of 1998 at the expense of other stakeholders, such as educators or libraries. Business associations representing industry segments that are subject to regulation by specialized agencies, such as the telephone, cable television, or broadcasting industry as well as industries whose destiny is affected by these regulations – in particular, potential new entrants into these markets – operate simultaneously at the legislative, regulatory, and judicial levels.

A further hypothesis therefore holds that associations have different influence targets according to their regulatory regime in which they are embedded. This can be checked by using the information that was used at an aggregate level in Figure 7.4. Our database then is a matrix containing information on the estimation of 32 political organizations (columns) by 19 associations (rows) with respect to their sectoral importance and targets of information provision. The entries of a row in this matrix than can be taken as an association's 'lobbying profile'. Our hypothesis then would imply that associations from the same sector have similar lobbying profiles, whereas associations from different sectors would exhibit rather dissimilar lobbying vectors. We can check this by computing a 'dissimilarity matrix' based on a systematic comparison of the matrix rows. A standard measure for this is Euclidian distance (Wasserman & Faust, 1994).

We used hierarchical cluster analysis to group associations according to the similarity of their lobbying profiles. This analysis partitions the various associations in three clusters:

- *Cluster I* includes the largest number of associations with very similar lobbying profiles, of which the two 'alternative' telecommunications associations are almost identical. The whole group embraces various information content providers such as AAP, NAA, MPAA, some telecommunications associations (ALTS, OPASTCO, NTCA), telecoms newcomers (PCIA and CTIA), but also AEA.
- *Cluster II* contains a rather diverse group of broadcasters and telecommunications associations and CEA.
- *Cluster III* covers exclusively associations representing the computer industry.

Although not all subsector associations are grouped together in the same clusters, there is a high degree of concordance. This means that lobbying profiles can be explained to a considerable degree by the institutional particularities of the various subsectors.

Table 7.3 Membership of domestic and international business associations

	Domestic associations	International associations
Members	TIA, CCIA	CEA, TIA, MPAA, NAB, NAA, AAP, ITAA

As mentioned above, a distinct feature of the American associational system is its non-hierarchical character. There are only few associations that are members of inter-sectoral peak associations. A considerable number of associations, however, are affiliated with international associations. Table 7.3 shows that these associations are, understandably, the most prominent and resourceful associations in the sector.

Why and when business associations become internationally organized is an interesting question. It is likely that only associations with sufficient resources will participate at an international level. However, resources are probably only a necessary and not a sufficient condition. To understand international activities fully, the action space of an association will also have to be examined. Some associations are primarily oriented to the national level and therefore do not see any need to invest in international lobbying and representation. There is some evidence that this geographic orientation is to a degree dependent on the specific industry characteristics. For instance, MPAA faces a global threat of piracy and therefore has to defend its members' interests at an international level. On the other hand, associations such as ALTS, which are primarily interested in their members' access to local networks, can pursue this objective at a national and subnational level.

Conclusions

The hypothesis that globalization and liberalization are leading to similar adaptations in the affected countries and their associational systems has gained widespread popularity. The magnitude of change associated with these transformations is theorized differently by deep impact and gradual change theories. However, both extreme positions expect similar responses across all affected nations. This overlooks the fact that every political system contains a specific set of organizing principles, that each is shaped by its own path and unique forms of institutional inertia. We hence proposed an intermediate position of recognizing that even in the presence of similar environmental challenges, national strategies and capacities to cope with these pressures may differ. We further hypothesized that existing approaches in association research fall short of grasping these changes and that our understanding of these responses would be enhanced if the existing literature were enhanced with concepts from complexity theory.

The US information and communication sector is a particularly interesting case for exploring these issues in detail. Its direct and indirect importance for society, its turbulent technological environment that continuously redraws industry boundaries, and the magnitude of national and global policy transformations from tightly regulated monopoly to lightly regulated competition illustrate the extent of the environmental pressures. At the same time, with the increased concern about privacy and security issues, hitherto unregulated segments such as consumer electronics and computing, are facing the prospect of more government regulation. Overall, these developments pose formidable challenges for all stakeholders.

In 2000, the sector was populated by more than 380 business associations, many with overlapping membership and interest domains. The number of associations is strongly associated with major events in the history of these industries: growth spurts occurred in the early part of the twentieth century during the formative years of the state and federal regulatory systems and the emergence of new technologies, such as data and mobile communications, in the 1970s and 1980s. The most influential associations were identified with the help of an expert survey. Interviews were requested from 20 of the top focal organizations; 19 organizations were willing to fill out detailed questionnaires and were also available for complementary structured interviews. Association representatives identified national economic and political changes as well as global technological developments as the predominant sources of environmental challenges. Overall, economic changes were seen as more daunting than technological and political factors. Associations responded to these developments in various ways, most importantly by expanding their scope of activity and shifting their expenditures from membership to lobbying investments.

In contrast to that in other nations explored in this book, the US associational system is often seen as a prototype of a pluralist model. Our analysis revealed that these accounts fall short of the richness of the US associational system in I&C. While we detected strong pluralist features, it became clear that a pure pluralist approach focusing on the 'logic on influence' would overlook important features of the overall system. We found much more cooperation than expected by a pluralist approach and only few examples of competition between associations. Moreover, there was more hierarchy (or at least heterarchy) than expected in the system: whereas there are no formal peak associations, two players (CEA and TIA) informally appear to take on strong coordinating roles. Main targets of lobbying activities are the national legislature and regulatory agencies. Nevertheless, international and global organizations such as WIPO and the European Commission rank prominently among lobbying targets, reflecting the increased importance of international policies for large segments of the I&C industries.

Several aspects seem to characterize the specific American response to technological turbulence, globalization, and liberalization. Despite the relative stability of the overall population of associations, membership by industry players shifted between associations in response to the issues of the day and the positions taken by associations. Most associations encourage their members to pursue independent lobbying activities. Associations with declining memberships – such as PCIA in the late 1990s, which had achieved its major political goals – redefined the scope of their activities to rejuvenate themselves. Associations regularly form varying coalitions to pursue political objectives, but they also complete head-on for members during certain periods. Although this was not a primary focus of this paper, our information also reveals that, with a few exceptions such as the Digital Millennium Copyright Act of 1998, US I&C associations generally are more successful at blocking undesired policies than at achieving specific desired outcomes. As traditional forms of regulation have been phased out, new contested battlegrounds, including network neutrality, protection of intellectual property, information security, and privacy have emerged as key issues, creating continuing environmental adaptation pressure.

Our findings challenge existing pluralist and neocorporatist approaches. We conclude that concepts first developed in expansions of systems theory, such as organizational ecology or neoinstitutional approaches, and in particular concepts stemming from complexity theory can fruitfully be combined with these earlier frameworks to yield a richer understanding of the organization of business interests in the US I&C sector.

Note

1. Funding by the German Research Council (Deutsche Forschungsgemeinschaft, DFG) for the field research reported in this chapter is gratefully acknowledged.

8
Complex Associations in the Dairy Sector: A Comparison of Development in Four Countries

Claudius Wagemann

This chapter examines the change of organizational communities, organizational populations, and individual associations in the dairy sector of four countries, namely Austria, Britain, Germany and Switzerland.

The dairy sector has not just been selected in order to enrich the other chapters of this volume with a somewhat 'folkloristic' example, but – as will be explained in the next section – it can add some important insights to our central question of the evolution of organized business, and it therefore provides more than a study of a single sector. In fact, the dairy sector had been regulated in the past as a 'private interest government' (PIG), which has also been described as 'the most advanced form of neocorporatism' (Traxler, 1985: 150). It can, furthermore, be characterized as a very traditional sector that – although being exposed to enormous politico-economic changes at the European and global level – is still embedded in national niches.

Thus, the present chapter can be seen as an exemplary study of how this very specific and highly peculiar form of an interest group arrangement evolves further, when it is faced with political, economic, and social globalization, internationalization, and Europeanization (see Chapters 1 and 3). The results presented here go back to a more detailed investigation comprising 10 Austrian associations, 17 British associations, 29 German associations, and 55 Swiss associations (112 in total; on the exact process, see Wagemann, 2005a: 47ff).

I will first lay out the framework of the analysis, presenting the model of a PIG in more detail and giving some ideas about the research design. I will then discuss the changes at the levels of the organizational community; the organizational population; and the individual organizations themselves. In the conclusion, I will put the dairy sector in the context of the other studies presented in this volume.

The dairy sector in four countries

One central insight of neocorporatist approaches to interest group systems is that different forms of corporatism can be observed in economic governance (Czada, 1994: 45f). These can be typologized according to both various strengths and various forms. The first distinction refers to the attempts to define different intensities of corporatism (as done in Siaroff, 1999). The second differentiation is about variants of corporatism, such as the 'tripartism' between the state and two (usually competing) interest groups (Cawson, 1985a: 9), or a 'social partnership' (as most famously in Austria), where the state is not actively involved in a corporatist arrangement at all and leaves the floor exclusively to the associations (Karlhofer, 1996).

In an even more particular kind of interest group involvement in public policy making, the state delegates power to interest associations, leading to associational self-regulation. This form of corporatism has also been called 'private interest government' (abbreviated as PIG) (Streeck & Schmitter, 1985a). Empirically, PIGs have mainly been observed at the sectoral level and are, therefore, examples of 'meso' rather than economy-wide 'macro' corporatism. In the case of PIGs, the state not only integrates private associations into public policy making but even hands over its (monopolistic) political authority to them (*ibid.*: 10ff; Schmitter, 1994: 661). The decisions of the associations are authoritative (*allgemeinverbindlich*) for both members and non-members (Jacek, 1987: 48). The prerequisites of such an arrangement are 'a limited and fixed set of interest organizations that mutually recognize each other's status and entitlements and are capable of reaching and implementing relatively stable compromises (pacts) in the pursuit of their interests' (Streeck & Schmitter, 1985a: 10). Not only is more than a single organization usually involved in a PIG structure, but a PIG is also created out of other types of interrelated organizations (Voelzkow, 2000: 190). This could be called the 'organizational community' of a PIG.

Of course, this arrangement has an effect on the associations themselves. Associational action is not determined so much by membership, but rather by the quasi-public tasks of the association. This can significantly influence the balance between the 'logic of membership' and the 'logic of influence'. These two expressions go back to the classic terminology used in the early 1980s to capture the two main, basically contradictory aspects of associational action that determine the organizational properties of an association (Schmitter & Streeck, 1999 [1981]: 19, 21). The two logics represent the '*Janus*-like nature of ... associations in their role as intermediaries between at least two independently constituted, resourceful and strategically active sets of actors' (*ibid*.: 19), namely, association members on the one hand, and state agencies or competing associations on the other. The strong orientation of PIG associations toward maintaining their own influence can lead to substantial neglect of the direct needs of the membership (Traxler, 1985: 167; Farago, 1987: 41f).

Nevertheless, in order to maintain the associational basis, membership may be obligatory or, if this is not appropriate or simply prohibited by law, 'quasi-obligatory' (Voelzkow, 2000: 190). 'Quasi-obligatory' means that certain goods that are indispensable or at least highly important for the economic activities of the members (selling rights and so on) are the incentive making it necessary for businesses to join. Thus, the free-rider problem is completely solved, and the 'logic of membership' is not notably important.

PIGs usually emerge when this model achieves functional advantages over other models of social order, such as dispersed competition in markets, hierarchical control by the state, or spontaneous solidarity within communities (Streeck & Schmitter, 1985a: 1, 22ff). A social order based on markets often fails 'to produce certain collective or categoric goods which are a necessary precondition for an effective functioning of the market' (*ibid*.: 23). The state can fail because of lack of expertise (*ibid*.: 16, 23) and insufficient capacity to govern complex economic processes. Communities often 'authoritative means to mobilize resources above and beyond what can be obtained on a voluntary basis' (*ibid*.: 24). In this way, PIGs represent a fourth type of social order in those sectors where it is especially important to avoid the failure of any of the other models.

The perfect example of such a sector for which any failure of sectoral governance must be avoided is the dairy sector (Jacek, 1987: 50). Reasons for a PIG arrangement in the dairy sector are the importance of the sector for public welfare (*ibid*.: 37; Traxler & Unger, 1994: 199ff);[1] the economic importance of dairying for the primary sector and therefore for the balance of payments of a country (Traxler & Unger, 1994: 185); the high interdependence (and therefore vulnerability) between the economic actors (Grant, 1992: 63); the special characteristics of the products, especially their perishability, which necessitates rapid (smooth) production, transport, and marketing (Jacek, 1987: 48); the especially strong requirement for detailed expertise (Jacek, 1987: 37f); and sector-inherent historical traditions, related to the symbolic importance of milk and dairy products (Grant, 1991b: 20).

It goes without saying that economic globalization is an enormous challenge to arrangements such as PIGs. It is well known that 'the processes involved in the internationalization of economic activity do not appear to favor associational governance' (Coleman, 1997: 132) As a consequence, current developments have been interpreted as a first steps toward an increased convergence of national policy-making styles that will wipe out existing national arrangements (Crouch & Streeck, 1997: 13). This process of convergence is mainly described as a liberalization of national economies and a general retreat of the state or state-like institutions from economic governance (Crouch & Streeck, 1997: 14, 17). Alternatively, it has been argued that the different forms of capitalism, economic governance, and public policy making will fundamentally survive (Hall & Soskice, 2001a: 57f).

Linking this discussion to interest groups, the 'convergence view' entails the risk for interest associations that existing actor constellations would be replaced by new structures in a more 'liberalized' economy, and that traditional actors – above all, those that oppose liberalization – would be weakened. New forms of interest intermediation would emerge that would be less formal and less institutionalized (Mach, 1999: 430ff). In our case, this would mean that deeply embedded and highly domestic institutional arrangements, such as the sectoral governance and the structure of the associational system in the dairy sector, would be negatively affected by internationalization processes.

The reasoning behind internationalization in general can be easily enlarged to European integration. Since the EU is basically described as a neoliberal project (Streeck, 1998: 429ff), there is no reason to believe that arrangements such as PIGs, which are the exact opposite of a neoliberal arrangement, do not fit into this policy.[2]

The most natural conclusion from this is that – due to a general liberalization, which can be traced back to internationalization in general or European integration in particular – PIGs might not exist any longer, and PIG associations will be deprived of their privileged and specific status. In such a case, it is obvious that the organizational community and the associational population will undergo substantive changes and, moreover, that at the level of the individual organizations the specific organizational properties that reflected the special status of the PIG associations will have to be replaced by something else; alternatively, the associations that were part of the PIG would simply disappear. Using the terminology of the 'logic of membership' and the 'logic of influence', and the insight that PIG associations can easily concentrate on the logic of influence, we may assume that in such a scenario the logic of membership would be emphasized more.

The countries under analysis are Austria, Britain, Germany, and Switzerland. The four main countries have been selected with the most different system design of cases (Przeworski & Teune, 1970: 34).

First, the spectrum of different forms of interest intermediation is covered. The Austrian social partnership is regarded as the most important example of a corporatist arrangement (Siaroff, 1999: 179, 184). Germany counts as a medium-level corporatist system (*ibid.*: 184), whereas Britain has a pluralistically organized associational system (Ronit & Schneider, 1997: 37; Siaroff, 1999: 184).[3] Switzerland is very difficult to classify (*ibid.*: 182f, 186f) and has been labeled a 'non-corporatist associational state' (Abromeit, 1993: 171), because of the *Vernehmlassungsverfahren* that assigns special power to interest associations in the policy-making process (Armingeon, 2001: 412ff).

Second, the countries differ in size. Britain and Germany are large, Austria and Switzerland small. This also means that communication (above all before the rise of electronic communication) was much easier in Austria and Switzerland than in Britain or Germany. The smaller size of Austria and Switzerland also makes it easier to create communication networks. This is a central aspect for inter-organizational structures and the perception of external processes.

Third, the countries feature different political 'macro-institutional' arrangements. Britain is characterized by 'classic' parliamentarism; Austria by a deeply rooted proportionalism; Switzerland by strong elements of direct democracy, a strong federal structure, and linguistic heterogeneity (for the effects of the latter on associational systems, see *ibid.*: 412f); and Germany by its federal and highly interconnected structure that affects the activities of interest groups (Kohler-Koch, 1993: 24, 44f), amplified by the problems arising from reunification.[4]

Fourth, the countries differ with regard to their relationship and attitudes toward the European Union. Germany is part of the core founder-member group; Great Britain shows a notable euro-skepticism; Austria joined the EU only recently; and Switzerland is not even a formal member. However, Swiss politics cannot be decoupled from the European integration process (Kux & Sverdrup, 2000: 238, 251f).

Fifth, in the 1980s the dairy sector was regulated in different ways in each of these countries (Van Waarden, 1987: 67), as will be shown in more detail in the following section.

Change at the level of organizational communities

As mentioned, PIG arrangements can be seen as equivalents to 'organizational communities' of the dairy sector, defined as 'functionally integrated systems of interacting populations' (Baum, 1996: 77), since they do not only consist of the population of the relevant interest groups, but also include state authorities, which license associational governance, or the general public, which critically follows and evaluates PIG arrangements. However, it would be misleading to assume that there was a single form of PIG in the dairy sectors of the countries under research. Instead, PIG forms and structures varied among countries.

The former Swiss dairy sector can be seen as the perfect example of a PIG (Farago, 1987: 88). It emerged during the First World War as a reaction to rising food-supply problems, which made the collaboration of all (originally opposed) groups necessary (Popp, 2000: 24). It concentrated on the regulation of the cheese subsector. The organizations involved were the ZVSM (*Zentralverband schweizerischer Milchproduzenten*, Central Association of Swiss Milk Producers), which comprised the farmers as raw milk suppliers, and the SMKV (*Schweizerischer Milchkäuferverband*, Association of Milk Buyers), being the association of dairy manufacturers (Farago, 1987: 54f). The acquisition of raw milk, to be processed as cheese products, was regulated by a complex system of contracts, which empowered SMKV and ZVSM to establish who could sell how much milk, to whom, and at what price (*ibid*.: 134f). The cheese manufacturers were completely dependent on the decisions of the associations and were not allowed to alter either the quantity or the quality of their products (*ibid*.: 135f). However, their sales and prices were simultaneously guaranteed by the associations (*ibid*.: 136, 152). Subsequently, the dairy producers were obliged to sell their cheese[5] to the *Käseunion* (Cheese Union). This fully fledged organization with its own infrastructure fixed quantities and prices (to be formally legitimized by the federal parliament), bought the cheese from the processors, and then sold it to the retailers and the cheese exporters. It was entirely dominated by the central associations, also including cheese exporters and the two big Swiss retailers, COOP and MIGROS. Thus, the entire production chain from the supply of raw material for the processing of milk into dairy products, to the retailing of the final product (both on the internal and the external markets) was regulated by the central associations, with regard to prices as well as quantity and quality.[6]

The so-called Milk Marketing Boards were the basic institutions of the British sector. Differently to Switzerland, they were state-imposed dairy farm cooperatives (Grant, 1985: 183), created from the early 1930s onwards in various parts of Britain (England and Wales; Northern Ireland; Aberdeen and District; North of Scotland; rest of Scotland), in response to the dominant position of large, oligopolistic processing plants. Their functioning was quite simple. They bought raw milk from farmers, who were obliged by law to register with the MMBs and to sell their raw milk to these entities (Traxler & Unger, 1994: 187; *Dairy Facts and Figures*, 1996: 8). Then they pooled the milk, sold it to the producers, and distributed the earnings among the farmers in proportion to the share of raw milk delivered. Within this scheme every farmer was assigned a maximum volume of milk, which the MMB would buy. These quotas were subject to a trade system (Grant, 1997b: 109). The advantages for the farmers were that, in the end, all milk was bought and a market found for it by the MMBs (Traxler & Unger, 1994: 187), despite the geographic location of the farmers. From 1954 on, the processors participated in the fixing of raw milk prices, since the 1970s in a Joint Committee of the MMBs and the DTF (Dairy Trade Federation, the processors' association). Prices were binding for both raw milk suppliers and producers (Grant, 1985: 185; Traxler & Unger, 1994: 188). The Joint Committee was also involved in fixing the price for the final dairy product on the retail market (Grant, 1991b: 54). Thus, similar to the Swiss structure, quantity, quality, and prices were fixed by the most important sectoral actors, and membership *de facto* was compulsory.

The situation in Austria was similar to Switzerland and Britain insofar as a similar involvement of interest groups in the governance of the dairy sector could be observed. However, whereas the Swiss and British associations operated within the boundaries of the dairy sector, a separate associational system for the dairy sector did not develop in Austria. Rather, its system of (associational) self-regulation is a special case of the regulation of economic affairs in Austria in general, since the Austrian dairy sector is a part of the macro-economic social partnership (*Sozialpartnerschaft*). This core of Austrian (economic) policy making (Karlhofer, 1996; Kittel & Tálos, 1999) includes the main social groups ('social partners').[7] These groups also dominated the PIG of the dairy sector (Traxler, 1985: 156; Traxler & Unger, 1994: 192). This macro arrangement of a social partnership made the emergence of specific PIG associations for the dairy sector unnecessary. The institutional frame for the dairy sector was given by the *Milchwirtschaftsfonds* (MWF). Similar to its counterparts in the other countries, this dated back to times of low food supply and had subsequently been maintained. The scope of the negotiations within its framework covered more or less the same issues as the equivalent arrangements in Switzerland and Britain. Thus, the Austrian dairy sector was a strong instance of a PIG (Jacek, 1987: 53); however, it was not maintained by specific dairy interest associations, but by centralized, all-encompassing, big macro-economic associations.

Sectoral regulation in the German dairy sector was notably different from the Swiss, British, and Austrian counterparts in that market forces played a far higher role in Germany (van Waarden, 1987: 68; Traxler & Unger, 1994: 190f). Above all in Germany, price and quantity negotiations were not regulated by associational governance. Consequently, there were no pure PIG associations in Germany. Nevertheless, some associations show certain characteristics of PIGs, namely, the *Landesvereinigungen der Milchwirtschaft* (LVs) and the two federal organizations GML (*Gemeinschaft der milchwirtschaftlichen Landesvereinigungen*, Community of the Dairy *Landesvereinigungen*) and VDM (*Verband der deutschen Milchwirtschaft*, Association of the German Milk Sector). These are higher-order organizations to which 'associations representing dairy interests along the entire food chain from farmers through processors to consumers' (Jacek, 1987: 43) are affiliated. Milk farmers and dairy processors are obliged to pay a fee toward maintaining the LVs, which mainly concentrate on quality and hygiene regulation and matters concerning sector coordination.

Today, however, the situation has changed in the countries under research. PIG structures have disappeared in (nearly) all the countries, for a number of reasons.

In Switzerland, the whole regulatory structure of the former PIG was dismantled as a consequence of agricultural reform in 1999 (Popp, 2000: 75ff). The reasons for this fundamental change were that technological change had led to overproduction; a general political aversion to subsidies had resulted in the wish to liberalize economic markets; and the public was increasingly dissatisfied with the spectacle of partially decrepit sectoral regulation in the dairy sector.[8] The main consequence of this was the abandonment of associational regulation in the milk sector. The sector was liberalized and competitive market structures were introduced. Neither associational price fixing nor sales guarantees were maintained. Price and quantity negotiations were decentralized and are no longer regulated by law. As an important consequence of giving up this structure, organizations such as the *Käseunion* and BUTYRA became superfluous and were disbanded in 1999.

In Britain, intense pressures for change arose at the beginning of the 1990s (Kirke & Anderson, 1995: 128; Banks & Marsden, 1997: 389f). The decisive factor was national economic policy choices, increasingly influenced by the idea of liberalizing all non market-governed sectors, which were perceived as being similar to a 'planned economy' style of governance (*Farmers Weekly*, 15 March 1995: 34). The economic involvement of the MMBs (*ibid.*; *Financial Times*, 16 August 1991) and the complicated situation of sectoral governance due to the EU quota system (Traxler & Unger, 1994: 188f; Kirke & Anderson 1995: 128)[9] contributed to the tensions. When farmers, wishing to express dissatisfaction with the MMB, finally started selling their raw milk outside of its scheme, the government did not discourage such (illegal) action (*Farmers Weekly*, 30 December 1994: 8). In view of these developments, several ideas for reforms were developed by MMB officials themselves, seeking to ensure the institution's continued existence (Schmitter, 1994: 670, 1997: 417, 426), but finally the attempts to save the regulatory system and the MMBs failed. The sector was liberalized by the end of 1994 (*Dairy Facts and Figures*, 1996: 11). The MMBs were dissolved and voluntary cooperatives and other organizations replaced them. Price negotiations are no longer centralized or controlled by state agencies.

The developments in the Austrian dairy sector have been similar to those in the other former PIGs in Britain and Switzerland, insofar as the Austrian PIG has ceased to exist as a consequence of Austria's accession to the EU in 1995. The effect of EU accession was indirect, however. In order to meet the requirement of adopting the *acquis communitaire*, Austria had to give up its system of so-called horizontal subsidies. Previously, earnings from the artificially high prices of dairy products in general had been used to subsidize selected 'weakly' performing dairy products, a strategy not respecting EU law. Giving up the system of horizontal subsidies meant depriving the MWF of its resources. Thus, the MWF was dismantled by the end of 1994. As in the other countries, prices and quantities are now largely determined by market forces. However, the MWF was not replaced by voluntary associations but by state agencies, such as the AMA (*AgrarMarkt* Austria) and its subordinate organization AMA Marketing.

With regard to the low importance of PIG structures in Germany, not much has changed. The tasks of the obligatory associations continue to be regulated by law and have not altered. Neither have attempts been made to introduce stronger PIG structures. Thus, Germany is a rather exceptional case compared with the other countries under research.

The process of dismantling PIGs is not necessarily irreversible, however. In Switzerland, a partial re-emergence of a kind of 'limited' PIG can be observed since early 2001, first for butter and milk powder. This arrangement was requested because the leaders of the respective

Table 8.1 Comparison of PIG structures

Country	Previous strength of PIG	Previous level of PIG	Changes	Situation today
Austria	High	Macro	Yes	State as the dominant form of social order
Britain	High	Meso	Yes	Market as the dominant form of social order
Switzerland	High	Meso	Yes	Limited PIG re-emerging
Germany	Low	Meso	No	Still weak PIG, still some importance of the market

organizations did not want to offer services for free, while the producers had the freedom not to join and not to contribute to the organization, but could nevertheless benefit from its marketing initiatives. Government agencies nonetheless play quite a strong role in this new form of limited PIG, and the issue areas to which this arrangement is applied are still quite narrow; most importantly, price fixing is not included. Later, this new system was – referring to even fewer issues – enlarged to the milk farmers' associationns. Furthermore, the envisaged end of the Swiss system of *Milchkontingentierung* led to the creation of a semi-official *Branchenorganisation Molkereimilch* (BOM), and a major economic crisis (the *Milchkrise*) to which the sector was exposed soon after its liberalization raised the public claim for a partial return to the previous situation (on this change in Swiss dairy governance, see Wagemann, 2005b: 15ff).

With regard to the dimension of European integration, the case of Switzerland, where the change was as notable as in Austria or in Britain but which is not a member of the EU, makes it clear that EU membership is not a necessary condition for the collapse of the regulatory system. The case of Germany, however, suggests that it is also difficult to maintain EU membership as a sufficient condition for the collapse of all elements of the regulatory system (for the logic of necessary and sufficient conditions, see Ragin, 2000: 98; for its application to our case, see Wagemann 2005a: 182).

Indeed, we have to limit our explanations to the insight that the similarity of the collapse of the PIG goes back to a general liberalization trend in the sectors under research, which followed specific and perhaps unique ways in the single countries. We are able to account for (in order to avoid the word 'explain') the breakdowns of PIGs in the single countries, but we have to attribute these changes to a very fuzzy notion of 'liberalization' trends in the associational environment.

However, the differences in the evolution of the changes at the level of the organizational community can be traced back to a fundamentally divergent situation at the level of organizational population, as the following section will show.

Change at the level of organizational populations

If an organizational community, such as the various PIG arrangements in Austria, Britain, and Switzerland, breaks down in such a rigid and definite manner, then it goes without saying that the organizational populations must also be affected by such a process. However, the causal direction is not necessarily limited to the statement that the changes in the organizational community have provoked changes in the organizational population. Additionally, variations with regard to the organizational populations have contributed to a different evolution at the level of the organizational community. We can see this very clearly in a comparison between Switzerland and Britain:

In Switzerland, the already existing 'division of labor' of the main organizations (basically, differentiating between raw milk producers and dairy processors; that is, the former ZVSM – today's SMP – and the former SMKV – today's FROMARTE[10]) has been further intensified by the emergence of new associations, which either represent new membership domains or differentiate existing domains further. Examples of associations in which new memberships are organized are the organizations of organic milk producers, which rival the traditionally oriented raw milk producers' association, SMP. Their roots date back to before the agricultural reform, but, of course, they were considerably strengthened in their importance when the state-assured representative monopoly of raw milk producers was abolished. Examples of a further differentiation of the existing organizational population are new associations for industrial producers (some differentiated by plant size, others differentiated by the dairy product they produce); Prolait as a new layer between the federal SMP and its regional subunits from the French-speaking part of Switzerland; a new type of organization (the *Sortenorganisationen*) which organizes actors across the production chain of dairy products and does not differentiate between raw milk processors, producers, retailers, scientists, public authorities, and so on (in fact a radical innovation for the Swiss sector); and some marketing organizations. Summarizing, the

Swiss organizational population has expanded, widened, and is much more differentiated and numerous than before.

In Britain, however, although being exposed to a similar kind of change at the level of the organizational community, the situation is very different. Milk farmers, having been securely organized into Milk Marketing Boards (MMBs), now had to choose among the privatized successor organizations of the MMBs; other milk groups; spontaneous initiatives for collective action; and options for individual action. The domain of raw milk suppliers was then aggregated into broader, higher-order associations, namely, the Federation of Milk Groups (FMG) and the Federation of Milk Producers (FMP). The FMP quickly disappeared, so that the FMG was left as the most important organizer of milk groups. The development of the former producer organizations was even more dramatic. The main producers' organization, DTF, did not only change its name to the DIF (Dairy Industry Federation), but also merged with the NDA (National Dairymen's Association), an organization of small dairy businesses and of the traditional British doorstep delivery sector, in early 2002. The new organization, called DIAL (Dairy Industry Association Limited), combined all previously separately organized branches of dairy manufacturing. However, at this point the distinction remained between raw milk suppliers on the one hand and producers on the other. The great upset occurred in late 2004, when the FMG, as the main representative of milk groups and milk suppliers, merged with DIAL, to form Dairy UK as a new sectoral association. For the first time, milk suppliers and dairy producers were no longer organized in two different 'camps' (as nicely seen in the antagonistic construction of the PIG Joint Committee), but were united under a common organizational roof. Moreover, the Dairy UK merger was extended to the Scottish and Northern Irish producers' organizations. Thus, the merger not only dissolved the organizational division between suppliers and producers, but also abolished regional differentiation. A highly differentiated associational system has been converted into an umbrella organization, to which a very heterogeneous set of members is affiliated.

Without doubt, the British and Swiss organizational populations have developed in two completely different directions: the British associational system has become highly concentrated, whereas the Swiss associational system appears highly differentiated. The main reason for this is that preconditions for a strengthening of the organizational population as a response to the breakdown of the organizational community existed in Switzerland, whereas in Britain these preconditions were absent.

First, it can be observed that the Swiss associational system has always been far more densely interconnected than the British system. Mutual membership and jointly composed committees were (and are) more diffused in Switzerland than in Britain. Combined with the fact that Switzerland is a small country (the main associations of the Swiss dairy sector are located within a walking distance from one another), this leads to very intensive regular personal contacts among associational decision makers.

Second, the public and social roles of the sector are different in Switzerland and Britain. Whereas the Swiss cheese-producing industry receives strong support from the public and from government authorities, the British dairy sector is exposed to rising pressure from big supermarkets, consumers (as visible in the volatile product spectrum in Britain, see Kirke & Anderson, 1995: 121f, 146), other sectors, and even the government. Put simply, cheese is a product with which Switzerland is identified, but this is not the case for British milk. A decline in the success of Swiss cheese production is, therefore, socially much more relevant than the problems of British milk production will ever be. The Swiss cheese-producing industry's interest in its own survival could even become a national interest. This also relates to the high number of dairy businesses in Switzerland (compared to Britain).[11] Thus, not only is the Swiss government aware of the importance of the dairy sector, but, moreover, public awareness is high. Note that this problem is also linked to the failure of individual businesses, the number of which is higher in Britain than in Switzerland, and to the fact that Britain is the only country in this study where the total amount of milk production has decreased since the early 1980s.

Third, the British logic of adaptation after the end of the PIG can be labeled 'competitive', 'pluralist', or 'leading to a liberal market sector', whereas the Swiss process rather reflects a 'consensual' or 'corporatist' adaptation, which is associated with a 'coordinated market sector'. This is in perfect accordance with the characterization of politics and the political economy in the two countries in general, so that a certain level of 'isomorphism' with the already existing structures in the environment can be assumed. Whether one wishes to emphasize this analogy or not, it is indisputable that, both in the Swiss and the British case, typical and nationally specific examples in other policy areas were on hand when the PIG collapsed to serve as models for the new structure of the regulatory system.

As mentioned at the outset of this section, not only do changes in the organizational community explain changes in the organizational

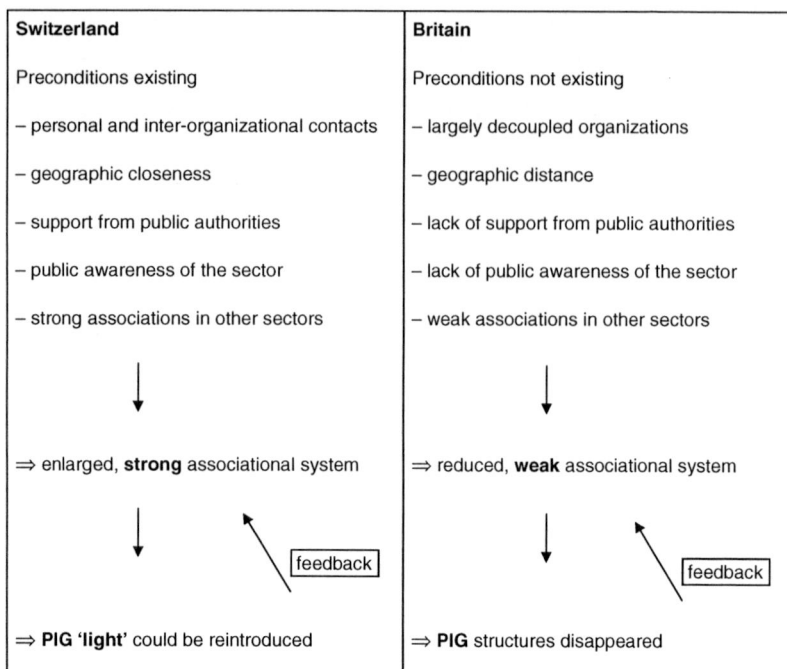

Figure 8.1 Enlarged Swiss associational system vs. shrinking British associational system

population, but different characteristics of the organizational population also help us to explain different developments in the organizational communities. For example, this comparison between Switzerland and Britain makes it clear why the *Milchkrise* (see above) was a 'window of opportunity' for reintroducing some institutions of the former PIG, whereas such a window of opportunity – even if it had occurred – would not have been used in Britain because the structural preconditions for a re-emergence of the PIG were not met.[12]

For reasons of completeness, let me briefly mention the changes within the organizational populations of Austria and Germany:

In Austria, no specific dairy PIG associations had existed before the breakdown of associational governance. The few existing associations (mainly implementation agencies at the subnational level) were mostly converted into free-market higher-order cooperatives, and the VÖM (*Vereinigung Österreichischer Milchverarbeiter*, Association of Austrian Milk

Processors) was created. VÖM organizes milk processors (but not milk farmers) of any size or legal form. However, since this association duplicates the existing compulsory structure of the Austrian *Sozialpartnerschaft*, all its members are also either a member in the WKÖ or of the Chambers of Agriculture, so that the incentive to join the VÖM as a voluntary organization is low, and membership rates hardly reach 20 percent.

In Germany, there has been hardly any effect on the (already very weak) PIG associations. This is altogether surprising, since not even the most expected changes happened, namely, the transfer of the obligatory *Landesvereinigungen* structures to East Germany. Only two out of the five new *Länder* adopted the principle of a *Landesvereinigung*, whereas the other three *Länder* either preferred pure state regulation or left the issue of an LV in the hands of the farmers' association. In a similar way, the interest group formed by the East German dairy industry merged with the most important Western voluntary (that is, not part of any regulatory system) association, the MIV (*Milchindustrieverband*, Milk Industry Association). Other smaller organizations also ceded their daily business to the MIV, or to other stronger associations. In sum, the MIV has strengthened its position as one of the most important (if not the most important) interest groups in the German dairy sector. However, this minor concentration of interest domains in the MIV did not affect the important differentiation between Bavaria and the rest of Germany. Bavaria still features a highly independent system of interest groups in the dairy sector, which, in part, continue to rival the MIV.

Nevertheless, apart from these differences between the countries, there are also some similarities as far as the development of organizational populations is concerned.

First, new associations are often not classic direct membership interest groups. They are, rather, higher-order organizations of already existing organizations, to which the existing organizations outsource certain policy outputs.

Second, these new organizations consequently become, in effect, service organizations under the umbrella of a larger interest association. This often results in an arrangement in which staff, offices, and strategies are shared between the new actors and the established organizations, although these are legally distinct.

Third, there is also a tendency to unite the different actors in the dairy sector into one single association (and thus to create very broad interest domains). This was already popular in case of the German *Landesvereinigungen*, but it was subsequently imitated in Switzerland and in

Britain. An observable tendency becomes clear: The sectors in all these countries are trying to 'speak with a single voice'. It seems that the only way to deal with pressure from outside (international challenges for all countries; national liberalization policies in Britain and Switzerland; ecologically inspired agricultural reform in Germany; structural change in all countries; pressure from supermarkets in Britain; lack of public support in Britain, and so on) is to collaborate within the sector, despite the diverging interests of the actors.

Change at the level of individual organizations

An interest group as such is a very complex social structure and therefore difficult to describe. There are so many parameters that characterize an association that a one-dimensional approach is not sufficient. With regard to interest groups, this problem was solved in a typological way: namely, by the definition of four different dimensions of so-called 'organizational properties'. These are the interest domains, the structure, the policy outputs, and the resources of an organization/interest group. Following this idea, 'the formal organizational properties of [systems of] interest associations can be conceived of as a behavioral expression of how the respective associations perceive and interpret the collective interest of their constituents' (Schmitter & Streeck, 1999 [1981]: 46). 'Analyzing the organizational properties of interest associations, therefore, and relating them to the structural conditions existing in the society-at-large may yield important insights into the dynamics of politicization of social interests and into the way social structures, economic resources and political processes influence each other' (*ibid.*: 13). I will now present the changes with regard to these four organizational properties.

The interest domains have undergone a change in many associations. Usually they were broadened. Most spectacular is the development in Britain, where milk farmers and dairy processors are organized in one single association after a century of opposition between two (or even more) separate organizations. However, Germany is an exception. Although a differentiation of interest domains could have been expected as the result of reunification, the associational system of the dairy sector has not responded.

Concerning structures, the most important change is that (quasi) compulsory membership in dairy interest associations has only been maintained in very selected instances. Only Germany has not undergone changes in this respect. Interestingly enough, the opening has not led to high levels of free-riding in the other countries. Most associations still represent over 90 percent of the dairy industry.

Another rather new structural phenomenon is that, since associational subsystems that differentiate between raw-milk suppliers, dairy processors, and other sectoral actors are no longer so dominant, parity structures have gained importance. The new organizations unite all kinds of sectoral actors (and also overcome regional boundaries and combine businesses of different sizes or legal forms). This heterogeneous membership has required changes in internal structures (Schmitter & Streeck, 1999 [1981]: 67), such as parity decision-making boards.

With regard to the organization of working processes, insights from private management theory regarding personnel, administration, and organization are increasingly common within interest associations of the dairy industry. The (openly pronounced) attempts of the German MIV (*Milchindustrieverband*, Milk Industry Association) to imitate its members and their organizational behavior is the most visible example of this phenomenon and can also be observed in other organizations.

There were also notable changes regarding the integration of economic activities in the associational structures.[13] Depending on the country, a complete organizational split between interest group and economic activities in two or more separate organizations (Britain); a dismantling of interest group activities and a continuation of dairy production (Austria); or various forms of institutional arrangements, including stockholding or a subordination of interest group activities (Switzerland) are all observable.

Inter-organizational links have been considerably strengthened. This has led to the emergence of densely woven webs and 'umbrella' associations that control and coordinate the other organizations.[14]

With regard to the policy outputs, the similarities of the associations across all the countries and across all levels of change of the regulatory system and the organizational population are striking. Above all, the (externally induced) loss of regulatory capacities has been compensated for in those associations that were involved in the PIG structures. Most of them partially achieved this through a strengthening of lobbying activities. These initiatives were more or less successful, according to the respective political conditions. For example, the declining support of the British government made British associations explore lobbying channels involving British aristocracy, even the House of Lords and the royal family. The continuous changes of German national and Bavarian agricultural policy after 1998 also made lobbying there more difficult.

However, services and advice are entirely novel policy outputs that the associations provide. Basically, two variants have to be distinguished. On the one hand, services are provided directly to members (e.g., technical advice, management consultancy, quality control, and so on). On the other hand, services are offered to the general public on behalf of the members and in order to strengthen the public recognition of the sector and its products (e.g., provision of teaching material, nutrition help lines).

These services regularly take the form of marketing and public relations work. The associations have become very creative in performing these policy outputs. Indeed, there is a marked difference if an organization, such as the Swiss FROMARTE that was (as SMKV) one of the most important actors in price negotiations in the old PIG system, is today organizing public events such as the Swiss Cheese Awards.

Another important service that should be mentioned separately is the offer of further education to employees in the sector. This takes into account that the traditional professions related to the dairy industry are under pressure. The most illustrative example of this kind of service is the offer of computer courses for British milkmen.

With regard to associational resources, empirical research revealed itself to be more difficult. It was hard to get any information about this, and the information that was given was not always reliable or comparable across cases.

These observations can be revisited in three more general points, which are less limited to a discussion of single properties, but more to the changes of the organizations as a whole.

First, associations that have undergone a change or associations that are newly founded emphasize the logic of membership much more than the logic of influence. An 'increasing independence of interest associations with respect to their members' (Kriesi & Baglioni, 2003: 23) has not been observed. Above all, this new emphasis on the logic of membership is visible in the provision of internal and external communication such as policy outputs that have recently been strengthened or introduced, but also structural reforms toward more 'lean management'; a higher level of participation of members in associational decision making; and more parity structures of decision-making bodies are examples of this trend.

Second, many interest associations take on organizational properties that would be more typical of other kinds of corporate actors, such as industrial firms, professional service providers, lawyer bureaux, PR agencies, or organizers of public events. This also means that the status of an organizational member becomes more and more that of a client.

This concerns both the structural dimension and policy outputs. With regard to the latter, associational 'goods' that are offered by the associations could also be offered by other actors (e.g., commercial agencies). In order to be able to compete with profit-oriented actors, the associations have to reform their structures. Indeed, as mentioned above, the German MIV explicitly states the desire to become similar to its own members. Both legitimacy vis-à-vis the members (DiMaggio & Powell, 1991: 73) and increased competitiveness might be reasons for this. Thus, an isomorphic process can be observed, as it is a fairly well-known phenomenon for organizations that are densely linked to other actors of their environment (*ibid.*: 63; Crouch, 2003: 193).

Finally, the local and subnational contexts are increasingly important. This is less visible in interest domains, but very apparent in organizational structures. Subnational differentiations are increasingly respected in decision making, but the nature of policy outputs, above all with regard to marketing and public relations, shows the importance of the subnational level. Campaigns, forms of advertisement, and product development take local markets and local audiences into account. Whenever possible, politicians or local VIPs are asked to collaborate with subregional associations or subnational organizational units of nationwide associations. This strengthens a certain common identity, which is not only based on the product, but increasingly on the region. Scotland in Britain, Bavaria in Germany (above all the Allgäu), Vorarlberg in Austria, and most regions in Switzerland are classic examples, but other – less agriculturally specialized regions – in Britain, Germany, and Austria increasingly emphasize the local component in their policy outputs.

In this case, the 'logic of goal formation' (Schmitter & Streeck, 1999 [1981]: 21)[15] also gains some importance over the 'logic of effective implementation', since these subnational initiatives touch on the creation of consensus around solidaristic goals.

This phenomenon seems to be opposed to 'globalization', which is perceived as dominating our current societies (Brose & Voelzkow, 1999: 9). Since it is claimed in the literature that this new discovery at the local and subnational levels is a consequence of globalization, the term 'glocalization' (Brose & Voelzkow, 1999: 20) has been coined for this phenomenon. The dairy sector is an obvious example of such a trend. It is, of course, not possible to infer this finding automatically for other sectors. Given the different natures of the production and the products, and the different degrees of internationalization of the market, such glocalization cannot be generalized to all sectors.

Conclusion: Complex associations in the dairy sector – What are they a case of?

With regard to the central question of this volume, namely, the development of individual interest groups, their organizational populations, and their organizational communities in an era of rising international social, economic, and political interdependence, the dairy sector is a fruitful example.

First of all, it reminds us that internationalization does not determine the actions and properties of interest groups in every case. Without denying the importance of global and European processes, domestic settings and processes should not be discredited too quickly. Rather, a process of glocalization seems to be one of the survival strategies for interest groups in a globalizing world. Admittedly, glocalization as a concept might work better for the dairy industry than for other, less locally bounded sectors, but its role should not be underestimated. The fact that we cannot confirm a clear trend of Europeanization for the dairy sector seems surprising, since milk quota and an ever intensified Common Agricultural Policy suggest the contrary. Although the impact of European integration on the sector can certainly not be negated, at least it does not play the central role for dairy interest groups that could be assumed.

Second, considering other important elements of complex associations, we have seen that the changes were caused by a combination of political, economic, social, and technological processes (with the latter being constant among all cases). Politically, we could see some variation with regard to the involvement of state policy makers (recall the difference between the supportive Swiss government and the less helpful British government), even at the subnational level (both visible in Switzerland and in the case of Bavaria); therefore, analytical categories such as federal government structures should not be discarded too easily. Economically, different actor constellations (such as the dominance of the retail sector in Britain, coinciding with a strong concentration process in the production field) have been identified to play a role. Also, the impact of the social embeddedness of the sector should not be ignored. This means that the study of the dairy sector can help us to detect environmental factors that could be overlooked too easily if we concentrated only on seemingly more modern sectors.

Third, the dairy sector shows us that a shift of 'associational logics', both from the logic of influence to the logic of membership and in part from the logic of effective implementation to the logic of goal formation, can happen in a considerably short time frame. Therefore, we can conclude that interest groups can have the flexibility to change the main principles of their structure and their activities, if this is needed. Indeed, the deprivation of their quasi-public status hit the associations in a very rigid manner, but some of them showed a surprisingly good ability to cope with the new situation. However, this cannot be generalized to every association under research; some of them also died.

This takes our attention to the fourth point, namely, the conflict between path dependence (Mahoney, 2000: 513) and the capacity for institutional adaptation to which interest groups might be exposed. We can observe that – although institutional adaptation is a dominant feature – path dependence applies once a window of opportunity opens. The reaction of Swiss associations to the *Milchkrise* demonstrates that legacies of the past cannot simply be abandoned.

Fifth, the discussion of the question of a convergence or divergence of economic governance in the dairy sector leaves us with a differentiated conclusion: Whereas there is a convergent trend toward change, this trend can follow national specifics. There is no clear convergence into a single model, but an adaptation process that takes national settings into account. Again, this is a disconfirmation of an overly rapid conclusion that followed the idea that internationalization and Europeanization would have an exclusive weight in economic governance.

Finally, the divergence of national adaptation processes makes us reconsider the role of institutions that have always played an important role in economic sociology and the study of systems of production and interest intermediation (Streeck, 1992: vii). Certainly, the term 'institution' is used in an inconsistent manner in today's social sciences, but the dairy sector seems to be a case to which it can be very broadly applied. Political, economic, and historical institutions play as much of a role as cultural ones. The deep embeddedness of the dairy sector in the economy and the society of a country (or even of a subnational region) and its historical pathways make institutions an especially valuable factor in the analysis of the development of the dairy sector.

In conclusion, we have seen that the dairy sector serves as an interesting extreme case of the dynamics of complex associations. It is specific in many respects, but it might also prevent us from coming to sweeping (and rapid) generalizations. It teaches us that even less 'fashionable' cases should be studied in order to get an idea about a specific pattern.

Notes

1. The necessity of remaining independent from economically oriented market mechanisms and untouched by state or community failure is reinforced by the fact that consumers, nowadays, are increasingly critical regarding the quality of food (Grant, 1991b: 2).
2. Furthermore, the impact of European integration can be more direct. The Single European Act (SEA), for example, explicitly questions the existence of PIG arrangements. 'On paper, ... the Single European Act of 1986 placed in jeopardy all 'private interest governments' ... Only if it could be shown ... that these practices were needed to serve some higher public purpose, ... and that they did not discriminate against products or services from other member states, would these ... arrangements ... be safe' (Schmitter, 1994: 660, emphasis in the original). This basically means that PIGs are not compatible with EU law (*Financial Times*, 6 August 1991).
3. Note that the highly corporatist dairy sector is exceptional in the British case (Grant, 1985: 186), since the meso-corporatist system of the British dairy sector is embedded in a macro-pluralist system of interest intermediation.
4. Federalism is generally seen as an important factor for the organization of interest groups. Even Britain shows a considerable level of subnational associability, which is due to administrative structures rather than regional identities (Grant, 1989).
5. Strictly speaking, this was only the case for Emmental, Gruyère, and Sbrinz cheeses (accounting for nearly half of the Swiss cheese market). However, similar arrangements existed for other brand marks (Farago, 1987: 175). In addition, the BUTYRA was the equivalent for the butter subsector (on this see Pestoff, 1987: 106).
6. However, ZVSM and SMKV were not the only important actors in the Swiss dairy sector. It is also important to mention the SMV (*Schweizerischer Milchwirtschaftlicher Verein*), which can be seen as the administrative heart of the PIG system (Farago, 1987: 54, 69, 73, 103).
7. These are the WKÖ (*Wirtschaftskammer Österreich*; Economic Chamber Austria), in the past called BWK (*Bundeswirtschaftskammer*, Chamber of Trade and Industry); the Chamber of Agriculture; the Chamber of Labor; and the ÖGB (*Österreichischer Gewerkschaftsbund*, Austrian Trade Union Federation).
8. The (symbolic) turning point that radicalized public opinion was the failure of the *Käseunion* to protect brand names for Swiss cheeses.
9. Note that PIGs existed despite the EU milk quota system, since this left considerable space for domestic adaptations (Fouilleux, 2003: 253).
10. These two central associations changed their names after the breakdown of the PIG structures. SMP stands for *Schweizerische Milchproduzenten* (Swiss Milk Producers).
11. Whereas there are little more than two dairy businesses per 1,000,000 inhabitants in Britain, the comparative figure for Switzerland is 125, so that the dairy sector is part of the daily neighborhood of Swiss people (Wagemann, 2005a: 81f).
12. In fact, it could be argued that there were developments similar to the Swiss *Milchkrise* in Britain as well, such as the crisis of the successor organizations

to the MMBs; the breakdown of major companies; and the rapid changes in the structure of the industry.
13. Some PIG associations not only served as interest groups and para-state agencies in the PIG arrangement, but were also active in the production of dairy products. Whereas this practice originally dated back to the need to process low-quality or surplus items, over the years this associational segment of the dairy sector became more and more dominant. Switzerland is a perfect example of this (Wagemann, 2005b: 16), but also the former British dairy business Dairy Crest (Grant, 1991b: 54; *Farmers Weekly*, 10 February 1995: 19).
14. Note that the 'umbrella' organizations are very often led by associational policy *entrepreneurs* (individual people or groups of individuals, often from more than one association) who are also responsible for the creation of the organizational webs and occupy powerful positions within the new structures. This is facilitated by the high degree of elite continuity in the dairy sector.
15. Recall that the competition between the logic of membership and the logic of influence is only one (but admittedly the more famous) dimension of the scheme of associational logics (Schmitter & Streeck, 1999 [1981]: 21).

Part III
Business Associations at the European Level

9
Europeanized Convergence? British and German Business Associations' European Lobbying Strategies in the Formulation of REACH[1]

Arndt Wonka

In February 2001 the European Commission published the *White Paper on the Strategy for a Future Chemicals Policy* (European Commission, 2001b), in which it outlined its plans for REACH (Registration Evaluation Authorization of Chemicals), the future regulation of chemical substances in the EU.[2] The publication provoked a shocked outcry among Europe's chemical industry business community, which saw its international competitiveness decline and predicted a large-scale loss of jobs if the Chemicals White Paper were to be translated into EU law. As a consequence, firms as well as business associations took action to influence the EU's future chemicals policy. In this chapter I will comparatively analyze how British and German chemical industry business associations organized their strategic lobbying activities from the publication of the Chemicals White Paper until the publication of the European Commission's legislative proposal.

The institutional environment in which national business associations interact is conceptualized as a two-level arena. It consists of multiple national arenas, plus the EU arena. National business associations' lobbying strategies are discussed with respect to the choices they face when organizing their lobbying of the EU policy process. I will consider two aspects of this choice: the kind of public actor that is targeted by an association; and the degree of coordination of lobbying activities with the national peak and branch associations, as well the supra-national business association and its branch associations. Special attention will be paid to how the structural configuration of the associational configuration in which British and German business associations are embedded respectively affects their European lobbying activities. Thus in the terminology introduced in the introductory chapter of this volume, the chapter combines a view of both the organizational community level – lobbying at the domestic and the EU level – and of the organizational level – that is, choices made by individual associations. The data on business associations' lobbying activities following the publication of the Chemicals White Paper reported in this chapter was gathered through 12 semi-structured interviews in Brussels in January 2002 and through standardized questionnaires that were collected from British and German business associations between December 2001 and April 2002.

What might be the possible findings on national business associations' European lobbying strategies in the context of the research framework underlying the contributions to this volume? If the Europeanization hypothesis discussed in the introductory chapter applies, British and German business associations, although embedded in different national contexts, will show no differences in their lobbying strategies. If, on the other hand, the 'varieties of capitalism' hypothesis is valid, one would expect both countries' business associations to vary in their delegation of European lobbying interactions to the European peak and business associations.

This chapter is structured as follows. First I will define the central concepts and outline the actors and institutions that constitute the EU's two-level system of policy making. Then I will give a concise overview of the European chemical industry's economic situation and the regulatory status quo of chemicals policy in the EU. In addition, the structural properties of the British and German associational system of chemical industries' business associations will be highlighted (see also Grote, this volume). The next section presents this chapter's central empirical analysis of British and German chemical industry business associations' European lobbying strategies.[3] After that I will discuss the chemical industry's European business associations in EU interest intermediation vis-à-vis national business associations. A short discussion concludes the chapter.

Actors and lobbying in the European Union

Three public actors play a central role in EU policy making: the European Commission, which has the monopoly power to introduce legislative proposals;[4] the European Parliament (EP), which is a co-equal legislator in the co-decision procedure (Hörl *et al.*, 2005); and finally the Council, which has to approve any legislative proposal for it to become EU law.

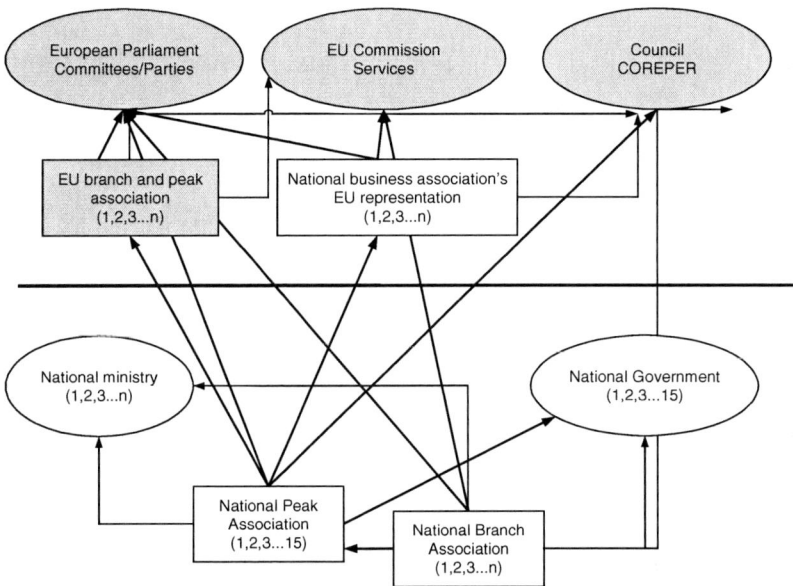

Figure 9.1 Ideal-type two-level arena of EU interest intermediation

In the Council, member state ministers come together to take decisions. Accordingly, member state ministries in which Council decisions are prepared, as well as the prime ministerial offices, are important actors in EU legislative decision making.[5] The EU's system of interest intermediation is made up of European and national associations (Greenwood, 2003; Hix 2005: 208–31).

Figure 9.1 depicts an ideal-type representation of the EU's two-level system of policy making and interest intermediation, in which all hypothetically possible (lobbying) paths between national business associations and those public actors that are relevant in EU policy making are represented. In addition, the figure accounts for the possibility that national business associations delegate their lobbying activities to their EU counterparts. The lower level currently consists of 27 national systems of interest intermediation. These national systems vary with respect to the form of their respective political system as well as the structural configuration of their associational systems. In the following I will only take into account the latter. While the associations in some countries show pluralist characteristics in which co-equal associations interact competitively, in other countries interest intermediation is organized in a corporatist fashion; that is, associations are integrated in a hierarchical associational system and interact in a coordinated fashion (Schmitter, 1979: 13–15).

As Grote shows (this volume), the British system of chemical industry business associations exhibits pluralist characteristics. The British peak association, the *Chemical Industry Association* (CIA), does not occupy a central role. The associational system of Germany's chemical industry, on the other hand, shows strong corporatist characteristics. The national peak organization, the *Verband der Chemischen Industrie* (VCI), is the focal association around which German branch associations group. Whether these structural differences in the make-up of national associational systems actually do have an impact on business associations' lobbying strategies will be investigated in the empirical sections below. Earlier studies, however, show that national associations' EU lobbying activities consist of extensive interactions with other associations and public actors in their national arena. Yet, they are not simply restricted to the national arena but extend to the EU (Pappi & Henning, 1999: 278–9; Beyers, 2002: 607), which can be expected to attract interest groups' attention because of the EU's successively extended legislative competences that increasingly shape the political and economic environment in which domestic groups operate (Börzel, 2005). Moreover, Eising (2004) shows that the extent to which national interest groups complement their national lobbying activities with EU-level activities is heavily affected by the groups' resource endowment and the structural conditions of interest intermediation prevailing in their country.

At the same time, both national interest groups' internal organization as well as the structural properties of national systems of interest intermediation do not seem to be fundamentally transformed through interest groups' behavioral adaptations to the EU's multi-level lobbying arena (Kohler-Koch, 1999; Grote & Lang, 2003; Beyers & Kerremans, 2007). Thus, existing empirical evidence does not lend empirical support to Streeck and Schmitter's speculation (Streeck & Schmitter, 1994), which was recently reformulated by Bartolini (2005): "[T]he indirect effect of integration produces changes in the modalities of interest intermediation at the national level and in the stability and cohesion of individual organizations. Changes in the predominant national interest intermediation structures are likely to occur whenever the national modalities of interest intermediation are in conflict with those prevalent in the same area at the European level" (Bartolini, 2005: 293). This chapter complements the work discussed in this paragraph by investigating how the structural conditions in which they are embedded affected British and

German chemical industry associations' lobbying behavior in the early stages of the EU chemicals policy (REACH).

The national business associations' inclination to rely on associations from their national context for their European lobbying activities could be explained by the transaction costs of establishing and activating relationships with other organizations. While considerable resources need to be invested to form new strategic partnerships, activating existing domestic ties is comparably inexpensive. Moreover, existing and stable domestic relationships reduce an association's uncertainty about the likely behavior of its potential lobbying allies. In addition, these relationships allow associations to penalize non-compliance by other associations, thus reinforcing the mutually cooperative domestic configuration (Axelrod, 1984). Finally, domestic associations can politically put their respective governments under considerable pressure by claiming that a political decision will deteriorate the economic situation of their members, eventually resulting in job losses and accompanying negative political campaigns in the respective country. To prevent this, governments will refer to information from their country's interest groups in advance, reinforcing the national interaction patterns of domestic business associations.

Let us now shift the analytical perspective from the EU's multilevel system of policy making and interest intermediation to the organizational level of individual business associations. Schmitter and Streeck (1999) analytically distinguish two logics driving a business association's actions, the 'logic of membership' and the 'logic of influence'. According to the former, business associations 'have to structure themselves and act so as to offer sufficient incentives to their members to extract from them adequate resources to ensure their survival' (Schmitter & Streeck, 1999: 19). The logic of influence forces business associations to react to public actors 'in such a way as to offer sufficient incentives to enable them to gain access to and exercise adequate influence over public authorities' (Schmitter & Streeck, 1999: 19). Yet, why should public actors allow interests groups such access to and influence on their decisions? Public actors rely on the technical as well as political information provided by interest groups because it allows them to formulate efficient policies; that is, policies whose implementation raises little political opposition and eventually generates constituencies' political support. Such a proceeding is not only likely to reduce the costs of implementing a political decision. Associations' support helps a public actor to legitimize a political decision vis-à-vis the general public, thereby improving its bargaining position vis-à-vis political opponents

(Wonka & Warntjen, 2004). Interest groups provide such information.[6] In this chapter, I denote the logic of influence by the term 'lobbying'.

The concept of lobbying as understood in this chapter captures a business association's strategic reasoning about which actors to interact with in order to influence the outcomes of decision-making processes (Knoke, 1990: 3). An important restriction in a business association's lobbying capabilities is the fact that it only has a limited amount of material and time resources at its disposal. As the contributions in Part II of this book showed, business associations allocate a considerable share of their resources to member services, such as consultation and information services. Thus, taking into account the limited resources that business associations can invest in political activities,[7] it is safe to assume that they plan the allocation of their lobbying resources strategically. In this chapter national business associations' European lobbying strategies are defined by two procedural characteristics:[8] first, by a national business association's choice of the type of public actor that it targets with its European lobbying activities and the level on which the respective public actor is situated; secondly, by the degree to which national business associations coordinate their lobbying activities with national business associations of the same country, with business associations of other EU member states and, finally, with EU branch and peak business associations.

Before analyzing British and German chemical industry business associations' European lobbying strategies, I will give a concise overview of the economic situation of the EU's chemical industry as well as the current regulatory development in terms of the planned chemicals legislation as proposed by the Commission in its Chemicals White Paper. The following section is intended to inform about politico-economic incentives for the chemical industry to mobilize lobbying resources in order to influence REACH. It shows that British and German business associations act under comparable economic and regulatory conditions. Differences in these actors' European lobbying strategies are therefore unlikely to be caused by major differences in the sectoral-economic or regulatory environment in which these actors act.

The reformulation of the EU's chemicals policy

In terms of employment, trade and turnover, the chemical industry is one of the European Union's most successful manufacturing industries. It accounts for approximately 30 percent of the world's chemicals turnover (VCI, 2003: 104) and directly employs 1.7 million people, with an estimated 3 million jobs directly depending on the chemical industry (European Commission, 2001b: 4). Within the EU, the British and the German chemical industries play a leading role. Their share in the EU's chemical industry turnover rose steadily for the last two decades. While in 2002 the British chemical industry accounted for 10 percent of the EU's chemical industry turnover, the German chemical industry accounted for 25 percent (VCI, 2003: 104). In the same year the British chemical industry employed 231,000 employees, whereas in Germany 462,000 employees worked for the chemical industry (VCI, 2003: 112). The figures show that in economic terms, British and German chemical industry firms operate on a similar basis, relative to the overall size of their respective economies. Differences in British and German business associations' European lobbying strategies are therefore unlikely to be related to differences in their members' economic incentives.

In February 2001 the European Commission published the Chemicals White Paper. Its publication was the starting gun for an enormous lobbying campaign initiated by chemical industry business associations in all member states as well as in the EU capital Brussels. What happened? The White Paper was initiated by the EU member states at the informal Environmental Council meetings in Chester (April 1998) and Weimar (May 1999). The EU member states advised the Commission to develop ideas on how to reformulate chemicals regulation in the European Union (EU).[9] The Directorate General (DG) Environment, headed by the Swedish Social Democratic Commissioner Margot Wallström, was mandated to draft the Chemicals White Paper. Its core is the REACH program. REACH aims to abolish the present distinction made between 'existing' and 'new' substances. While under the current regulatory system new substances have been tested with respect to negative effects on human health and the environment according to their production tonnage, existing substances have been largely exempted from these tests. As opposed to the EU chemicals regulations in force presently, REACH aims at a test of all substances produced at a certain yearly tonnage. The testing of substances shall be carried out by industry itself, not by public agencies, thus reducing the public costs of the regulation as well as very likely increasing the speed of testing. Finally, unlike the chemicals regulatory regimes in Japan and the US (Fleischer, 2001) and in line with the EU's precautionary principle (Wepler, 1999), chemicals will only be admitted to the market after previously fixed tests have been conducted and the substances have been registered by a European regulatory agency, to be founded in the course of the implementation of the new EU chemicals policy. However, the chemical industry claims that implementation of REACH as outlined in the Chemicals White Paper would not only weaken the European chemical's industry competitiveness internationally, but also destroy a great number of jobs in the chemical sector itself as well as in branches attached to it (Arthur D. Little, 2002). That is why chemical industry business associations invested a lot of resources in their lobbying efforts.

The Commission reacted to the huge resonance of its Chemical White Paper by staging a stakeholder conference as well as a conference on the business impact of the new chemicals policy. Both conferences were meant to assess the level and character of conflict with respect to the planned chemicals policy. Commission representatives, MEPs as well as ministerial bureaucrats from the member states participated in the stakeholder conference. In addition, US and Japanese representatives also participated. The private actor representatives taking part in the stakeholder conference represented the whole range of affected interests ranging from environmental and consumer interest groups to business associations as well as representatives of large firms (European Commission, 2001a). In line with the policy officially propagated by the Commission, the private actor representatives were almost exclusively representatives from supra-national EU associations.

By now, the Commission, other EU public actors and member state governments were fully aware of the (explosive) political potential contained in the reformulation of the chemicals policy. Taking this into account, it is remarkable that the European Commissioners decided that the DG Environment as well as the DG Enterprise shared responsibility in drafting the legislation. Both DGs have different constituencies and are likely to pursue diverging interests in preparing the draft legislation. The DGs Environment and Enterprise formed seven technical working groups, in which representatives of EU and member state public actors as well as representatives of EU associations participated. In general, the Commission uses working groups extensively to fathom conflicting interests as well as political compromises among a diverse set of private and public actors (Larsson, 2003). The official task of the seven working groups in the case discussed here was to prepare proposals on specific aspects of the planned chemicals regulation. The management responsibilities for the technical working groups and the subgroups they formed rested with DG Environment for some working groups and with DG Enterprise for others.

The 'double assignment' of the DG Environment and the DG Enterprise on developing a legislative proposal on the new EU chemicals policy indeed allowed the Commission to fathom the widely diverging interests of different stakeholders. However, the Commission's strategy backfired on itself. The assignment of two DGs with different constituencies forced the Commission to mediate publicly between the interests of two opposing types of interest groups. The double assignment constituted a strategic risk, since it meant the institutionalization of political conflict within the European Commission itself. As a consequence, it took the European Commissioners longer than they expected to come up with their legislative proposal. Before the legislative proposal was sent to the Council and the EP, an eight-week internet consultation was held. More than 6000 private and public actors participated and commented on the Commission's draft legislation. When the Commissioners finally did come up with their proposal (COM(2003) 644 final) on 29 October 2003 and opened the co-decision procedure, special interests as well as the media agreed that the chemicals industry had managed to account for their arguments in this first round of EU lobbying and interest intermediation (*Süddeutsche Zeitung*, 19 December 2003).

National business associations' European lobbying strategies in the reformulation of the EU's chemicals policy

The planning and realization of the investigation of national business associations' European lobbying strategies are affiliated to the research project introduced by Volker Schneider, Achim Lang, and Jürgen Grote in the introductory chapter of this volume, the core results of which are presented in Part II. The research population is therefore the same as Grote's (this volume). The data analyzed in this chapter was collected by standardized questionnaires. I excluded those associations that stated in his survey that they are not actively involved in the reformulation of the EU chemicals policy from Grote's research population. VCI-*Fachvereinigungen*, which are organizational subunits of the German chemical industry peak association VCI and directly integrated into its hierarchical structure, cannot be expected to engage in their own lobbying activities. They have accordingly been excluded from the sample. The target population of my investigation was thus reduced from 61 to 51 (24 British and 27 German) business associations; 25 of these 51 associations completed the questionnaire. On the basis of the answers provided by the business associations, I excluded another two organizations that noted that they are not involved in the reformulation of EU chemicals policy. This left me with a final sample of 23 chemical industry business associations, 12 of which are British and 11 German associations. In addition to the questionnaire survey, five members of the European Parliament as well as one representative of the secretariat of the European Parliament's environment committee who are involved in the chemicals policy-making process were interviewed. Finally, three representatives of environmental and consumer NGOs, three representatives of the European chemicals industry peak business association, as well as one representative of a national chemicals industry peak association's office in Brussels were also interviewed. Representatives of all interviewed organizations, except the national business association's Brussels representatives, were taking part in the Commission's stakeholder conferences.

The analysis of British and German chemical industry business associations' European lobbying strategies in the reformulation of EU chemicals policy centers around three hypotheses, which are derived from the theoretical discussion earlier in this chapter.

Hypothesis 1 (H1) relates to the type and level affiliation of the public actors that national business associations address with their European lobbying. National associations often have stable relationships to their country's public actors. For national interest groups' European lobbying activities, using these existing relationships means saving transaction costs. In addition, a country's public actors depend directly, in the case of voter, and indirectly, in the case of interest associations on their national constituencies for their political survival. This is, for example, not true for the European Commission, which therefore might gain more independence from interest groups and is able to choose more freely with which interest group it will interact. National associations can use the political dependence of their country's public actors to exert influence. Accordingly, hypothesis 1 states that

> H 1: *National business associations primarily target their respective country's executive with their European lobbying activities.*

Hypothesis 2 (H2) speculates about the effect that a national association's (informal) institutional context, represented by the respective national associational system's pluralistic (as in the case of UK) or corporatist (as in the case of Germany) configuration, has on an individual association's European lobbying strategy. Just as in interactions with public actors, this could be explained by the lower transaction costs related to the activation of existing relationships and coalitions as opposed to building new ones. Hypothesis 2 therefore states that

> H (2): *National business associations national interest intermediation styles persist in EU interest intermediation. Thus, the configuration of the*

national associational system has a structuring effect on national business associations' European lobbying strategies.

Finally, the last hypothesis shifts the focus to the role that the EU branch and peak business associations play in national business associations' European lobbying. In contrast to the national bias inherent in Hypotheses 1 and 2, Hypothesis 3 (H3) states that

(H3) The European peak association (CEFIC) and its branch associations are supranational actors that represent a European chemical industry position and engage in direct interactions with public actors. Thus they have a strong position vis-à-vis their national counterparts and monopolize lobbying interactions on the EU-level.

Before I discuss national business associations' European lobbying strategies on the basis of Hypotheses 1 to 3, let me turn to the role that different resources play for business associations' European lobbying. Two questions are of special interest with respect to exchange resources in EU interest intermediation: Which resource is of value for a national business association in EU interest intermediation? Is there a difference in the value of a specific exchange resource when used on the national and the EU level? I want to draw attention to the fact that Table 9.1 provides a supply-side perspective on the value of specific resources, since the information reported in it was provided by business associations.[10] However, the interviews with public actor representatives indicated that the supply is matched by public actors' demand. Technical expertise especially was considered a highly relevant resource by MEPs.

British and German chemical industry business associations consider 'technical expertise' as a 'very important' exchange resource in national-level interest intermediation. This changes slightly with respect to EU interest intermediation. Whereas German chemical industry business associations still consider technical expertise as a very important resource, British associations consider it 'less important'. However, in relative terms technical expertise is considered as the most valuable exchange resource in interest intermediation by British and German chemical industry business associations – on the national as well as the EU level. This supports the speculation that public actors in general are very dependent on external expertise in order to be able to formulate policies.

In addition, the authority to make members comply with a political decision is considered a valuable resource. British business associations

Table 9.1 National business associations' exchange resources in EU interest intermediation

	Total	British associations	German associations
National level			
Technical expertise	1.3 (SD 0.7) N = 21	1.3 (SD 0.9) N = 12	1.3 (SD 0.5) N = 9
Compliance by an association's members	2.1 (SD 1.0) N = 20	1.8 (SD 0.6) N = 11	2.4 (SD 1.2) N = 9
Political information	3.1 (SD 1.2) N = 20	2.9 (SD 1.1) N = 11	3.2 (SD 1.2) N = 9
Public legitimation of political decisions	3.2 (SD 0.9) N = 20	2.9 (SD 0.9) N = 11	3.6 (SD 0.7) N = 9
European level			
Technical expertise	1.8 (SD 0.9) N = 18	2.1 (SD 1.1) N = 9	1.4 (SD 0.5) N = 9
Compliance by an association's members	2.6 (SD 1.0) N = 17	2.3 (SD 0.9) N = 8	2.9 (SD 1.1) N = 9
Political information	3.4 (SD 0.9) N = 17	3.6 (SD 0.5) N = 8	3.2 (SD 1.2) N = 9
Public legitimation of political decisions	3.5 (SD 0.7) N = 17	3.4 (SD 0.7) N = 8	3.6 (SD 0.7) N = 9

Notes: 1 = very important, 2 = less important, 3 = not important, 4 = not important at all. The values of individual resources are reported as mean values. SD is the standard deviation for the average value.
Source: Own data.

consider this resource more important than German associations do. This might well be attributed to the pluralistic character of interest intermediation in the UK. Since public actors cannot rely on centralized coordination and cooperation among the individual associations with which they interact, they rely on individual associations when it comes to honoring political deals.

Political information and legitimizing support are considered relatively unimportant resources in national as well as EU interest intermediation by both British and German chemical industry business associations. One interpretation of this finding is that public actors use business associations as technocratic interaction partners rather than political interaction partners in interest intermediation. If public actors are in need of political information, they fall back on those actors on which they directly depend given a certain formal insitutional situation, be

Table 9.2 British and German chemical industry business associations' interaction partners in the reformulation of EU chemicals legislation

	Total (N = 23)	British associations (N = 12)	German associations (N = 11)
National government and ministries	82.6	75.0	90.9
Members of the national parliament	21.7	16.7	27.3
European Commission	39.1	16.7	63.6
European Parliament committees	30.4	16.7	45.5
Member of the European Parliament, MEP (same nationality)	52.2	50.0	54.5
Business associations (same country)	82.6	66.7	100.0
National peak association (CIA and VCI)	82.6	66.7	100.0
Business associations (other EU member states)	39.1	41.7	36.4
European peak association (CEFIC)	34.8	25.0	45.5
European branch associations	26.1	41.7	9.1

Notes: Multiple namings were allowed. The percentages represent a positive response to the question of whether the business associations are interacting with the respective actor in order to influence the outcome of the re-regulation of the EU chemicals policy.
Source: own data.

it voters, the parliament or in case of the European Union their member state principals. However, another explanation for the low exchange value of political information and legitimizing support is that business associations have no competitive advantage over other private actor suppliers of these resources, such as the media or political parties. As a consequence, public actors can acquire political information 'more cheaply' from private actors other than business associations.

Let me now turn to the procedural characteristics of British and German chemical industry business associations' European lobbying strategies in the reformulation of EU chemicals legislation. As said before, national business associations' European lobbying strategies are defined by two characteristics: first, by a national business association's choice of the type and level affiliation of the public actor that it targets with its European lobbying activities; second, by the degree of national business associations' coordination with national business associations of the same country, business associations of other EU member states and, finally, the EU branch and peak business associations (Table 9.2).

Table 9.2 shows that British and German business associations primarily target their respective national executive (government and ministries) with their lobbying to influence the outcome of REACH. Hypothesis 1, which speculated that national business associations primarily target their country's public actors with European lobbying activities, is thus corroborated in principle. This is especially true for the British associations: only few of them target the European Commission or the EP's committees in which legislative proposals are discussed and amended. Yet, British associations frequently rely on their country's MEPs to communicate their position to the European Parliament. German associations also extensively target their country's executive. At the same time, however, the Commission is a popular target of German chemical industry business associations' European lobbying activities. An explanation for this finding lies in the hierarchical and coordinated character of Germany's chemical industry associational system, with well-established contacts to the government. Due to this fact, individual associations can direct a considerable part of their lobbying resources to other public actors, who still have to be 'belabored' in order to get the association's interests recognized in the final outcome of the chemicals policy.

With respect to the level of coordination of their European lobbying activities with other business associations, British and German associations' statements reveal a clear pattern. Considerably more chemical industry associations in both countries report coordinating their lobbying activities with business associations from the same national context than with business associations from other countries or with European business associations. In line with the hierarchical structure of the German chemical industry's associational system, all German business associations consider their country's peak business association, the *Verband der Chemischen Industrie* (VCI), as a partner in their lobbying efforts to influence REACH. German business associations EU lobbying strategies thus confirm the central role played by the VCI in national interest politics. With respect to German associations' coordination of activities with CEFIC, one should emphasize that in most questionnaires associations noted that their interactions with the EU peak association CEFIC take place via the VCI.

British associations' coordination of European lobbying with other business associations also closely corresponds to the speculations of Hypothesis 2. The British CIA cannot substantially improve its position vis-à-vis British branch associations when shifting from national to European processes of interest intermediation: two-thirds of associations already report cooperation with the CIA. At the same time, considerably more British than German associations consider the European branch associations as strategic partners to influence the outcome of REACH.

To sum up the empirical results discussed so far, it seems safe to say that the European lobbying strategies of British and German chemical industry business associations show a national orientation with respect to interactions with public actors as well as other business associations (Table 9.2). 'National interactions', however, are complemented by interactions with EU public actors as well as business associations of other EU member states and the EU chemical industry peak and branch associations. Furthermore, when treating EU public actors as collective, rather than unitary, actors, it shows that the national logic again applies within these supra-national EU public actors. Business associations approach their country's MEPs instead of functional subunits of the EP, such as the relevant EP committee (Table 9.2). The same seems to be true for the Commission: On the working level national experts, A-level bureaucrats in the DGs as well as a Commissioner's cabinet member with the same nationality are preferred and seemingly privileged access points for national business associations (see also Egeberg, 1996; Beyers & Kerremans, 2004).[11]

The structural characteristics of a business association's national associational context also proves highly relevant (cf. Hypothesis 2). In line with the make-up of the German chemical industry associational structure, the European lobbying strategies of German business associations are hierarchically coordinated by the German peak association VCI (Table 9.2). British associations, on the other hand, show a greater proneness to coordinate their European lobbying strategies with business associations of other EU member states as well as EU-level branch associations. Thus, even under high political pressure from the EU level, the British peak association CIA could not substantially increase its centrality in (EU) interest intermediation when compared to its general role in the British associational system (Grote, this volume). The German peak association VCI, on the other hand, managed to transfer its central national role to the lobbying activities of German associations in EU interest intermediation.

Finally, the naming of the 'primary coalition partner' confirms the pluralist and corporatist orientation of both countries' business associations in lobbying over the reformulation of EU chemicals legislation. 64 percent of the 11 German business associations named the VCI as their primary coalition partner. Neither other national nor European chemical industry business associations were named as the primary coalition partners, nor any national or EU public actor.[12] In contrast to that, only 25 percent of the 12 British associations stated that the CIA is their primary coalition partner. Another 17 percent of British associations named other national branch associations as their primary coalition partner. European branch associations were mentioned by still another 17 percent of the British associations.

The chemical industry's European business associations: Limitations and capabilities

If what I am suggesting is true, namely that national business associations occupy a prominent role in EU interest intermediation and that national business associations' national lobbying paths are not replaced but complemented by European lobbying paths, what then is the role that EU branch and peak associations play in EU interest intermediation? I will argue below that there are no indications for the neofunctionally inspired 'transcendence scenario' discussed in the third chapter of this volume, according to which CEFIC and its branch associations would replace national business associations in EU interest intermediation. Before that, however, let me briefly outline the organizational characteristics of the chemical industry's European business association, CEFIC, and its branch associations. The goal of sketching the organizational properties of the EU associations is to give the reader an idea of the sheer size of the European chemical industry's EU associations, which complement the national associational systems.

Since 1972 CEFIC has represented the interests of the European chemical industry in Brussels. It is widely considered as one of the strongest EU-level sectoral peak associations (Grant *et al.*, 1988). Currently CEFIC's staff comprises approximately 140 employees. Its membership includes 25 fully entitled national peak associations, 4 associated national peak associations, 42 large multinational firms, and 20 delegates representing 500 small and medium-sized European chemical industry enterprises. To represent the diverse product-specific interests of the chemical industry, CEFIC has available around 120 branch associations, so-called sector groups, in which more than 700 enterprises as well as national branch and peak associations cooperate. To coordinate the activities of the branch associations effectively, CEFIC implemented 'program councils'. These consist of one representative of CEFIC's management board as well as representatives of member firms and associations. In addition, 18 organizationally independent chemical industry associations, which represent interests between the product and the branch level, are affiliated to CEFIC (CEFIC, 2002a, 2002b).

CEFIC and its branch organizations play an important role in the EU's chemical industry lobbying on the reformulation of EU chemicals policy with respect to three functions. First, they provide their members with valuable information about political developments in the EU. Second, they build an institutional framework in which their national members can coordinate their European lobbying strategies and find out about common as well as diverging interests. Third, CEFIC and its branch organizations have stable links to EU public actors, which their representatives themselves use for direct interactions with public actors and which they provide to their national members as 'access channels'.

Let me take up the third point first. The interactions of CEFIC and its branch organizations focus on the Commission.[13] The Commission's stakeholder conferences exemplify its official policy of interacting primarily with supra-national associations. According to two CEFIC representatives, CEFIC mainly interacts with Commission policy specialists. The European peak association provides these bureaucrats with the technical expertise they need when preparing policy proposals dealing with technically complex policies such as the new EU chemicals regulations. Since national associations extensively lobby their country's MEPs and government (Table 9.2), CEFIC and its branch organizations engage in a division of labor with these as concerns direct interactions with public actors. The division of labor between the complementary interactions of national and supranational associations in EU interest intermediation systematically runs along the supra-national and intergovernmental institutions respectively. There are no indications that the supra-national business association replaces national interest groups in EU interest intermediation, as supra-nationalists and neofunctionalists claim.

An important reason we do not observe the supra-national transcendence of national associations is that CEFIC organizes heterogeneous members, both in terms of organizational characteristics and in terms of interests. As outlined above, among CEFIC's members are large multinational firms whose economic perspective is global, as well as small and medium-sized enterprises that are embedded in their respective national economic structures and whose economic perspective is primarily directed toward national markets as opposed to a global one. Finally, CEFIC is the peak organization of 25 national chemical industry peak organizations that themselves represent diverse interests based on the structural make-up as well as the economic relevance of the chemical industry in their respective country. The formation of a uniform European chemical industry position is accordingly severely limited in cases where CEFIC's members' interests diverge widely.[14] Consequently, there might simply not be such a thing as a uniform European chemical industry position that CEFIC can represent vis-à-vis public actors.

Since CEFIC does not have the means to (hierarchically) impose a position on its members and since its member organizations do have the means to engage in political action themselves, CEFIC can be interpreted as a supra-national organizational structure, which coordinates rather than aggregates the policy positions that its national members pursue in EU interest intermediation. In addition, it provides its members with up-to-date information on political developments in the EU rather than prescribing a strategy for lobbying on a specific policy process. CEFIC therefore allows its members to find out about those cases where the formulation of a common European policy position is possible. Yet, its potential to work toward the generation of such a uniform position is limited.

Nevertheless, its coordination function puts CEFIC in a privileged position to acquire information on diverse national policy positions as well as public actors' policy positions on current political developments. This informational function on political developments in the EU is of special relevance to the majority of CEFIC's members who cannot afford their own representation in Brussels. The supra-national business associations' informational capacities thus reduce the costs of national business associations' information gathering and should have positive effects on the effectiveness of national business associations' European lobbying strategies.

To sum up the arguments made in the previous paragraphs on the role of supra-national business associations for national business associations' European lobbying strategies: CEFIC and its branch organizations do fulfill important functions in EU interest intermediation. However, rather than being autonomous supra-national actors engaging in 'European' interactions and therefore building a kind of European counterweight to national actors in EU interest intermediation, CEFIC and its branch associations play an important coordinating and informational role in national chemical industry business associations' European lobbying strategies.

Discussion

The aim of this chapter is to make a statement about the (procedural) characteristics of national business associations' European lobbying strategies. European lobbying strategies have been analyzed by means of national business associations' interactions with public actors and business associations of the same national population, other EU member states and at the EU level. The results of the analysis of British and German business associations' European lobbying strategies shows that national business associations' primary focus of action is directed toward private and public actors embedded in the same national context or having the same national background, as is the case with MEPs (Hypothesis 1). In the conceptual language employed by the editors of this volume, the configuration of an association's national population strongly influences the procedural characteristics of national business associations' European lobbying strategies. One could say that national business associations extend the core characteristics of their national interest intermediation to EU interest intermediation (Hypothesis 2).

However, national business associations' strategic thinking and politico-economic awareness are highly Europeanized, in that national business associations are very well aware of the politico-economic effects that EU regulatory policies have on their members' economic operations. Thus, national business associations pay close attention to political developments at the EU level. In this regard, European associations play an important role. Rather than being autonomous supra-national actors, they are information and access brokers for their members. They do not replace national business associations as important actors in EU interest intermediation, but are important complements to national business associations, helping them to gather information relatively cheaply and negotiate strategies in the institutionalized framework provided by supranational associations (Hypothesis 3).

As a consequence, neither the Europeanization nor the 'varieties of capitalism' approaches (Schneider, Lang & Grote, this volume) fully apply to the findings of this chapter. Even under the (top-down) impact of European integration and the political and regulatory challenges associated with it, national business associations' European lobbying strategies do not converge to identical patterns of lobbying interactions, as the Europeanization scenario predicts. Furthermore, European business associations do not 'transcend' their national counterparts as primary actors in EU interest intermediation in the way that 'BIAs originally organized at the national level simply "transfer" their activity and authority to a higher level of aggregation ... [while] [n]ational (or sub-national) BIAs might persist organizationally, but only as units of administrative convenience for newly empowered European or Global associations' (Schmitter, 2000). Rather European business associations 'complement' national business associations.

Yet, when applying a 'delimited' concept of Europeanization (Grote, 2003), restricted on *cognitive awareness* – that is, strategic considerations of the costs and benefits of engaging in or refraining from European lobbying activities as a response to EU policy developments – rather than *form* – that is, patterns of national business associations' European lobbying interactions – the concept could contribute to a better understanding of the strategic considerations that guide those actors' actions. This, however, requires that the sources of Europeanization – policies, the EU polity or EU politics – and the mechanisms through which the concept of Europeanization causally operates are identified and explicated.

Notes

1. I want to thank Jürgen Grote, Achim Lang, Dirk Lehmkuhl, Philippe C. Schmitter and Volker Schneider for helpful comments on an earlier draft of this chapter.
2. In the following I will refer to the *White Paper on the Strategy for a Future Chemicals Policy* as the Chemicals White Paper.
3. The exclusive focus on the lobbying activities of chemical industry business associations helps to prevent collective action problems that are related to the interest to be organized (Olson, 1970) from having a distorting effect on the findings.
4. The Commission can, however, be asked to formulate legislative proposals by the Council and the European Parliament.
5. Earlier analyses have shown that national parliaments play a minor role in EU policy making (Beyers, 2002; Schneider & Baltz, 2004).
6. Analytically, I distinguish four types of resources: technical expertise, the authority of an association to make its members comply with a political decision, political information and finally a business association's support in legitimizing a specific policy (cf. Pappi & Henning, 1999).
7. Grote shows that British and German business associations invest 30 percent of their resources in national and EU-level lobbying.
8. The procedural characteristics of lobbying as understood here have to be distinguished from the actual influence exerted by lobbying. While the former capture the way in which influence attempts are organized and executed by business associations, the latter capture the effectiveness that these interactions have in shaping the final content of a policy outcome. However, the procedural characteristics of business associations' lobbying are expected to have a decisive impact on their ability to get access to public actors, which again is an important condition for actually exerting influence on a policy outcome (Bouwen, 2004).
9. The reformulation of EU chemicals legislation aims at replacing the core of the currently valid chemicals legislation, which consists of the directives 67/548/EEC, 88/379/EEC, 76/769/EEC as well as the regulation 793/93.
10. The associations were asked to attribute values to the listed resources according to the respective resource's usefulness in gaining access to public actors at the national as well as the EU level.
11. Interviews with private and public actor representatives.

European Convergence? 199

12. Instead German chemical industry business associations considered the peak organization of German industry (BDI) as a relevant coalition partner.
13. In an interview, the CEFIC representatives estimated that 70 percent of interactions with the Commission are dealt with by CEFIC. The remaining 30 percent are carried out by national business associations. Council interactions, on the other hand, were said to be national business associations' job in 90 percent of cases. Finally, according to the CEFIC representative, the interactions with the European Parliament are dealt with in 40 percent of the cases by CEFIC and in 60 percent by national business associations. This again mirrors the double-edged institutional role occupied by MEPs, as described above.
14. In trading emission certificates, where the positions of national industries varied significantly, CEFIC for example had to give up any European activities and left the field of interest intermediation to national associations.

10
Business Interest Associations and Corporate Lobbying: Which Role for Brussels?

Marc Tenbücken

Corporate lobbying has become an important aspect of interest representation over the past decade. The ratification of the Treaty on European Union in 1993 led to a situation in which a growing number of interest groups wanted access to the political arena and made considerable efforts to enter into consultation with the European institutions. The Commission particularly experienced a heavy increase in lobbying activities by business interest associations (BIAs). The increasing shift of activities of interest representation to the European level soon caused a situation in which the respective political institutions were facing an overload of access and information. As a consequence, these institutions had to reduce the complexity of their consultation system and therefore began to regard multinational companies (MNCs) as their natural and proven partners in the business dialogue (Coen, 1997: 96). The result of this development was that more and more Euro groups became dominated by large enterprises and direct-firm lobbying increased significantly (McLaughlin *et al.*, 1993: 193).[1] The increase in the Commission's regulatory competencies and general institutional changes caused by the Maastricht Treaty have further facilitated direct lobbying. One visible result of the maturity of business was the establishment of policy forums by the Commission in which BIAs and, by special invitation, MNCs were asked to participate.[2] In such forums, the Commission, BIAs and large firms organize around specific issues, exchanging positions and discussing possible implications of new regulatory provisions (Cowles, 1998: 120). In sum, the 1990s marked a clear trend toward an intensified partnership between Community institutions and MNCs.

Direct lobbying as an important form of interest representation

This chapter focuses on interest representation of MNCs in the European policy arena and the role played by BIAs in the lobbying process. Following the overall approach in this book, the chapter differentiates between a *functional* and a *territorial* dimension. The former refers to the organizational hierarchy implicit in the representation of business interests. In general, any representational activity is based on the business interests of companies operating in a specific sector. In order to increase the chances of realizing these interests, individual companies are members of national BIAs. National BIAs are again organized in supra-national federations to facilitate interest representation at the EU level. However, as outlined above, large and powerful firms often are direct competitors of BIAs when it comes to the representation of interest vis-à-vis political institutions. Today, MNCs often possess better access to EU institutions than the respective BIAs of which they are members. They undertake direct representational activity and can therefore be conceptualized as an individual population acting beside the BIAs (Grote & Schneider, 2006: 119). The division of tasks during the course of a lobbying initiative between these two distinct populations at the community level is one central aspect that is dealt with in this chapter.

The territorial dimension inherent in the analytical approach points to the characteristics of the multilevel governance system in the EU (Hooghe, 1995: 4). As a consequence of European integration, a fundamental transformation of state–business relations has occurred due to the interconnectedness of political levels, the expansion of issue arenas and the multiplication of actors. The resulting complexity of the EU's multilevel system, including the existence of multiple centers of authority on the regional, national and European levels, makes it necessary for business to focus on all three levels simultaneously. While national BIAs predominantly target political actors at the domestic level, mainly ministries or other institutions of the executive branch, the task of Euro federations is to represent business interests to the EU institutions. Depending on the stage of the decision-making process at the EU level, the intensity of lobbying activity shifts back and forth between the Commission, the European Parliament (EP) and the Council of Ministers. In addition, we have witnessed the emergence of new forms of policy communities in which public and private actors work together to make binding decisions (cf. Greenwood & Ronit, 1994). At the European level, those networks often originate in the expansion of regulatory activities by the Commission.

Based on these two analytical dimensions, this chapter sheds light on the question of in which situations MNCs use forms of direct lobbying and bypass BIAs in the EU decision-making process. The focus lies on the identification of the conditions that favor direct lobbying and the corresponding strategies employed by MNCs. The hypothesis is that direct lobbying of MNCs becomes especially viable in the light of emergency situations. These are situations in which the policy-making process at the EU level is likely to result in costly regulatory provisions for business and in which traditional forms of interest representation did not lead to acceptable modifications of the original proposal. Such a situation is exemplified by the decision-making process of the Directive on end-of-life vehicles. The original proposal by the Commission included provisions that would have caused tremendous costs for the European automotive industry. During the course of the decision-making process, traditional forms of associational lobbying proved to be unsuccessful. Hence, a new strategy had to be found. The statistical analysis and discussion of the case will outline under which circumstances and with which strategies business was successful in modifying the original Commission proposal.

The chapter is organized as follows. In the next part, I will discuss the relationship between the two distinct populations of MNCs and BIAs as regards the organizational characteristics and the various strategies of corporate lobbying. The third part then briefly presents the cornerstones of the decision-making process of the Directive on end-of-life vehicles, a case that has caused a high-profile lobbying campaign by the automotive industry in the EU. Following this presentation, the fourth part analyzes the influence exerted by the various actors in the decision-making process of the Directive. It also analyzes the different influence routes that were used by MNCs and assesses the role played by national and European BIAs. The last part summarizes the results of this chapter and concludes by looking at institutional developments that might affect the lobbying strategies of MNCs and, thus, the role played by BIAs.

Corporate versus associational lobbying

The organization of business interests and the strategies employed for the representation of these interests at the EU level possess distinct characteristics. Usually, the representation of business interests is left to the responsibility of sectoral interest associations, whose members are either companies or national BIAs. However, interest representation via national or supranational associations is only one option among a variety of others that are viable and open to MNCs. In the past, large companies have shown increasing efforts to intervene directly in the decision-making process at the European level. Depending on the policy issue, MNCs possess different ways to influence the political institutions that are responsible for a certain proposal. They can either rely on the initiatives of BIAs or lobby these institutions directly.

However, forms of direct lobbying also require certain coordination and organization efforts from the public affairs managers in these firms. As a consequence, in recent years most MNCs have restructured their public affairs departments and developed new political strategies for the national and European level. Some even hire professional lobbying or law firms to represent their interests. An interesting question in this context regards the role played by national and supra-national BIAs. Certain institutional and organizational characteristics seem to catalyze direct lobbying and the bypassing of established BIA structures at the domestic and European levels. In the following, I will discuss the organization of interests of MNCs and their corresponding strategies.

Organizational characteristics

In general, large companies are able to finance and organize their own lobbying activities and do thus not rely on representation through BIAs. Smaller firms, however, are usually unable to organize their own campaigns because they lack sufficient financial resources. They cannot afford to maintain their own Brussels representation or to mandate law firms with the representation of their interests. As a consequence, they rely almost exclusively on their BIA membership and the representation of their interests through the respective associations. In recent years, we have been able to observe the emergence of vertical alliances between larger and smaller firms outside established interest associations. Their goal is to improve the representation of business interests of small and medium-sized enterprises that had previously been marginalized in the policy-making process. In addition, these alliances give large firms 'political legitimacy' (Coen, 1998: 80–81). However, critics argue that they are often dominated by these large companies, which only pretend to fight for the interests of the industry in order to legitimize their individual interest-maximizing activities.

Recognizing that MNCs possess the ability to organize their interests individually, we face the question of why large companies nevertheless join BIAs. The direct financial costs of BIA membership are usually not the central issue for accession. The answer to this question lies in the relational complexity between politics and business and is based on

Salisbury's argument that the various institutional embeddings of a company are the driving force behind its decision to join a BIA. This BIA membership helps a company to structure or even reduce the complexity of these embeddings (Salisbury, 1984: 69). Political incentives also make the accession to an interest association attractive for MNCs. One example of such a political incentive would be the common belief held by large companies that 'if we do not take action, no one else will' (Cowles, 1998: 120).

A further reason for the accession of MNCs to interest associations regards the legitimizing effects of a BIA membership. It can facilitate the situation if a company is able to mask unpopular demands by hiding behind the representational claims of a BIA instead of pursuing its own lobbying activities. These activities are then attributed to the industry or the sector as a whole and not to an individual firm. This seems especially true in cases of such sensitive policy issues as environmental or consumer protection. Some authors argue that MNCs are unlikely to be influential in situations in which their policy positions differ from those of European BIAs (cf. Greenwood, 1997: 131). As we shall see, this does not necessarily need to be true. In the public debate on the provisions of the end-of-life vehicles Directive, the German car company Volkswagen took a different position than ACEA, the interest association of the automotive industry at the EU level. But instead of being isolated in the decision-making process, Volkswagen's lobbying initiative proved to be highly successful.

MNCs possess a special role based on their capacity to influence the strategies and actions of BIAs. Very often they are the driving force, the 'powerhouse' (*ibid.*, 1997: 125) behind the associations' activities. This can be explained by the fact that in order to achieve acceptable representational outcomes, a company has to be an active member of an interest group and cannot simply free ride (McLaughlin & Jordan, 1993: 151–2). The perspective of influencing the collective strategy and the representational policy of the interest group vis-à-vis the political institutions is definitely one of the most important incentives for MNCs to become BIA members. In addition, membership might help a MNC to redefine its own policy positions on the basis of new information gathered through horizontal exchange with other companies.

At the *associational* level, the peak association of the German automotive industry, the *Verband der Automobilindustrie* (VDA), represents about 500 companies, namely the large car manufacturers and their suppliers. In other European countries, car manufacturers and suppliers are organized separately in specialized BIAs and then grouped together in one common peak organization, as is the case in the German chemical industry.

With regards to the organizational *community* level, business interests are usually represented through national and European BIAs as well as large multinationals operating individually or in concert. In our particular case, the interests of European car manufacturers are represented through ACEA, the *Association des Constructeurs Européens de l'Automobile*. ACEA is the only European BIA in the sector of automobile production. Currently, 13 automobile companies are members of ACEA. The German members of ACEA are BMW, Daimler-Chrysler, MAN Nutzfahrzeuge, Porsche and Volkswagen. The numerical relationship of five German companies to one national BIA is well reflected in ACEA's policy positions. These are largely dominated by the interests of the companies rather than by the interests of national BIAs. The VDA has associative membership status in ACEA.

Within ACEA, the individual firms are the decision takers. One reason for the loss of acceptance by the Commission of the association's predecessor, CCMC, was that it was unable to find a common position among its members on certain policy issues.[3] In order not to be confronted with the same problem of internal stagnation as its predecessor, ACEA adopted a three-fourths qualified majority voting rule. This qualified majority voting has facilitated the formulation of a common position. A solid common position, in turn, is the basis for a successful dialogue with the Commission. As a consequence, the strong position of the new association finally urged the PSA group to join ACEA. It felt that retaining an 'outsider status' meant losing valuable influence at the EU level (Greenwood, 1997: 75).

In general, it is said that BIAs at the European level are very effective in cases of 'damage limitation' (Sargent, 1993: 235). One example of such a strong BIA is the *Comité des Organisations Professionnelles Agricoles* (COPA), an association that rather successfully defends farmers' interests at the EU level. The BIA of the chemical industry at the EU level, the *European Chemical Industry* Council (CEFIC), is another very effective sectoral association (Grant, 2000: 85–9). However, this effectiveness is dependent on the sector and on the specific policy issue. In the case of the Directive on end-of-life vehicles, for example, we find that the sectoral BIA was not strong enough to win important political concessions during the decision-making process at the EU level. In fact, ACEA was too weak to lobby successfully and as a result the German car manufacturers entered the arena and lobbied directly at the national level. This process is presented in more detail later in this chapter.

Lobbying strategies of MNCs

The central argument made in this chapter is that MNCs possess various influence routes for the representation of their interests vis-à-vis the institutions of the EU. In doing so, large companies generally base their strategy on the simultaneous use of these influence routes in order to maximize their effectiveness. Depending on the issue, MNCs can either employ an orthodox strategy, rely on established access routes and leave interest representation to national or European interest associations with little or no direct lobbying effort. In this case, the key role is played by the European interest association, which acts as the legitimate partner and spokesperson for business interests to the EU institutions. Or MNCs can enforce their own initiatives parallel to those of national and supranational BIAs. This applies especially in emergency situations (cf. Averyt, 1977). In such a situation, MNCs use their good contacts with national ministries or even heads of states. Thus, interest representation via BIAs constitutes only a subset of all potential influence routes open to business in the policy-making process. In order to obtain an overview of all possible influence channels, we need to consider the activities of BIAs and the direct lobbying efforts of MNCs together at the organizational community level.

Every strategy consists of a distinct mix of influence routes. The necessity of employing several routes simultaneously originates in the uncertainty about political conditions and in the question of whether a certain route is indeed accessible and successful in the end. The theoretical assumption in this context is that each lobbying strategy and the corresponding use of certain influence routes is determined by the institutional configuration in the decision-making process and the organizational characteristics of the respective sector (cf. Tenbücken, 2002). Depending on the issue, business possesses multiple points of access to the important political institutions in the complex multilevel system of the EU. Often, large and powerful companies establish networks and create their own direct contacts with key political actors and institutions at the domestic and at the European level.

Based on Europeanization and globalization trends, MNCs can exert an immense influence on the political institutions at the national level.[4] Today, large firms can coordinate their business from almost anywhere in the world and use these possibilities as a structural advantage. Threats of reducing employment in the home market or of completely relocating production serve as effective means of political pressure. What is more, national access channels remain the lowest-cost options relative to other lobbying alternatives.[5] Most of the time, the CEOs of large companies can even rely on their good contacts to the heads of government.[6] As the case shows, Ferdinand Piëch, the CEO of Volkswagen at that time, was able to influence the position of German Chancellor Gerhard Schröder in such a direction that the latter started a political campaign against the Directive on end-of-life vehicles.

These national political strategies take on a European dimension when MNCs are able to use their cross-national alliances to form a broad front of resistance in the Council of Ministers. It seems true that '[t]he importance of government relations in subsidiary management affects the extent to which each subsidiary is coordinated centrally versus managed locally' (Lodge, 1990: 29). In other words, the multilevel character of the EU and the distribution of competencies between institutions demand the strategic coordination of activities between the company's headquarters and its subsidiaries in other EU countries. In the decision-making process of the Directive on end-of-life vehicles, Volkswagen could rely on its Spanish subsidiary Seat, which put pressure on the Spanish government. Thus, complex ownership relations within internationally operating companies can result in simultaneous lobbying activities of MNCs and their subsidiaries in different EU member countries, expanding the spectrum of influence routes.

Regardless of their domestic impact, in times of growing competencies of EU institutions MNCs began to increase their direct lobbying activities at the European level. Often, MNCs bypass long established representational structures that include national and European BIAs. Instead of mandating the national association with the representation of their interests, MNCs increasingly try to influence EU legislation directly (Cowles, 1998: 109).[7] Currently, on the side of business, the Commission, the Council and the EP possess most frequent contacts with MNCs (Kohler-Koch & Quittkat, 1999: 3). In their presence at the European level, MNCs are often supported by the Permanent Representatives of the member state governments. These representatives with ambassadorial status provide access to EU institutions and to political resources for MNCs in return for technical information on an issue (Coen, 1997: 105).

MNCs have experience of political exchange with national and international regulators (Greenwood et al., 1992a: 21) and with operating in international politico-economic environments. This international experience of MNCs and their good contacts with high state officials and politicians could lead to the assumption that MNCs are better equipped for lobbying EU institutions than are most of the BIAs (cf. McLaughlin & Jordan, 1993: 153). Most MNCs have set up their own pubic affairs offices in Brussels, whose main function is to establish contacts with Commission officials and national deputies in the EP. It should be noted, however, that the Commission tries to avoid overextensive bilateral contacts with firms; it rather tries to further the involvement of European BIAs in negotiations (McLaughlin *et al.*, 1993: 200). Often, the Commission consults with industry on the basis of ad hoc groups, including MNCs and sectoral European BIAs.

BIAs are not marginalized in the decision-making processes at the EU level. On the contrary, there are four major reasons why BIAs are still important channels of influence for MNCs, even if today large companies use multiple strategies to lobby EU institutions:

1. The Commission prefers collective bodies in order to built a large basis of consent.
2. The Commission wants to act 'even-handedly', not favoring some firms over others.
3. The Commission appreciates sectoral self-regulation.
4. MNCs can use European BIAs to avoid strict regulation of their general business environment.

Despite these important functions of European BIAs, MNCs have managed to gain acceptance even in areas that have traditionally been reserved for collective interest representation. Examples are new forms of micro-corporatism in which policies are determined and implemented through bargained agreements between the Commission and major European companies (Cawson, 1992: 117). In some sectors large MNCs even monopolize the representation of industry interests. Often, these companies operate under an associational mask to conceal the existence of their individual power and influence (*ibid.*: 101).

We can thus summarize that MNCs possess various channels of influence for the representation of their interests in course of policy-making processes at the EU level. The impact of national and European BIAs largely depends on the respective policy issue. The following example will exemplify the coexistence of MNCs and BIAs as lobbying actors at the European level. It will make clear that the institutional configuration and the organizational characteristics of the sector are the decisive determinants for the involvement and the impact of BIAs in the decision-making process.

The Directive on end-of-life vehicles

The decision-making process of the Directive on end-of-life vehicles is outstanding in many respects. First and foremost, basic institutional rules have changed in the course of the process. Some MNCs switched their lobbying strategy from orthodox to emergency. Thus, the lobbying process can be regarded as a good example for comparing traditional interest representation through BIAs and alternative lobbying activities through MNCs. This part of the chapter presents a comparison of the Directive's major regulatory provisions before and after direct lobbying pressure exerted by MNCs. Secondly, it briefly summarizes the different phases of the decision-making process at the EU level and the corresponding lobbying activities employed by MNCs.

Major elements of the Directive

The goal of the Directive on end-of-life vehicles is to prevent the creation of waste from vehicles and, in addition, to promote the reutilization, recycling and other forms of recovery of end-of-life vehicles and their components. It seeks to reduce the quantity of waste from vehicles taken off the road and dumped or incinerated with energy recovery. Technically, the Directive regulates the disposal of old cars. Since 2002 all end-of-life vehicles in the EU have to be disposed of at special processing centers. The owner or the last holder of the car may claim the cost of disposal from the manufacturer. It was exactly this provision of 'producer liability' that made the decision-making process of the Directive so difficult.

A brief comparison between the original proposal (European Commission, 1997) and the final version (European Parliament, 2000) will help us to understand what significant changes the Directive on end-of-life vehicles underwent during the course of the decision-making process. It becomes obvious that several original regulatory provisions of the Directive were modified in favor of the automotive industry after MNCs changed their lobbying strategy. As we can see in Table 10.1, there were important changes between the original Commission proposal of 1997 and the final position of the Council and the EP in summer 2000.

According to industry representatives, changes made to the original Directive reduced the costs for the automobile industry by about 40 percent. The most important of these changes refer to the ban on heavy metals, the dates concerning the beginning of producer liability and the recycling and recovery quotas.

Table 10.1 Comparison of original proposal and final version

Issue	Original proposal 7/1997	Final version 9/2000
Prevention	Heavy metals[8] in vehicles placed on the market after 1 January 2003 *must be recycled or eliminated from new vehicles*.	Vehicles put on the market after 1 July 2003 *must no longer contain* heavy metals.
	Manufacturers must make an effort to reduce the use of dangerous substances, if possible at the vehicle design stage.	Same.
Collection	From *1 January 2000*, all vehicles must be taken to licensed processing centers.	*18 months after entry into force of the Directive*, all vehicles must be taken to licensed processing centers.
	Owners receive a certificate of destruction.	Same.
	From *1 January 2003*, owners may claim the cost of taking their vehicle to a professional dismantling installation from the manufacturer.	For *new* vehicles, put on the market after *1 July 2002*, producers should be liable for dismantling and recycling from that date.
		For *existing* vehicles, put on the market before 1 July 2002, producers should be liable from *1 July 2007*.
Reutilization, recovery and recycling	By *1 January 2005*, the rate of reutilization/recovery must be 85% of the weight of the vehicle and the rate of reutilization/recycling must be 80%.	By *1 January 2006*, the rate of reutilization/recovery must be 85% of the weight of the vehicle and the rate of reutilization/recycling must be 80%. *For vehicles produced before 1 January 1980*, the member states can set lower quotas, but not lower than 75% for recovery and 70% for recycling.
	By *1 January 2015*, the rate of recovery must be 95% and the rate of recycling must be 85%.	Same.
Information	Vehicle manufacturers must supply information on the rate of reutilization, recovery and recycling achieved during the *past* year.	Every *three* years, the member states must send a report to the Commission about the execution of this Directive.

Stages in the decision-making process

The Commission issued its proposal for a Directive in July 1997. Up to December 1998, all members of ACEA basically agreed on this proposal. At the beginning of 1999, Ferdinand Piëch, at that time CEO of Volkswagen, became the new President of ACEA. He immediately began to launch attacks against the Directive, and from this moment on the constructive atmosphere between the EU institutions and the industry began to vanish (*Franfurter Allegmeine* Zeitung, 26 June 1999). In what followed, we were able to observe one of the most spectacular cases of direct lobbying by MNCs in the history of the EU.

The EP held its first reading on the Commission proposal on 11 February 1999. Its members voted generally in favor, but made 43 amendments to the original proposal. The meeting of the Council of Ministers for adopting a Common Position was scheduled for 11 March 1999. When the ACEA President started to realize the costly provisions for the automotive industry foreseen by the Directive, he addressed German Chancellor Gerhard Schröder. In a letter of 3 March 1999 he expresses his deepest concerns about the Directive, trying to convince the Chancellor that producer liability should only be applied to new vehicles and not old ones.[9]

Hence, on 11 March 1999, the day the Council of Ministers was supposed to formulate a Common Position on the proposal, the German Minister of the Environment, Jürgen Trittin, cancelled the corresponding point from the agenda[10] based on the instructions he had been given by Chancellor Schröder (*Frankfurter Rundschau*, 11.3.1999). Thus, Volkswagen's approach was successful and the industry had won valuable time for reconsidering its strategy. The following phase was characterized by the fact that neither the Commission nor the industry made any compromises to the other side. On 27 April 1999, the Commission accepted 17 of the 43 amendments demanded by the EP in its first reading either partially or entirely and so introduced the first modifications to the original proposal.

On 1 May 1999, based on the provisions of the Treaty of Amsterdam, the decision-making procedure for environmental legislation changed from cooperation to *co-decision*, giving the EP a more powerful position. Thus, the EP held a new first reading on the Commission proposal in which it confirmed its vote of 11 February 1999. On 24 June 1999, the Council of Ministers of the Environment met in Luxembourg to find a Common Position on the modified Commission proposal. When it came to the vote, Germany was against, Spain and the UK abstained. Hence a qualified majority of 62 or more votes was not reached and a Common Position was not formulated. The three countries formed a blocking minority based on a total of 28 votes not in favor of the proposal.

How was this development possible when in late 1998 all 15 member states had basically signaled the acceptance of the original Commission proposal? The German voting behavior seems clear: Volkswagen managed to raise the Chancellor's doubts about the proposed Directive and its adverse effects on the German car industry (*Handelsblatt*, 23/24 July 1999). During the car summit in Bonn, the German automobile industry as a whole was able to convince the Chancellor that such a Directive was too costly for the industry. But what about Spain and the UK?

The interviews I conducted reveal two factors behind the voting behavior of the Spanish government. First, Seat, the biggest car producer in Spain, is a 100 percent subsidiary of Volkswagen. The experts agreed that this relationship was an important factor for the position of the Spanish government (Interviews Frankfurt, 21 August 2000, and Brussels, 1 February 2001). The second factor was an interesting package deal: the German government agreed to support Spain in the question of fishing rights around the coast of Morocco if, in turn, Spain supported Germany concerning the Directive on end-of-life vehicles. With regard to the voting behaviour of the UK, there are also two explanations. In 1999 the British car producer Rover was a 100 percent subsidiary of BMW. If we consider the importance of jobs in the automotive sector, it becomes plausible that corresponding pressure was likely to be successful. Nevertheless, issue linkage was also at work in the British case. The German government promised the UK support in the question of the harmonization of art trading, an important issue for the British government at that time (Interview Brussels, 8 September 2000).

Based on the negative vote in Luxembourg another Council meeting was needed. In preparation for this meeting on 22 July 1999, the COREPER[11] headed by the new Finnish presidency reached a compromise integrating 20 of the 43 amendments proposed by the EP in its first reading, 13 of which had previously not been accepted by the Commission. The most important modification to the original proposal was that of producer liability, which charges the costs of the disposal to the producer. It now applied two different dates. The first date, 1 January 2001, covered liability of the manufacturer only for new vehicles and the second date, 1 January 2006, was for vehicles that are already on the market. The Council of Ministers of the Environment finally agreed on the Common Position on 29 July 1999, with only Germany voting against.

After the critical questions had been solved, the co-decision procedure continued according to the Treaty. The EP basically approved the Common Position of the Council, but made some technical amendments in its second reading on 3 February 2000 so that the Conciliation Committee was called.[12] In May 2000, it reached agreement on a joint text for the Directive, setting the date of producer liability for existing vehicles to 1 January 2007. The new text was finally accepted in September 2000 by the EP and the Council.

Actor salience and routes of influence

Based on the information presented above, I conducted an empirical analysis in order to identify the salience of the actors and the major routes of influence chosen by MNCs for their lobbying strategy. In the following I will first analyze the *effective influence* of the various actors in the decision-making process of the Directive. This will give us an idea of the salience of each actor in the lobbying game. In a second step, I determine the importance of each *influence route* for the lobbying strategy of MNCs. This tells us about the significance that MNCs attribute to national and European BIAs in emergency situations. However, before I present the results of the empirical analysis, I shall briefly explain the methodology that has been used for data collection and statistical analysis.

Methodology

For the collection of the data I consulted ten experts, one from each of the major actors that were involved in the decision-making process. A list of all actors and the corresponding experts who were interviewed can be found in the appendix to this chapter. Based on the answers of the experts to a standardized questionnaire, it is possible to assess the actors' influence and to identify the most important influence routes. In addition, I conducted non-standardized interviews with the chief lobbyists of the three largest German automobile producers, BMW, Daimler-Chrysler and Volkswagen in their Brussels public affairs offices. The interviews provided valuable background information on the case as well as explanations for results obtained in the quantitative analysis.

Actor influence

The assessment of *effective influence* of the various actors is based on a model by Stokman *et al.* (1999). During the interviews, the experts had to identify the relevant actors, their potential power relative to the other actors and the salience that each actor attributes to the Directive. In the context of the analysis, *actors* are defined as individuals or organizations that possess power resources that allow them to exert influence on other actors. Some actors use their influence directly – that is, governments or public institutions – other actors use it indirectly – that is, interest associations or companies. *Potential power* is defined as the ability of an actor to change the behavior of other actors in a direction that is advantageous for it. This potential is based on distinct resources such as information, access to other important actors, financial resources or the formal authority to take decisions. The values of the different resources may vary according to the issue. And finally, *salience* is defined as the level of importance an actor attributes to an issue in relation to other issues. It indicates the extent to which an actor is willing to mobilize its potential power in order to exert influence.

The values for potential power and for salience can vary between zero and 100 (Thomson *et al.*, 1999: 6ff.). For the calculation of effective influence, I took the average of these values across the ten interviews. The effective influence (INF) that each actor x(i) exerted in course of the decision-making process is the product of its potential power (POW) and the salience it attributes to the issue (SAL):

$$INF_{X(i)} = POW_{X(i)} * SAL_{X(i)}$$

In other words, INF describes how much of the actor's potential power has been activated for influencing the decision-making process. The INF values we obtain for each actor give us an indication of whether MNCs were indeed more effective in the decision-making process than domestic or European BIAs. Table 10.2 presents a listing of all relevant actors and their INF values. An actor is termed 'relevant' if its effective influence is higher than 0.3.

From the information presented above, we could expect that the MNCs show a higher value of effective influence than the sectoral BIAs, namely VDA and ACEA, either because MNCs attributed a higher salience to the Directive or because their potential power was indeed bigger. Let us consider salience first. It is seems to be the case that Volkswagen's attack on the original proposal in early 1999 made the other car companies aware of the enormous costs inherent in the provisions of the Directive (Interview Brussels, 8 September 2000). The companies were especially interested in modifying the provisions regarding the cost responsibility. The inclusion of all existing vehicles, it was argued, would result in an enormous financial burden for the industry. Hence, at the beginning of 1999 the MNCs changed their lobbying strategy from orthodox

Table 10.2 Relevant actors

No. i	Actor x	Potential power $POW_{x(i)}$	Salience $SAL_{x(i)}$	Effective influence $INF_{x(i)}$
1.	Council of Ministers of the Environment	0.93	0.89	0.83
2.	European Parliament	0.86	0.88	0.76
3.	European Commission	0.76	0.90	0.68
4.	**Volkswagen AG**	0.62	1.00	0.62
5.	German Ministry of the Environment	0.57	0.92	0.52
6.	German Ministry of the Chancellor	0.63	0.79	0.50
7.	VDA	0.51	0.94	0.48
8.	**Bayerische Motorenwerke AG**	0.50	0.91	0.46
9.	**Daimler-Chrysler AG**	0.50	0.80	0.40
10.	Ford of Europe Inc.	0.47	0.84	0.39
11.	General Motors Europe AG	0.47	0.84	0.39
12.	ACEA	0.43	0.90	0.39

to emergency. This is reflected by the relatively high salience values attributed to the German MNCs in Table 10.2.

As can be seen from Table 10.2, Volkswagen possessed the fourth strongest effective influence in the decision-making process ($INF_{VW} = 0.62$). It was thus stronger than the national BIA ($INF_{VDA} = 0.48$) and the supra-national BIA ($INF_{ACEA} = 0.39$). While BMW possessed about the same influence value as VDA, the influence of Daimler-Chrysler was at 0.40 around the level of ACEA. The INF value of Volkswagen is mainly due to its high value for potential power *and* salience, where it got the maximum value of 1.0.

A further interesting observation is that the horizontal BIAs in Germany and at the EU level, BDI and UNICE, possessed only very low INF values. This result is confirmed by interviews with the experts, who ascribe to both BIAs only minor importance in the decision-making process. What is more, environmental groups seem to have played a rather unimportant role. Their effective influence was very low ($INF_{ENV} = 0.03$), so that they cannot be regarded as relevant actors in the decision-making process.

Influence routes

The lobbying strategy of MNCs usually includes the use of various routes of influence. An influence *route* is composed of a sequence of multiple influence *channels*. The central question is whether the MNCs have used influence routes that included the BIAs in their lobbying strategy or if these organizations have been bypassed. The importance of each influence *route* is based on the information given by the experts. They were asked to assess the relevance of each influence *channel* in course of the decision-making process. For doing so, the experts had to draw arrows indicating the influence actor A had exerted on actor B. The importance of each influence channel in the decision-making process is expressed through its density. The density of each channel is calculated as the average of the values attributed to the channel by each of the ten experts.[13] On the basis of this calculation, it is possible to identify the most important influence channels and, thus, the central influence routes used by the MNCs to reach the respective political institutions.

The results are presented in Figure 10.1. The densities correspond to the average values that have been attributed to each influence channel by the experts.[14] The results are clear. First, Volkswagen has indeed exerted a strong influence on the *Bundeskanzleramt*, the Ministry of the Chancellor (DENS$_{\text{VW-BKA}}$ = 2.0). The *Bundeskanzleramt*, in turn, had

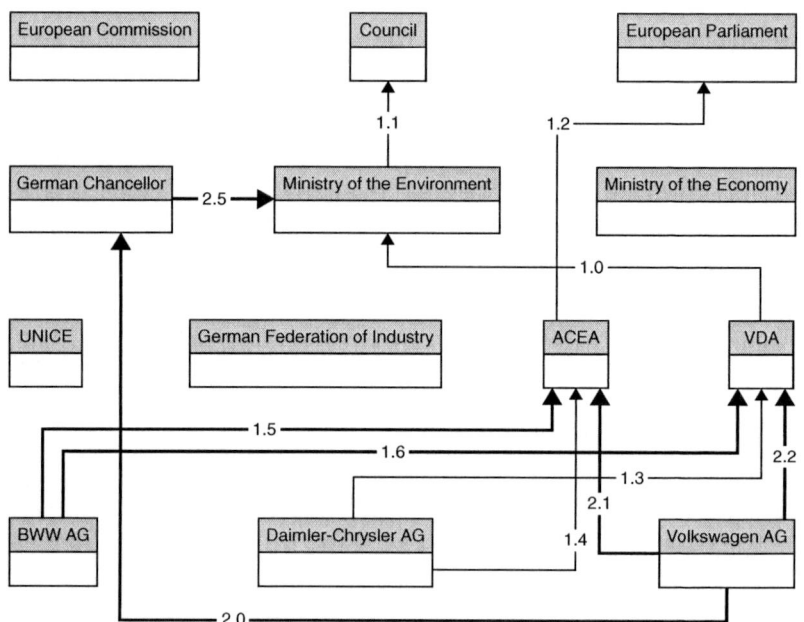

Figure 10.1 Influence channels

a very strong impact on the position of the German Ministry of the Environment ($DENS_{BKA-BMU} = 2.5$), which in turn used its influence in the Council of Ministers ($DENS_{BMU-Council} = 1.1$). The combination of these three individual influence channels leads to the first influence route: *from Volkswagen over the Chancellor over the Ministry of the Environment to the Council.*

Secondly, all three German car companies either had a medium or a strong impact on VDA ($1.3 < DENS_{X-VDA} < 2.2$). VDA again had a medium influence on the Ministry of the Environment, which again had medium influence on the Council. These channels constitute the second influence route: *from the German car companies over VDA over the Ministry of the Environment to the Council of Ministers.* Finally, a third influence route is clearly visible. With almost the same density as toward VDA, the German car manufacturers influenced ACEA ($1.4 < DENS_{X-ACEA} < 2.1$). ACEA, in turn, exerted a medium influence on the EP ($DENS_{ACEA-EP} = 1,2$). The third and only pure European influence route then goes *from the German MNCs over ACEA to the EP.*

The results show that the BIAs did indeed play a role in the lobbying strategy of the MNCs. However, the most important influence route was the national route over the head of state and the responsible ministry bypassing VDA, the national BIA. The car companies nonetheless included VDA in their strategy, but this constituted merely a safeguard against possible setbacks to their direct lobbying approach. The emphasis was evidently placed on a lobbying strategy that included domestic influence channels such as ministries or heads of state. ACEA, the European BIA, was only active in lobbying the EP, an institution that is naturally more difficult to approach for a single company because of its internal organization, during the third and last phase of the decision-making process. This task was gratefully left to the European BIA, which spends many of its resources on establishing good contacts with MEPs.

Conclusion

From the evidence presented in this chapter, we can conclude that in emergency situations the lobbying strategies of MNCs shift, first, from associational to direct lobbying and, second, from the European to the national level. Such a situation emerges if a Commission proposal foresees heavy financial burdens for the industry and if the BIAs responsible for the representation of the industry's interests are not capable of modifying the proposal in a direction that is advantageous to MNCs. The interviews confirm that the multilevel structure of the EU demands simultaneous lobbying activities at the national and at the European level. However, direct lobbying activities in emergency situations are usually aimed at political institutions at the national rather than at the EU level. This was shown in Figure 10.1: the two most important influence routes involve actors and institutions at the national level. Central to the direct lobbying campaign were the initiatives of the German automotive companies. They focused on building cross-national alliances at the highest executive level, even personally involving heads of state. However, the national interest association, VDA, played an important role in accompanying these direct lobbying efforts through parallel initiatives at the domestic level.

The interviews further confirm that sector characteristics are important variables for the lobbying strategy of MNCs. The concentration of companies, for instance, affects the role of national and supranational BIAs. The fact that the automotive industry is a classic oligopoly might explain why VDA and ACEA were mainly active on the technical issues and why the highly political issues, such as cost responsibility and recycling quotas, were targeted by the German MNCs themselves. As one expert argued, member-driven interest associations rely much more on the input of their members than those that are driven by professional functionaries. ACEA and CLEPA, the *Comité de Liaison de la Construction d'Équipements et de Pièces d'Automobile*, serve as examples here.

Although ACEA is a direct member of BIA, during the second and decisive phase of the decision-making process the lobbying strategy of the German MNCs was characterized by an emphasis of activities at the national level. Obviously, national influence channels were more promising for the modification of important provisions such as cost responsibility and recycling quotas. The reason for the significance attributed to the influence route from the MNCs over ACEA to the EP can be explained by the fact that ACEA became active *after* the central questions had been resolved in the Council. The dialogue between ACEA and the EP during the third decision-making phase focused mainly on technical details of the Directive. The conclusion that in emergency situations large companies rely on strategies that prefer domestic over supra-national influence channels should lead to a refinement of propositions that emphasize the growing relevance of EU-level interest representation. Processes of corporate lobbying are more complex and possess more variants than are posited by several contributions on interest intermediation in the European Union.

Considering the significance of the institutional configuration for the lobbying strategy of MNCs, it is obvious that a shift from European to national influence routes is most promising if the Treaty demands unanimity in the Council. In such situations a single country is capable of blocking the entire decision-making process. Based on the revisions of the Treaty in Amsterdam and Nice, however, fewer and fewer policy fields require unanimous Council decisions.

What is more, the role of the EP has been significantly strengthened over the past decade. Today, the Treaty foresees co-decision rights for the Parliament for many policy fields. In general, BIAs possess better and more effective access to MEPs than do the public affairs offices of MNCs in Brussels. All these developments taken together mean that lobbying strategies that emphasize national instead of European influence routes should become less viable to MNCs. As a consequence, supranational BIAs could regain importance thanks to their privileged position vis-à-vis the Commission and the EP. It will be interesting to observe if this development leads to an erosion of the position of national BIAs and their corresponding reactions in the long run. Most probably, however, there will be an expansion of forms of cross-national alliances between MNCs and national governments, as was the case in the decision-making process of the Directive on end-of-life vehicles.

Notes

1. Coen identifies three main phases of MNCs' action at the EU level. First, the time prior to the Single European Act (SEA) when a small number of firms monitored the European Community (EC) but left most lobbying activities to their interest associations. During the period between the SEA and the Maastricht Treaty lobbying in the EC boomed, and MNCs became more aware of the relevance of European affairs and established their first direct links to supra-national institutions. Finally, the post-Maastricht era was characterized by developments in which firms created horizontal alliances, built up their own Brussels public affairs offices and established direct contacts with the Commission (Coen, 1997: 92).
2. Further reasons for the establishment of these forums were the increase in the Commission's regulatory competencies and general institutional changes through the Maastricht Treaty that facilitated direct lobbying.
3. Jacques Calvet, President of the French Peugeot-Citroën (PSA) group, regularly used his veto position, which rendered a coherent and reliable position of CCMC on important European issues impossible. As a consequence of this internal blockade and the resulting lack of a reliable policy position, the Commission classified CCMC as a less important partner. It is also worth noting

that when ACEA was formed in 1991, the PSA group initially did not join the association.
4. It is interesting to note that national institutions are still more frequently contacted than European institutions.
5. Furthermore, national governments retain a key role when it comes to the implementation of EU Directives in the member states. Thus, MNCs have a chance to use the national influence route to modify certain technical details even after the Directive has been adopted at the EU level.
6. In some cases national BIAs act as, sweetener lobbyists' and provide the grounds for further corporate lobbying at the national level (Coen, 1998: 84).
7. However, for lobbying the EP firms still prefer the activities of the respective European BIA (McLaughlin & Jordan, 1993: 128).
8. Considered as heavy metals are lead, mercury, cadmium and hexavalent chromium.
9. He argued, for instance, that from the approximately 150m vehicles in the EU, almost 29m were from Volkswagen.
10. During the first half of 1999 Germany held the Presidency of the European Union.
11. Comité des Représentants Permanents.
12. According to Art. 251 (3, 4) of the Treaty establishing the European Community, the Conciliation Committee is called on by the President of the Council in accordance with the President of the EP. It consists of the members of the Council and the same number of MEPs. On the side of the Council members the Committee decides with qualified majority and on the side of the MEPs with simple majority.
13. The experts were asked to assess the relevance of each influence channel according to a 'medium', 'strong' and 'very strong' influence that actor A had exerted on actor B.
14. $DENS_{X-Y} = 1.0$ corresponds to 'medium influence', $DENS_{X-Y} = 2.0$ to 'strong influence' and $DENS_{X-Y} = 3.0$ to 'very strong influence'. Only influence channels with a DENS value above 1.0 are considered.

11
The Complexity of Adaptation: Conclusions

Achim Lang and Volker Schneider

This book is a comparative study of sectoral systems of business associations and their adaptation to changes in their political, economic, and technological environments. The previous chapters presented a systematic description and analysis of the activities and structures of national business associations. The contributors to this volume have offered a realistic description of associational networks that consists of multiple, sometimes contradictory relationships, and of associational activities that not only involve lobbying but also the provision of services. The country chapters have also revealed major changes and adaptation processes that have taken place during the last 20 years. We relate these changes in associational activities and structures to transformations in sectoral governance as well as in market structure. According to our theoretical framework, the country chapters are basically organized in two sections, covering, on the one hand, the inter-organizational relations within the associational system and, on the other, the organizational properties of business associations.

At the level of the associational system we are interested in competitive, neutral, and cooperative relations. Such ecological networks indicate degrees of integration within associational systems. Furthermore, we investigate the extent to which business associations develop centralized hierarchical networks in which information flows and other activities are coordinated.

At the level of organizational properties, the chapters highlight lobbying as well as member-oriented activities of business associations. In this respect we go beyond traditional public choice and rent-seeking approaches, as well as some versions of neocorporatist theory that either conceive of associational activities as a pure search for particularistic goals, or focus on aspects and capacities of associational governance, widely ignoring the complex mixture of functions that business associations perform. These functions contain, for example, services and products for firm members as well as their own business activities. Furthermore, we explore the different facets of lobbying strategies that today also include general societal lobbying or 'political gardening', as we have labeled these novel strategies.

In the introductory chapter the drivers of associational change were scrutinized and located in the economic, technological, and political environments, which consist either of actual or potential firm members, collaborating and competing business associations, and public authorities and organizations as lobbying targets.

This chapter summarizes the empirical findings of the previous country chapters and analyzes the changes in the activities and structures of business associations over two decades from 1980 to 2000. Our analysis covers three economic sectors: the chemicals industry, the information and communications sector, and the dairy industry. We have chosen these research objects according to their varying degree of affectedness by environmental forces. In the dairy industry Europeanization is the main external force triggering change at the level of associational systems. The chemicals sector is primarily affected by processes of market extension and global competition. Europeanization there is related to a changing regulatory environment. In the information and communications sector, technological revolutions have changed the sector's make-up completely. These effects have been accompanied by globalization and Europeanization. In order to control for Europeanization effects, we included non-European Union countries such as the US and Switzerland in our research design.

Inter-associational structures

Inter-associational relations cover a broad array of topics and measures, ranging from competition and cooperation patterns to structures of formal and informal hierarchy and subordination (Baum & Amburguey, 2002). Associational theories rarely conceptualize or even mention inter-associational relations. An exception is pluralism, which views ties between business associations as attempts to influence other associations, or as efforts to organize coalitions between interest groups in order to affect public policy making (McFarland, 2004). Neocorporatism contrasts pluralist pressure politics with a more hierarchy-centered perspective, in which business associations are tied together by affiliation and subordination (Schmitter & Streeck, 1999 [1981]). However, the case studies in this volume demonstrate that empirical findings are more complex than the broadbrush accounts of pluralist or neocorporatist approaches indicate. Ties to other associations are frequently multiplex and multilayered, and are often structurally not consistent. Furthermore, associational systems cannot be reduced to single logics such as competition in pluralism or hierarchy in neocorporatism. Real existing associational systems may contain different logics at different network positions. Associational change is therefore not limited to organizational properties alone, but includes also the foundation and disbandment of business associations as well as changes in their embeddedness in inter-associational networks.

Ecological relations

Chemicals associations in the US, UK, and Germany have experienced highly similar patterns of foundings and mergers and form comparable ecological networks that are characterized by dense cooperation and few competitive links, predominantly located at the periphery of the ecological network.

The German ecological network is structured in a star-like configuration in which the national sectoral peak association, VCI, occupies a central position and is connected to almost all other business associations by mutual cooperative ties. Competitive relations are only located at the periphery and include newly founded associations such as the sector group for biotechnology companies (DIB) and the association of research-intensive pharmaceutical manufacturers (VFA). These examples document that changes have taken place primarily at the biotech sub-branch and have led to an increase in competition between associations (Chapter 4).

In the British landscape similar ecological networks have developed, in which only a few changes occurred, predominantly due to newly founded associations (Chapter 4). The British network consists of various cooperative ties that, in contrast, are not centered at the sectoral peak association, CIA, but are more evenly distributed in the overall network. The few competitive relations are located at the periphery of the network and include the 1992 founded *Specialised Organic Chemicals Sectors Association* (SOCSA).

The US associational landscape generated higher population dynamics compared to its British and German equivalents (Chapter 5). Six out of nineteen focal business associations experienced mergers or splits in the 1990s that led to the establishment of four independent associations. The ecological network consists primarily of cooperative ties centered at

Table 11.1 Ecological relations and structural changes in comparison

Sector	Country	Ecological relations	Changes (since 1980s)
Chemicals	Germany	Cooperative networks, medium density, competition at the periphery	Low population dynamics (some foundings), few changes in the overall network structures, changes at the periphery (competition in biotech and pharmaceuticals)
	UK	Cooperative networks, medium density, competition at the periphery	Low population dynamics (few foundings), few changes in the overall network structures, changes at the periphery (competition in pharmaceuticals)
	US	Dense cooperative networks, competition at the periphery	Medium population dynamics (foundings and mergers), few changes in overall network structures (cooperation as well as competition)
	EU – GER, UK	Strong cooperation between EU and national business associations. German associations favor peak associations, British other branch associations	
I&C	Germany	Highly competitive in communications, cooperation within information domain	High population dynamics (foundings, mergers and splits), increase in competition
	UK	Mainly cooperative/neutral relations, low competition density	Low population dynamics (foundings), few changes in relational structures
	USA	Mainly cooperative/neutral relations, low competition density	High population dynamics (foundings and mergers), some changes in relational structures

the *American Chemistry Council* (ACC). Competitive ties are less frequent. They emanate from newly founded associations, such as the *Chlorine Chemistry Council* (CCC), or are directed to these newcomers, as is the case for the *American Plastics Council* (APC). Interestingly, both the CCC and the APC are closely affiliated to the sectoral peak association ACC.

EU-level associations cooperate closely with national business associations. However, the intensity with which EU-level associations cooperate with (affiliated) national associations varies greatly between countries. Wonka's (Chapter 9) comparison points out that German associations clearly favor their domestic peak association VCI as an intermediary to EU institutions or interact with the EU peak association *European Chemical Industry Council* (CEFIC). British business associations, on the other hand, prefer to interact with EU branch associations than with CEFIC.

In the information and communications sector, technological, economic, and political changes generated strong population dynamics and increased competition between business associations. However, this evolutionary path is not as clear-cut as in the chemicals sector.

The German associational landscape experienced fundamental changes in the last two decades. Half of the focal business associations, particularly in the communications sector, have been established since then or have experienced mergers or splits. These newly established associations have positioned themselves between sub-branches of the I&C sector, thereby entering into competition with long-established business associations. As a result, the ecological network is subdivided into a cooperative cluster that includes information and media associations and into a competitive one that is made up mainly of communications and equipment associations.

The transformation of the British landscape of business associations in the I&C sector was comparably less profound. Related population dynamics unfolded earlier due to the earlier market liberalization. Changes have therefore been less dramatic. Some business associations were established in the 1990s, mainly in the communications sector. These associations are positioned at more peripheral sites in the ecological networks, or even maintain isolated positions. Only in one instance did the emergence of a newly founded association cause a competitive reaction from a long-established business association. The core of the ecological network is made up of media associations that have developed cooperative and neutral relations to each other.

I&C business associations in the US have developed cooperative or neutral relations over the last 20 years. As a result of early market liberalization, the US system was established in the 1970s and 1980s.

Subsequent consolidation processes led to some mergers within the last two decades. The ecological network is, compared to the other associational systems, the densest. On average each business association is linked to four other associations. Competitive ties are located at the network periphery and include, on the one hand, newly established associations such as the *Cellular Telecommunications & Internet Association* (CTIA) and the *Software & Information Industry Association* (SIIA) and, on the other, communications associations such as the *Personal Communications Industry Association* (PCIA).

Hierarchy

Business associations are not only embedded in ecological ties of cooperation and competition that integrate the individual association into a system of similar organizations, but also into a network of information exchange facilitating the coordination of activities. In this respect the sectoral systems of business associations have developed, in varying degrees, hierarchical networks of information exchange, where few associations occupy central and intermediary positions.

Most clearly, the German chemical business association landscape resembles a perfect hierarchy, in that all business associations are members of the umbrella association of the chemical industry (VCI). Moreover, the VCI is located at the center of a star-like configuration (Chapter 4) and thus is in a position to control information flows. Other associations rarely exchange information directly. This situation has not changed through the integration of newly founded associations. Instead, they have been smoothly integrated into the existing structure.

Likewise, British chemical business associations have developed a star-like information network, but this is far less hierarchical than the German network. The center of the star is occupied by the sectoral peak association the *Chemical Industry Association* (CIA). This is due to the fact that the density of information exchange is higher than in the German case, which implies that most business associations have additional contacts with other associations than the CIA. Again, the integration of newly established associations has not changed the overall configuration.

In the US, business associations in the chemicals sector show remarkably similar features compared with the British and German associational systems (Chapter 5). The sectoral peak association ACC occupies the central role within the information exchange network, although the ACC is not able to monopolize information flows. The density of exchange is considerably higher than in the German case but equals the British

Table 11.2 Associational hierarchies in comparison

Sector	Country	Inter-associational structures	Changes (since 1980s)
Chemicals	Germany	Almost perfect formal and informal hierarchy	Few changes in overall network structures
	UK	No formal hierarchy (but high informal coordination)	Few changes in overall network structures
	US	Some formal hierarchy with respect to functionally specific tasks (otherwise informal coordination)	Few changes in overall network structures
I&C	Germany	Low to medium hierarchy (in the information domain), none in communications	Reduction of hierarchy (communications sector)
	UK	Low hierarchy (information domain)	Few changes in hierarchical structures
	US	Low to medium hierarchy (communications domain)	Increase in hierarchy (communications)
Dairy	Austria, Switzerland, UK	Independent business associations, no hierarchical integration	High population dynamics, dismantling of hierarchical structures and associational governance
	Germany	Independent business associations, some associational self-regulation	No changes concerning hierarchical structures and associational governance

network. Newly established associations have been seamlessly integrated into the existing network.

In the information and communications sector, hierarchical patterns of information exchange are less frequent and less intense than in the chemicals sector. The German information exchange network is characterized by a polycentric structure, in which three associations occupy a more prominent position (Chapter 6). The centrally positioned associations link different subnetworks with each other. The subnetworks consist either of telecommunications associations or of media associations or of hardware and infrastructure associations. However, none of these business associations is capable of monopolizing information flows. The present network structure departs significantly from former analysis (Schneider & Werle, 1991) which demonstrates that the associational system was much more hierarchical at the end of the 1980s than it is now.

Information flows rather sparsely in the British associational population. Almost half of the focal business associations are not involved in information exchange, while the others frequently send and receive information. Due to the lack of ties, the associational network does not display any hierarchy. Newly founded associations are positioned at the periphery of the sparsely connected network.

I&C business associations in the US developed a polycentric informal hierarchy with two prominent actors, the *Telecommunications Industry Association* (TIA) and the *Consumer Electronics Association* (CEA). TIA and CEA connect the whole network by cross-linking the remaining business associations that are located at the network periphery. However, despite their central position, TIA and CEA cannot be said to have acquired more than an informal coordination capacity. Due to the lack of newly founded business associations, the US sectoral landscape has not experienced major changes (Chapter 7).

Wagemann's comparative study of associational systems representing the dairy industry (Chapter 8) analyzes transformations of associational self-regulation over the last 20 years. Prior to the 1980s, associational systems in the dairy industry were organized as private interest governments in Austria, Germany, the UK, and Switzerland (Traxler & Unger, 1994). Business associations were integrated into public policy making and fulfilled a number of governmental tasks. However, due to processes of internationalization and Europeanization, the hierarchical structure of these self-regulatory arrangements has been dismantled and a new associational system has emerged. Interestingly, the most rigid hierarchical structures have experienced the most profound transformations. In these cases completely new business associations emerged; others were dissolved or merged with potential competitors. Nevertheless, the most flexible arrangement in Germany, which only carried out limited governmental tasks and displayed less hierarchical structures, survived the political and economic turmoil of the 1990s largely unaffected.

In summary, business associations representing the chemical industry have developed similar network patterns in terms of ecological relations and information exchange. In all three countries ecological networks are predominantly made up of cooperative relations. Competition exists at the periphery of networks and is mainly inserted by newly established business associations. So far, changes within networks are due to population dynamics that have altered the composition of associational landscapes. However, these changes are restricted to peripheral locations in the ecological networks. Information exchange clearly shows hierarchical patterns in each country. The degree of hierarchy is somewhat lower in the Anglo-Saxon countries. It is thus not surprising that national associations favor either EU branch associations, as is the case for UK business associations, or the EU peak chemical industry association CEFIC, as is the case for German business associations.

I&C industry associations have developed distinct networks structures that neither resemble the patterns found in the chemicals sector nor make up a comparably consistent structure. Ecological networks in this sector are governed by different national logics. Cooperation clearly dominates in the US and British associational systems, where competition only looms at the periphery. In contrast, the German ecological network is characterized by a split between a cooperative and a competitive subnetwork. Centralization of information flows is clearly less pronounced than in the chemicals sector. In all countries there are some associations that control a limited amount of information exchange. Again, informal hierarchy is rather limited in the Anglo-Saxon countries compared to Germany.

In the dairy industry all forms of central coordination of associational activities by a system of peak associations has ceased to exist. Business associations now form a 'pluralistic' interest group system in which cooperation nevertheless still dominates and competition is less frequent.

Organizational properties

In the introductory and theoretical chapter we distinguished two major organizational properties of business associations: service for members and political activities directed toward public authorities or other sociopolitical actors. At the level of organizational properties, adaptation takes place when business associations adjust their activities to new environmental demands. Environmental demands and pressures arise from changes in the composition and structure of the political system or from transformations within the economic sectors that the associations represent. Changes in the political environment are said to lead to modifications in influence investments and access routes, while changes in the market structure should lead to adjustments in service provision to members.

In the chemicals sector, business associations have fairly homogeneous activity profiles. In Germany, business associations spend about 44 percent of their resources in lobbying activities at the national and international level, while the rest is invested in member services. Cluster analysis shows three kinds of activity profiles. The largest cluster consists of *service providers*, while the other clusters contain *multilevel lobbyists* that invest the resources in lobbying activities at the domestic and European level, and *domestic lobbyists and political gardeners* that primarily try to influence domestic policy makers and public opinion. Representatives of these business associations reported a tremendous reorganization of activities and indicated a clear shift toward political representation instead of providing services to members.

In the British case, business associations spend 34 percent of their resources in lobbying activities. Compared to the German associations, differences are mainly due to the minor importance of societal lobbying in the British context. As a result, British associations form just two different clusters: *multilevel lobbyists* and *service providers*. Similarly to their German equivalents, major changes are reported about the increases in influence activities while service provision remains at the same level.

The average resource allocation of the US chemical industry associations of 38 percent to lobbying activities ranges between German and British average values (Chapter 5). US business associations can be broadly separated into two types. One category of business associations is predominantly service oriented. The other primarily seeks to influence policy makers or attempts to alter public opinion in their favor. Representatives of US business associations reported a drastic increase in lobbying over the last few years, while increases and decreases in membership investments are balanced.

In the information and communications sector, business associations expanded their activities in various directions. Comparative case studies (Chapters 6 and 7) point out that within-population diversity is considerably higher than in the chemicals sector.

Table 11.3 Organizational properties in comparison

Sector	Country	Influence/membership activities	Changes (since 1980s)
Chemicals	Germany	Prevalence of multilevel lobbyists, some political gardeners, relatively homogeneous population	Increase in influence investments, particularly in European lobbying
	UK	Prevalence of multilevel lobbyists and service providers, relatively homogeneous population	Increase in influence investments, particularly in European lobbying
	US	Separation between membership-oriented and lobbying-oriented associations	Increase in influence investments, particularly in international and societal lobbying
I&C	Germany	Prevalence of multilevel lobbyists, relatively homogeneous population	Increase in influence investments, domestic as well as European lobbying
	UK	Prevalence of service providers and multilevel lobbyists, heterogeneous population	Increase in influence investments, domestic as well as European lobbying
	US	Prevalence of domestic lobbyists, some multilevel lobbyists	Increase in influence investments, particularly in domestic lobbying, strong decrease in membership activities
Dairy	Austria, Switzerland, UK	No regulatory tasks, high service orientation	New development of influence and membership activities
	Germany	Few regulatory tasks, high service orientation	Few changes in activities
Automotive	EU – Germany	Renationalization of lobbying strategies in case of emergency situations	

Lang's comparative analysis (Chapter 6) indicates that German I&C associations on average spend 45 percent of their resources on lobbying activities, but more than 50 percent on membership services. However, only a minority of business associations can be characterized as *service providers*. Among them are two of the largest and most centrally positioned German business associations, the DMMV and the ZVEI. German business associations are mostly *multilevel lobbyists*. Almost three-quarters of the German associations belong to this associational type. British business associations spend around 30 percent of their resources on lobbying activities. Therefore, *service providers* clearly dominate in the British system. Almost half of the associational population belongs to this category, while only four British associations have a *multilevel lobbyist* profile. The German as well as the British associational systems have developed a small number of specialist associations that focus either on domestic or on societal lobbying. Since the 1980s some activities have clearly lost or gained in importance. In the British and German associational systems the investments of lobbying activities increased considerably, both at the national and the European level. Membership activities also gained in importance, but not to the extent of lobbying investments.

In the US, business associations in the I&C sector invest more than 40 percent of their resources in lobbying activities, particularly at the national level (Chapter 7). International lobbying efforts are exceptional. Thus, most business associations fall into the categories of *domestic lobbyists* and *service providers*, while *multilevel lobbyists* are still the exception. However, among those *multilevel lobbyists* are some of the most prominent and resourceful associations, such as the *American Electronics Association* (AEA), the *Telecommunications Industry Association* (TIA), and the *Motion Picture Association of America* (MPAA).

In the dairy industry, business associations had to redesign their activities virtually from scratch, since their former quasi-governmental functions have ceased to exist. New access routes to policy makers had to be established and novel services to members had to be launched. Wagemann (Chapter 8) shows in detail how changes in the regulatory system have strengthened lobbying activities. By way of example, he states that British business associations explored new access channels to public policy making, which not only included Whitehall but also the Royal Family. Additionally, dairy industry associations have developed counseling services as new outputs, and intensified marketing and public relations.

In the automotive sector, Tenbücken (Chapter 10) stresses the emergence of particular lobbying patterns when multinational companies

(MNCs) and business associations face a situation of emergency; that is, an 'unexpected' European directive. In these circumstances, interest representation changes from associational intermediation to direct lobbying. At the same time, the MNCs shift their lobbying efforts from European to national access channels.

In summary, in all systems of business associations a clear distinction between lobbying- and service-oriented associations exists. However, in the I&C sector lobbying displays a greater variance. It includes not only domestic and multilevel lobbying, but also 'political gardening'. In the chemical industry the degree of specialization in certain lobbying activity is significantly lower than in the I&C sector.

The complexity of adaptation: A theoretical model of associational change

In the previous sections we have summarized the major findings of several case studies. We found that political internationalization – particularly Europeanization – fits very well with our expectations. In the introductory chapter, we hypothesized that growth in international policy making at the European as well as at the global level leads to an increase in international or European lobbying activities of national business associations, as well as an increase in membership of international and European branch associations. We found these hypotheses to be confirmed.

Political internationalization

Increasing European/global governance → increasing European/
global lobbying activities

Our findings confirm prior analysis by Beyers (2002) and Eising (2004), who found a similar relationship between governance and lobbying activities. In their analysis they found various types of domestic and European lobbying strategies, ranging from complete absence in European policy making as compensation for lacking domestic access to a dominance of European lobbying efforts. Eising (2004), however, explains differences in the degree of involvement in European public policy making by associational inertia ('laggards') and differences in resource procurement. We found, instead, that differences can be explained by the degree to which the interest domains of business associations are affected by political internationalization. Quite revealing is also the fact that US associations are not poles apart in terms of lobbying activities.

For instance, one third of US I&C business associations have a *multilevel lobbyist* profile (thereby even exceeding their British equivalents).

The shifting of regulatory competencies to international organizations is not the only mechanism by which public authorities affect business associations. Wagemann's comparative analysis of the dairy industry (Chapter 8) reveals that the delegation of powers to business associations gives them some leeway regarding the immediate demands of their members. As a result, associational hierarchies develop in which some business associations hold political authority and thus are located at the top of the hierarchical pyramid (Schmitter & Streeck, 1999 [1981]).

State involvement

Guaranteed representation monopoly → associational hierarchy

Wagemann (Chapter 8) also points out that the loss of regulatory functions inevitably leads to a decomposition of hierarchical structures. He demonstrates that countries where associational systems have been intensely involved in self-regulation have undergone a fundamental transformation in associational structures as well as in behavior. Less centralized associational systems, however, find it easier to adapt or have no need to adapt since they have not specialized in certain activities. Thus, it is safe to say that flexibility increases the likelihood of survival and swift adaptation.

All the case studies in this book clearly indicate that members' market position is the most important factor shaping systems of business associations. In cases such as the dairy industry, in which the state is delegating regulatory functions to business associations and thereby guarantees resources to consolidate hierarchical structures, market coordination loses its dominant influence. In all other instances, systems of business associations reflect market structures.

Market structure

Diversification → increasing population dynamics (foundings, M&As)
→ higher competition

Economic stability → low population dynamics → higher
→ cooperation and hierarchy

Technological innovations as well as economic growth and decline affect market structure. Technological innovations lead to the development of new products and therefore to a diversification of markets. Innovations arise predominantly at the edge of existing product branches and give rise to a readjustment of the value chain. In such instances it becomes likely that new business associations are founded that represent these newly developed branches. The information and communications sector is an example of market diversification through innovation. In conjunction with high economic growth rates, market diversification leads to new product niches or branches in which new business associations have been founded. As a result, diversification leads to higher population dynamics, which in turn also affect ecological network structures. The information and communications sector is an illustration of how newly founded business associations distort established network structures and alter established niche partitioning (Gray & Lowery, 1996, 1997). Therefore it is not surprising that newcomers often compete with other associations for members and influence in order to acquire their share of the niche. Another example of population dynamics and competition can be found in the biotech branch. This part of the chemical industry experienced a significant transformation that was followed by a restructuring of affected business associations, either by splits or new foundations. As a result, competitive relations have been introduced into the highly cooperative ecological networks of chemical industry associations.

Economic stability, in contrast, has consolidating effects on systems of business associations due to low population dynamics. Associational populations that face few foundings, disbandings, mergers and splits are able to partition interest domains among the individual business associations. The chemical industry and the media sector are examples of consolidated associational systems in which all associations stick to their niche and thus barely any domain overlapping exists between business associations.

Surprisingly, we cannot confirm that a consolidated national interest group system leads to a similarly consolidated sectoral associational structure. This becomes obvious if one considers the contrary effects of enforced hierarchization in the German I&C sector, in which the national umbrella association BDI planned to establish a sectoral peak association, thereby alarming and confronting established business associations. These in turn have entered into competition with the designated peak association.

Most theories of business associability focus on external factors that affect the structure and behavior of associations. However, endogenous factors also account for changes in business associations. Organizational properties develop differently if associational populations are competitive or cooperative. The difference between the chemical industry and the I&C sector clearly indicates that cooperative chemical associations invest resources more similarly than do competitive I&C associations. In the chemicals sector, all business associations can roughly be divided according to their activity focus: either lobbying or service provision. In the I&C sector, business associations build much more diversified populations that contain multilevel lobbyists, service providers, political gardeners, and domestic lobbyists.

Isomorphism

Cooperation → greater homogeneity of associational forms

Sociological institutionalism explains homogenization of organizational fields by institutional mechanisms such as coercion, normative rules, and cognitive mimicry (Powell & DiMaggio; Scott). From an institutional perspective, cooperative populations offer much more possibilities for organizational imitation and learning and thereby generate greater similarity in associational activities. This observation is consistent with the arguments of ecological and complexity theory (Baum & Amburgey, 2002; Eisenhardt & Bhatia, 2002). Both perspectives emphasize that multiple constraints, which comprise exogenous and endogenous factors that business associations face, lead to differential and more specialized adaptation processes, while similar adaptation pressures exhibit a homogenizing effect. For example, if there is a uniform adaptation pressure toward more European lobbying, then most business associations will develop European lobbying activities (at least in the long run). However, if some associations face other adaptation pressures simultaneously or are confronted with competing associations, the likely strategy is to find a spezialized niche in which fewer constraints and competition exist (see also Gray & Lowery, 1997).

Conclusions

The main purpose of this book is to shed light on the networks and behavior of sectoral business associations and compare them across sectors and countries. We also explore associational adaptation strategies and relate them to processes of internationalization and Europeanization. In the introductory chapter we presented four major hypotheses on the driving forces of associational adaptation processes that varied with regard to the degree of internationalization.

The *modernization* hypothesis is the most universal postulate, stating that there is a universal process toward differentiation and higher complexity. Our case studies, however, do not identify a single pattern of associational change. This holds both within and between countries. Therefore the modernization hypotheses must give way to more fine-grained theoretical considerations.

The *internationalization* hypothesis is next to the modernization thesis in terms of universality. It asserts that economic sectors that are heavily involved in international trade or are affected by international governance react similarly to these exogenous changes. The country chapters in this volume confirm this expectation. Internationalization works sector-wide. Technological innovations, and their international diffusion, are the driving forces leading to changes in associational founding rates and in network structures of sectoral populations.

The *Europeanization* literature assumes that EU member countries are similarly affected by European governance. Our case studies point out that the main reaction of business associations to increasing European integration is the joining of European branch associations and the development of lobbying activities at the European level. They indicate that Europeanization is primarily restricted to the political dimension. The economic effects of European integration, such as the privatization and liberalization of state monopolies in the telecommunications sector, clearly led to a restructuring of markets. However, Schneider (2001) and Simmons & Elkins (2004) show that this transformation was based on diffusion, with the US as a starting point. European integration, however, has accelerated this spread of reform ideas and policy instruments between member states. Some US associations, nevertheless, have also developed lobbying activities at the EU level and have opened liaison offices in Brussels. This might indicate that European governance, although geographically limited, radiates at a global scale, thereby affecting the lobbying activities of US business associations.

Finally, the *varieties of capitalism* hypothesis states that national institutional settings are consistent and reasonably unique in terms of how national economies are coordinated. In the light of our empirical findings, the varieties of capitalism hypothesis must be modified, since the main variation is between sectors and not so much between countries. Market dynamics account for most changes in systems of business associations, thus leading to fairly similar network structures and similar patterns of resource utilization within each sector. However, in each sector corporatist countries exhibit higher degrees of centralization than Anglo-American countries, which basically confirms the varieties of capitalism hypothesis.

The review of our initial hypotheses makes clear that neither modernization nor internationalization and Europeanization are uniform social mechanisms that shape systems of business associations. In fact, underlying mechanisms must be related to either the structure of markets, properties of other political organizations such as state agencies, or endogenous mechanisms such as interaction patterns.

Our empirical chapters demonstrate that the market structure clearly outstrips the effects of political variables in most respects. Market structures and dynamics have a direct effect (although via firm members) on the composition of associational systems. Technological innovation (product innovations as opposed to process innovations) creates new business opportunities leading to a diversification of existing markets. This in turn opens up new interest domains into which established business associations may penetrate or in which new associations may be founded. In any case, a diversification of existing markets alters not only the composition but also the interaction patterns of associational systems. As the I&C sector demonstrates, newly founded business associations that are positioned in or at the border of new interest niches are likely to have competitive relations to surrounding associations.

The structure and behavior of other political actors have direct effects on the interest representation of business associations. Europeanization and global governance, meaning the delegation of power to supranational organizations, have changed the way in which interest representation is executed by domestic business associations. Associations have broadened their lobbying activities and have included membership in international branch associations and their own lobbying efforts in their asset allocation.

Market structure and dynamics → inter-associational dynamics
                                                      and structure
Political system ↑

Moreover, the behavior of other political organizations exerts an intervening effect on economic and technological factors. Systems of business associations are primarily oriented to the demands of member firms. The structure and behavior of other political actors, however, intervenes in the formation of associational systems. This becomes clear when we look at the dairy industry, in which a number of regulatory functions had been delegated to business associations. As long as these powers were granted, business associations were able to develop a hierarchical organization of interest intermediation. The withdrawal of these powers led to a complete collapse of associational systems. The subsequent reconstruction yielded much more pluralistic structures in which membership demands are much more important (see Chapter 8). Another example of intervening effects is the imposed hierarchization of the German system in the I&C sector by the national peak association BDI. As a result, other business associations opposed this 'imperial strategy', creating many competitive relations among I&C associations.

Market structure/political system → organizational properties
Ecological networks ↑

Finally, network structures have an intervening effect on organizational properties. Cooperative relations increase the similarity of activities within associational systems, whereas competitive relations lead to more diversity.

In this book we find comparative evidence that allows us to rethink and reformulate conventional associational theory and their major lines of argument. In line with pluralist and neocorporatist thinking, we can allocate the major drivers of associational change in their immediate environment, which consists of member firms as well as public authorities (see Schmitter & Streeck 1999, [1981]). However, our empirical findings suggest that adaptation processes are much more complex than existing theories have acknowledged, and that complexity is enhanced by ecological networks and informal hierarchies that affect the activities and strategies of business associations. As our country chapters make clear, market dynamics – the logic of membership – have a major effect on the network structures of associational systems. In contrast, the logic of influence accounts for the use of access channels to public authorities and the development of associational lobbying strategies, while having only intervening effects on other organizational properties.

To summarize, the adaptation of systems of business associations is driven by economic, technological, and political forces, and dynamics within inter-associational networks. Environmental complexity – that is, multiple and sometimes contradicting external constraints – push and pull the activities and strategies of business associations in different directions, leading to rather heterogeneous populations. Thus network complexity adds further differentiation to this adaptation process. The complexity perspective is very useful in explaining diverging processes of associational change across countries and sectors. Complexity is the key to inserting new insights into the apparently saturated field of interest group research.

References

Abromeit H. 1993. *Interessenvermittlung zwischen Konkurrenz und Konkordanz. Studienbuch zur Vergleichenden Lehre politischer Systeme.* Opladen: Leske + Budrich.

Aftalion F. 2001. *A History of the International Chemical Industry. From the 'Early Days' to 2000.* Philadelphia: Chemical Heritage Press.

Aldrich H. 1999. *Organizations Evolving.* London/Newbury Park/New Delhi: Sage.

Aldrich H, Staber U. 1988. Organizing Business Interests. Patterns of Trade Association Foundings, Transformations, and Deaths. In *Ecological Models of Organizations,* ed. GR Carroll. Cambridge, MA: Ballinger.

Aldrich H, Zimmer C, Staber U, Beggs J. 1994. Minimalism, Mutualism, and Maturity: The Evolution of the American Trade Association Population in the 20th Century. In *Evolutionary Dynamics of Organizations,* ed. JAC Baum, JV Singh, pp. 223–39. New York/Oxford: Oxford University Press.

Alexander JC, Colomy P, ed. 1990. *Differentiation Theory and Social Change. Comparative and Historical Perspectives.* New York: Columbia University Press.

Allen CS. 1989. Political Consequences of Change: The Chemical Industry. In *Industry and Politics in West Germany. Toward the Third Republic,* ed. PJ Katzenstein, pp. 157–84. Ithaca and London: Cornell University Press.

Almond GA. 1956. Comparative Political Systems. *Journal of Politics* XVIII: 391–409.

Almond GA. 1958. Research Note: A Comparative Study of Interest Groups and the Political Process. *The American Political Science Review* 52: 270–82.

Almond GA. 1983. Corporatism, Pluralism, and Professional Memory. *World Politics* 35: 245–60.

Almond GA, Powell GB. 1966. *Comparative Politics. A Developmental Approach.* Boston: Little, Brown and Company.

ACC. 2001. *Responsible Care: A History of Accomplishment, A Future of Promise,* Arlington, VA: ACC.

ACC. 2002. *Guide to the Business of Chemistry.* Arlington, VA: ACC.

Anderson P. 1999. Complexity Theory and Organization Science. *Organization Science* 10: 216–32.

Anderson P, Tushman ML. 1990. Technological Discontinuities and Dominant Designs: A Cyclical Model of Technological Change. *Administrative Science Quarterly* 35: 604–33.

Armingeon K. 2001. Schweiz. Das Zusammenspiel von langer demokratischer Tradition, direkter Demokratie, Föderalismus und Korporatismus. In *Verbände und Verbandssysteme in Westeuropa,* ed. W Reutter, P Rütters, pp. 405–26. Opladen: Leske & Budrich.

Arora A, Rosenberg N. 1998. Chemicals: A U.S. Success Story. In *Chemicals and Long-Term Economic Growth. Insights from the Chemical Industry,* ed. A Arora, R Landau, N Rosenberg, pp. 71–102. New York: John Wiley & Sons.

Arthur D. Little GmbH. 2002. *Economic Effects of the EU Substances Policy. Summary of the BDI Research Project,* Wiesbaden: Arthur D. Little.

Austen-Smith D. 1997. Interest Groups: Money, Information and Influence. In *Perspectives on Public Choice: A Handbook*, ed. D Mueller, pp. 296–321. Cambridge: Cambridge University Press.
Averyt WF. 1977. *Agropolitics in the European Community: Interest Groups and the Common Agricultural Policy*. New York/London: Praeger.
Axelrod R. 1984. *The Evolution of Co-operation*. New York: Basic Books.
Baggott R. 1995. From Confrontation to Consultation? Pressure Group Relations from Thatcher to Major. *Parliamentary Affairs* 48: 484–502.
Banks J, Marsden T. 1997. Regulating the UK Dairy Industry: the Changing Nature of Competitive Space. *Sociologia Ruralis* 37: 382–404.
Bartolini S. 2005. *Restructuring Europe. Center Formation, System Building and Political Structuring between the Nation-State and the European Union*. Oxford: Oxford University Press.
Bauer JM. 2004. Harnessing the Swarm: Prospects and Limits of Communications Policy in an Era of Ubiquitous Networks and Disruptive Technologies. Presented at European Communications Policy Research Conference, Barcelona, Spain, March 28–30.
Baum JAC. 1996. Organizational Ecology. In *Handbook of Organization Studies*, ed. JAC Baum, SR Clegg, pp. 77–114. London/Newbury Park/New Delhi: Sage.
Baum JAC, Amburgey TL. 2002. Organizational Ecology. In *Blackwell Companion to Organizations*, ed. JAC Baum, pp. 304–26. Malden, MA: Blackwell.
Baumgartner FR, Leech BL. 1998. *Basic Interests: The Importance of Groups in Politics and Political Science*. Princeton, NJ: Princeton University Press.
Baumol WJ. 2002. *The Free-Market Innovation Machine: Analyzing the Growth Miracle of Capitalism*. Princeton, NJ: Princeton University Press.
Beck U, Bonss W, Lau C. 2003. The Theory of Reflexive Modernization: Problematic, Hypotheses and Research Programme. *Theory Culture Society* 20: 1–33.
Beer SH. 1956. Pressure Groups and Parties in Britain. *American Political Science Review* L: 1–23.
Bennett RJ. 1998. Explaining the Membership of Voluntary Local Business Associations: The Example of British Chambers of Commerce. *Regional Studies* 32: 503–14.
Bennett RJ. 2000. The Logic of Membership of Sectoral Business Associations. *Review of Social Economy* 63: 17–42.
Bentley AF. 1967 [1908]. *The Process of Government*. Cambridge, MA: Belknap Press of Harvard University Press.
Berry JM. 1984. *The Interest Group Society*. Boston: Little, Brown.
Beyers J. 2002. Gaining and Seeking Access: The European Adaptation of Domestic Interest Associations. *European Journal of Political Research* 41: 585–612.
Beyers J, Kerremans B. 2004. Bureaucrats, Politicians, and Societal Interests: How Is European Policy Making Politicized? *Comparative Political Studies* 37: 1119–50.
Beyers J, Kerremans B. 2007. Critical Resource Dependencies and the Europeanization of Domestic Interest Groups. *Journal of European Public Policy* 14: 460–81.
Blau P. 1964. *Exchange and Power in Social Life*. New York: John Wiley & Sons.
Boléat M. 2000. *Models of Trade Association Co-operation*. London: Trade Association Forum.
Boléat M. 2002. The Changing Environment for Trade Associations and Strategies for Adaptation. In *The Effectiveness of EU Business Associations*, ed. J Greenwood. Basingstoke and London: Palgrave.

Börzel TA. 1998. Organizing Babylon: On the Different Conceptions of Policy Networks. *Public Administration* 76: 253–73.
Börzel T. 2005. Mind the Gap! European Integration between Level and Scope. *Journal of European Public Policy* 12: 217–36.
Börzel TA, Risse T. 2000. When Europe Hits Home: Europeanization and Domestic Change. *European Integration Online Papers* 4: online at http://eiop.or.at/eiop/texte/200-015.htm.
Bouwen P. 2004. Exchanging Access Goods for Access: A Comparative Study of Business Lobbying in the European Union Institutions. *European Journal of Political Research* 43: 337–69.
Brandes U, Kenis P, Raab J, Schneider V, Wagner D. 1999. Explorations into the Visualization of Policy Networks. *Journal of Theoretical Politics* 11: 75–106.
Brickman R, Jasanoff S, Ilgen T. 1985. *Controlling Chemicals: The Politics of Regulation in Europe and the United States*. Ithaca/London: Cornell University Press.
Brittain JW, Wholey DR. 1988. Competition and Coexistence in Organizational Communities: Population Dynamics in Electronic Components Manufacturing. In *Ecological Models of Organizations*, ed. GR Carroll, pp. 195–222. Cambridge, MA: Ballinger.
Brock GW. 1981. *The Telecommunications Industry: The Dynamics of Market Structure*. Cambridge, MA: Harvard University Press.
Brock GW. 1994. *Telecommunications Policy for the Information Age: From Monopoly to Competition*. Cambridge, MA: Harvard Business School Press.
Brock GW. 2003. *The Second Information Revolution*. Cambridge, MA: Harvard University Press.
Brophy J. 2000. *The Impact of Chemicals Industry Mergers, Acquisitions and Restructuring on the UK Chemistry Infrastructure*. Available online at: www.rsc.org/pdf/general/mergers.pdf.
Broscheid A. 2002. *When Groups Break Up: A Formal Model of Organizational Change in German Pharmaceutical Interest Representation*. Cologne, MPIfG Working Paper.
Brose H-G, Voelzkow H. 1999. Globalisierung und institutioneller Wandel der Wirtschaft. In *Institutioneller Kontext wirtschaftlichen Handelns und Globalisierung*, ed. H-G Brose, H Voelzkow, pp. 9–23. Marburg: Metropolis.
Bunge M. 1996. *Finding Philosophy in Social Science*. New Haven, CN: Yale University Press.
Bunge M. 2003. *Emergence and Convergence: Qualitative Novelty and the Unity of Knowledge*. Toronto: University of Toronto Press.
Campbell DT. 1969. Variation and Selective Retention in Socio-Cultural Evolution. *General Systems* 14: 69–85.
Cawson A. 1985a. Introduction: Varieties of Corporatism: the Importance of the Meso-Level of Interest Intermediation. In *Organized Interests and the State. Studies in Meso-Corporatism*, ed. A Cawson, pp. 1–21. London/Newbury Park/New Delhi: Sage.
Cawson A, ed. 1985b. *Organised Interests and the State: Studies in Meso-Corporatism*. London/Newbury Park/New Delhi: Sage.
Cawson A. 1992. Interests, Groups and Public Policy-Making: The Case of the European Consumer Electronics Industry. In *Organized Interests in the European Community*, ed. J Greenwood, JR Grote, K Ronit, pp. 99–118. London: Sage.
CEFIC. 2002a. *CEFIC 21. A New CEFIC to Meet Tomorrow's Challenges*. Brussels: CEFIC.

CEFIC. 2002b. *Our Annual Review 2001*. Brussels: CEFIC.
CEFIC. 2006. *Global Insight*. Brussels: CEFIC.
CIA. 2000. *Annual Report and Accounts 2000*. London: CIA.
Clarkson S. 1998. Fearful Asymmetries: The Challenge of Analyzing Continental Systems in a Globalizing World. *Canadian-American Public Policy* 35: 1–66.
Coen D. 1997. The Evolution of the Large Firm as a Political Actor in the European Union. *Journal of European Public Policy* 4: 91–108.
Coen D. 1998. The European Business Interest and the Nation State. Large-firm Lobbying in the European Union and the Member States. *Journal of Public Policy* 18: 75–100.
Coen D, Dannreuther C. 2003. Differentiated Europeanization: Large and Small Firms in the EU Policy Process. In *The Politics of Europeanization*, ed. K Featherstone, CM Radaelli, pp. 255–78. Oxford: Oxford University Press.
Coleman JS. 1972. Systems of Social Exchange. *Journal of Mathematical Sociology* 2: 145–63.
Coleman JS. 1974. *Power and the Structure of Society*. New York: Norton.
Coleman JS. 1994 [1990]. *Foundations of Social Theory*. Cambridge, MA: Belknap Press of Harvard University Press.
Coleman WD. 1997. Associational Governance in a Globalizing Era: Weathering the Storm. In *Contemporary Capitalism. The Embeddedness of Institutions*, ed. JR Hollingsworth, R Boyer, pp. 127–53. Cambridge: Cambridge University Press.
Conlan T. 1988. *New Federalism: Intergovernmental Reform from Nixon to Reagan*. Washington, DC: Brookings Institution.
Cowles MG. 1998. The changing architecture of big business. In *Collective Action in the European Union*, ed. J Greenwood, M Aspinwall, pp. 108–25. London/ New York: Routledge.
Crouch C. 2003. Comparing Economic Interest Organizations. In *Governing Europe*, ed. J Hayward, A Menon, pp. 192–207. Oxford: Oxford University Press.
Crouch C, Streeck W. 1997. Introduction: The Future of Capitalist Diversity. In *Political Economy of Modern Capitalism*, ed. C Crouch, W Streeck, pp. 1–18. London/Newbury Park/New Delhi: Sage.
Culpin, D. 2000. *Development of the UK Chemical Industry. A Historical Review of the UK Chemical Industry, Including Reference to External Policy Issues and the Role of the Chemical Industries Association and its Forerunners*. London: CIA.
Cutler AC, Haufler V, Porter T, ed. 1999. *Private Authority and International Affairs*. New York: State University of New York Press.
Czada R. 1994. Konjunkturen des Korporatismus: Zur Geschichte eines Paradigmenwechsels in der Verbändeforschung. In *Staat und Verbände*, ed. W Streeck, pp. 37–64. Opladen: Westdeutscher Verlag.
DiMaggio PJ, Powell WW. 1991. The Iron Cage Revisited: Institutional Isomorphism and Collective Rationality in Organizational Fields. In *The New Institutionalism in Organizational Analysis*, ed. WW Powell, PJ DiMaggio, pp. 63–82. Chicago/London: University of Chicago Press.
Dolata U, Werle R. 2007. 'Bringing technology back in': Technik als Einflussfaktor sozioökonomischen und institutionellen Wandels. In *Gesellschaft und die Macht der Technik*, ed. U Dolata, R Werle, pp. 15–43. Frankfurt am Main: Campus.
Dosi G. 1982. Technological Paradigms and Technological Trajectories: A Suggested Interpretation of the Determinants and Directions of Technical Change. *Research Policy* 11: 147–62.

Dosi G. 1988. Sources, Procedures, and Microeconomic Effects of Innovation. *Journal of Economic Literature* 26: 1120–71.
Downs A. 1957. *An Economic Theory of Democracy*. New York: Harper.
Ebers M, Gotsch W. 1999. Institutionenökonomische Theorien der Organisation. In *Organisationstheorien*, ed. A Kieser, pp. 199–252. Stuttgart/Berlin/Köln: Kohlhammer.
Egeberg M. 1996. Organization and Nationality in the European Commission Services. *Public Administration* 74: 721–35.
Ehrmann HW. 1957. *Organized Business in France*. Princeton, NJ: Princeton University Press.
Eising R. 2004. Multilevel Governance and Business Interests in the European Union. *Governance* 17: 242–67.
Eising R. 2007. Institutional Context, Organizational Resources and Strategic Choices. *European Union Politics* 8: 329–62.
EITO. div. *European Information Technology Observatory*. Franfurt: EITO.
European Commission. 1997. Proposal for a Council Directive on End-of-Life Vehicles (COM/97/0358 final). *Official Journal of the European Communities* 337: 3–8.
European Commission. 2001a. www.europa.eu.int/comm/environment/chemicals/conference/014-final _list_of_participants.pdf. Accessed 10 January 2004.
European Commission. 2001b. *White Paper on the Strategy for a Future Chemicals Policy (COM (2001) 88 final*. Brussels: European Commission.
European Parliament. 2000. Directive 2000/53/EC of the European Parliament and of the Council of 18 September 2000 on End-of-Life Vehicles. *Official Journal of the European Communities* L 269: 34–42.
Evans P, ed. 1997. *State–Society Synergy: Government and Social Capital in Development*. Berkeley, CA: University of California Press.
Evenson RE. 2002. Agricultural Biotechnology. In *Technological Innovation and Economic Performance*, ed. B Steil, DG Victor, RR Nelson, pp. 367–84. Princeton, NJ: Princeton University Press.
EWG. 2001. Chemical Industry Archives. The Inside Story: Responsible Care 3. www.chemicalindustryarchives.org/dirtysecrets/responsiblecare/3.asp. Accessed 10 March 2003.
Farago P. 1987. *Verbände als Träger öffentlicher Politik*. Grüsch: Rüegger.
Featherstone K, Radaelli CM, ed. 2003. *The Politics of Europeanization*. Oxford: Oxford University Press.
Fleischer M. 2001. Zwischen Innovation und Regulation. *Chemie Report* 6: 24–8.
Fouilleux E. 2003. The Common Agricultural Policy. In *European Union Politics*, ed. M Cini, pp. 246–63. Oxford: Oxford University Press.
Freeman C, Perez C. 1988. Structural Crises of Adjustment, Business Cycles and Investment Behaviour. In *Technical Change and Economic Theory*, ed. G Dosi, pp. 38–66. London/New York: Pinter.
Freeman LC. 1979. Centrality in Social Networks: Conceptual Clarifications. *Social Networks*: 215–39.
Furlong SR. 1997. Interest Group Influence on Rule Making. *Administration and Society* 29: 325–47.
Furlong SR, Kerwin CM. 2005. Interest Group Participation in Rule Making: A Decade of Change. *Journal of Public Administration Research and Theory* 15: 353–70.

Gais TL, Peterson MA, Walker JL. 1984. Interest Groups, Iron Triangles and Representative Institutions in American National Government. *British Journal of Political Science* 14: 161–85.

Galunic DC, Weeks JR. 2002. Intraorganizational Ecology. In *Blackwell Companion to Organizations*, ed. JAC Baum, pp. 75–97. Malden, MA: Blackwell.

Grant A. 1997a. *The American Political Process*. Aldershot: Ashgate.

Grant W. 1985. Private Organizations as Agents of Public Policy: the Case of Milk Marketing in Britain. In *Private Interest Governments*, ed. W Streeck, PC Schmitter, pp. 182–96. London/Newbury Park/New Delhi: Sage.

Grant W. 1989. The Regional Organization of Business Interests and Public Policy in the United Kingdom. In *Regionalism, Business Interests and Public Policy*, ed. WD Coleman, HJ Jacek, pp. 95–112. London/Newbury Park/New Delhi: Sage.

Grant W. 1991a. Associational Systems in the Chemical Industry. In *International Markets and Global Firms. A Comparative Study of Organized Business in the Chemical Industry*, ed. A Martinelli, pp. 47–60. London/Newbury Park/New Delhi: Sage.

Grant W. 1991b. *The Dairy Industry*. Aldershot: Dartmouth.

Grant W. 1992. Models of Interest Intermediation and Policy Formation Applied to an Internationally Comparative Study of the Dairy Industry. *European Journal of Political Research* 21: 53–68.

Grant W. 1997b. *The Common Agricultural Policy*. Houndmills: Palgrave Macmillan.

Grant W. 2000. *Pressure Groups and British Politics*. Houndmills: Macmillan Press.

Grant W, Paterson WE, Whitston C. 1988. *Government and the Chemical Industry. A Comparative Study of Britain and West Germany*. Oxford: Clarendon.

Gray V, Lowery D. 1996. A Niche Theory of Interest Representation. *The Journal of Politics* 58: 91–111.

Gray V, Lowery D. 1997. Life in a Niche: Mortality Anxiety Among Organized Interests in the American States. *Political Research Quarterly* 50: 25–47.

Gray V, Lowery D. 2000. *The Population Ecology of Interest Representation: Lobbying Communities in the American States*. Ann Arbor, MI: University of Michigan Press.

Greenwood J. 1997. *Representing Interests in the European Union*. Houndmills: Palgrave Macmillan.

Greenwood J. 2002. *Inside the EU Business Associations*. Basingstoke: Palgrave Macmillan.

Greenwood J. 2003. *Interest Representation in the European Union*. Basingstoke: Palgrave Macmillan.

Greenwood J, Jacek HJ, ed. 2000. *Organized Business and the New Global Order*. Basingstoke: Palgrave Macmillan.

Greenwood J, Ronit K. 1994. Interest Groups in the European Community: Newly Emerging Dynamics and Forms. *West European Politics* 17: 31–52.

Greenwood J, Grote JR, Ronit K. 1992a. Introduction: Organized Interests and the Transnational Dimension. In *Organized Interests and the European Community*, ed. J Greenwood, JR Grote, K Ronit, pp. 1–41. London/Newbury Park/New Delhi: Sage.

Greenwood J, Grote JR, Ronit K, ed. 1992b. *Organized Interests and the European Community*. London/Newbury Park/New Delhi: Sage.

Grier KB, Munger MC, Roberts BE. 1994. The Determinants of Industry Political Activity, 1978–1986. *The American Political Science Review* 88: 911–26.

Grote JR. 2003. Delimiting Europeanization. Paper presented at the ECPR conference in Marburg.
Grote JR, Lang A. 2003. Europeanization and Organizational Change in National Trade Associations: An Organizational Ecology Perspective. In *The Politics of Europeanization*, ed. K Featherstone, CM Radaelli, pp. 225–54. Oxford/New York: Oxford University Press.
Grote JR, Lang A. 2004. The Representation of Small and Medium-Sized Enterprises: Yet Another Logic of Collective Action? Paper presented at the Biennial Meeting of the Council for European Studies, Chicago: March 11–13.
Grote JR, Schneider V. 2006. Organizations and Networks in a Internationalizing Economy: British and German Chemical Interest Associations. In *Governing Interests: Business Associations Facing Internationalization*, ed. W Streeck, JR Grote, V Schneider, J Visser, pp. 117–48. London: Routledge.
Grote JR, Lang A, Traxler F 2007. Germany. In *Handbook of Business Interest Associations, Firm Size and Governance*, ed. F Traxler, G Huemer, pp. 141–76. London/New York: Routledge.
Habermas J. 2001. *The Postnational Constellation: Political Essays*. Cambridge, MA: MIT Press.
Hall PA, Soskice D. 2001a. Introduction. In *Varieties of Capitalism: The Institutional Foundations of Comparative Advantage*, ed. PA Hall, D Soskice, pp. 1–68. Oxford: Oxford University Press.
Hall PA, Soskice DW, ed. 2001b. *Varieties of Capitalism: The Institutional Foundations of Comparative Advantage*. Oxford: Oxford University Press.
Hannan M, Freeman J. 1977. The Population Ecology of Organizations. *American Journal of Sociology* 82: 929–64.
Henderson RM, Clark KB. 1990. Architectural Innovation: The Reconfiguration of Existing Product Technologies and the Failure of Established Firms. *Administrative Science Quarterly* 35: 9–30.
Hesse JJ, Benz A. 1987. 'New Federalism' unter Präsident Reagan. Teilstudie im Rahmen des Projektes 'Wohlfahrtsstaatliche Entwicklung und föderalstaatliche Reaktion'. Speyer: Forschungsinstitut für öffentliche Verwaltung bei der Hochschule für Verwaltungswissenschaften.
Hix S. 2005. *The Political System of the European Union*. Houndmills: Macmillan.
Holland JH. 1992. Complex Adaptive Systems. *Daedalus* 121: 17–30.
Hooghe L. 1995. *Subnational Mobilisation in the EU*. Badia Fiesolana, Firenze: European University Institute Working Paper RSC No. 95/6.
Hörl B, Warntjen A, Wonka A. 2005. Built on Quicksand? A Decade of Procedural Spatial Models on EU Legislative Decision-Making. *Journal of European Public Policy* 12: 592–606.
Hull DL. 1994. Taking Vehicles Seriously. *Behavioral and Brain Sciences* 17: 627–8.
Jacek HJ. 1987. Business Interest Associations as Private Interest Governments. In *Business Interests, Organizational Development and Private Interest Government*, ed. W Grant, pp. 34–62. Berlin/New York: de Gruyter.
Jacek HJ. 1991. The Functions of Associations as Agents of Public Policy. In *International Markets and Global Firms. A Comparative Study of Organized Business in the Chemical Industry*, ed. A Martinelli, pp. 145–88. London/Newbury Park/New Delhi: Sage.
Karlhofer F. 1996. The Present and Future State of Social Partnership. In *Austro-Corporatism*, ed. G Bischof, A Pelinka, pp. 119–46. New Brunswick/London: Transaction Publishers.

Kenis P, Schneider V. 1991. Policy Networks and Policy Analysis: Scrutinizing a New Analytical Toolbox. In *Policy Networks: Empirical Evidence and Theoretical Considerations*, ed. BM Marin, R Mayntz, pp. 25–59. Boulder, CO: Westview.

Kennelly B, Murrell P. 1991. Industry Characteristics and Interest Group Formation: An Empirical Study. *Public Choice* 70: 21–40.

King AA, Lenox MJ. 2000. Industry Self-Regulation without Sanctions: The Chemical Industry's Responsible Care Program. *Academy of Management Journal* 43: 698–716.

Kirke A, Anderson D. 1995. Evolution of Market Structure and the Demand for Dairy Products in the UK. In *The European Dairy Industry: Consumption Changes, Vertical Relations and Firm Strategies*, ed. D Rama, R Pieri, pp. 111–48. Milan: FrancoAngeli.

Kittel B, Tálos E. 1999. Interessenvermittlung und politischer Entscheidungsprozeß: Sozialpartnerschaft in den 1990er Jahren. In *Zukunft der Sozialpartnerschaft*, ed. F Karlhofer, E Tálos, pp. 95–136. Wien: Signum.

Knill C, Lehmkuhl D. 2002. Private Actors and the State: Internationalization and Changing Patterns of Governance. *Governance* 15: 41–63.

Knoke D. 1986. Associations and Interest Groups. *Annual Reviews of Sociology*: 1–21.

Knoke D. 1990. *Political Networks. The Structural Perspective*. Cambridge: Cambridge University Press.

Kohler-Koch B. 1993. Germany: Fragmented but Strong Lobbying. In *National Public and Private EC Lobbying*, ed. MCPMv Schendelen, pp. 23–48. Aldershot: Dartmouth.

Kohler-Koch B. 1999. The Evolution and Transformation of European Governance. In *The Transformation of Governance in the European Union*, ed. B Kohler-Koch, R Eising, pp. 14–35. London: Routledge.

Kohler-Koch B, Quittkat C. 1999. *Intermediation of Interests in the European Union*. Mannheim: Mannheimer Zentrum für Europäische Sozialforschung, Arbeitspapiere, Nr. 9.

Kriesi H, Baglioni S. 2003. Putting Local Associations into Their Contexts. Preliminary Results from a Swiss Study of Local Associations. *Swiss Political Science Review* 9: 1–34.

Kriesi H, Tresch A, Jochum M. 2007. Going Public in the European Union: Action Repertoires of Western European Collective Political Actors. *Comparative Political Studies* 40: 48–73.

Kux S, Sverdrup U. 2000. Fuzzy Borders and Adaptive Outsiders: Norway, Switzerland and the EU. *European Integration* 22: 237–70.

Landau R. 1998. The Process of Innovation in the Chemical Industry. In *Chemicals and Long-Term Economic Growth. Insights from the Chemical Industry*, ed. A Arora, R Landau, N Rosenberg, pp. 139–80. New York: John Wiley & Sons.

Landau R, Arora A. 1999. The Dynamics of Long-Term Growth: Gaining and Losing Advantage in the Chemical Industry. In *U.S. Industry in 2000. Studies in Competitive Performance*, ed. DC Mowery, pp. 17–43. Washington, DC: National Academy Press.

Lang A. 2006. *Die Evolution sektoraler Wirtschaftsverbandssysteme*. Wiesbaden: VS Verlag.

Lang A, Schneider V. 2007. Wirtschaftsverbände. Verbandspolitik im Spannungsfeld divergierender Interessen und hierarchischer Integration. In

Interessenverbände in Deutschland, ed. U Willems, Tv Winter, pp. 221–43. Wiesbaden: VS Verlag.

Langlois RN. 2002. Computers and Semiconductors. In *Technological Innovation and Economic Performance*, ed. B Steil, DG Victor, RR Nelson, pp. 265–84. Princeton, NJ: Princeton University Press.

Larsson, T. 2003. *Precooking in the European Union: The World of Expert Groups. A Report to ESO, The Expert Group on Public Finance*. Stockholm: Fritzes Offentliga Publikationer.

Latzer M. 1997. *Mediamatik: Die Konvergenz von Telekommunikation Computer und Rundfunk*. Opladen: Westdeutscher Verlag.

Laumann EO, Marsden PV, Prensky D. 1983. The Boundary Specification Problem in Network Analysis. In *Applied Network Analysis*, ed. RS Burt, MJ Minor, pp. 18–34. Beverly Hills, CA: Sage.

Layard R, Nickell S, Jackman R. 1991. *Unemployment: Macroeconomic Performance and the Labour Market*. Oxford: Oxford University Press.

Leech BL. 2006. Funding Faction or Buying Silence? Grants, Contracts, and Interest Group Lobbying Behavior. *Policy Studies Journal* 34: 17–35.

Lehmbruch G. 1984. Concertation and the Structure of Corporatist Networks. In *Order and Conflict in Contemporary Capitalism*, ed. J Goldthorpe, pp. 60–80. Oxford: Oxford University Press.

Lehmbruch G, Schmitter PC, ed. 1982. *Patterns of Corporatist Policy-Making*. London: Sage.

Lehmkuhl D. 2000. Under Stress: Europeanisation and Trade Associations in the Members States. *European Integration Online Papers (EIoP)* 4.

Levi-Faur D. 2004. On the 'Net Impact' of Europeanization. The EU's Telecoms and Electricity Regimes Between the Global and the National. *Comparative Political Studies* 37: 3–29.

Lodge GC. 1990. *Comparative Business–Government Relations*. Englewood Cliffs, NJ: Prentice Hall.

Lowery D, Gray V. 2004. A Neopluralist Perspective on Research on Organized Interests. *Political Research Quarterly* 57: 163–75.

Mach A, ed. 1999. *Globalisation, néo-libéralisme et politiques publiques dans la Suisse des années 1990*. Zürich: Seismo.

Mahoney J. 2000. Path Dependence in Historical Sociology. *Theory and Society* 29: 507–48.

Majone G. 1997. From the Positive to the Regulatory State: Causes and Consequences of Changes in the Mode of Governance. *Journal of Public Policy* 17: 139–67.

Marin B, Mayntz R. 1991. *Policy Networks: Empirical Evidence and Theoretical Considerations*. Frankfurt: Campus Verlag.

Marks G, Hooghe L, Blank K. 1996. European Integration from the 1980s: State-Centric vs. Multi-Level Governance. *Journal of Common Market Studies* 34: 341–78.

Marx K. 1966. The Poverty of Philosophy. Peking: Foreign Languages Press. www.marx2mao.com/M&E/PP47.html#c2s5).

Mathews JT. 1997. Power Shift. *Foreign Affairs* 76: 50–66.

May T, McHugh J, Taylor T. 1998. Business Representation in the UK Since 1979: The Case of Trade Associations. *Political Studies* 46: 260–75.

Mayr E. 2001. *What Evolution Is*. New York: Basic Books.
McFarland AS. 2004. *Neopluralism: The Evolution of Political Process Theory*. Lawrence, KS: University Press of Kansas.
McLaughlin A, Jordan G. 1993. The Rationality of Lobbying in Europe: Why are Euro-groups so Numerous and so Weak? Some Evidence from the Car Industry. In *Lobbying in the European Community*, ed. S Mazey, J Richardson, pp. 122–57. Oxford: Oxford University Press.
McLaughlin A, Jordan G, Maloney WA. 1993. Corporate Lobbying in the European Community. *Journal of Common Market Studies* 31: 191–212.
Moe TM. 1980. *The Organization of Interests*. Chicago, IL: University of Chicago Press.
Molina O, Rhodes M. 2002. Corporatism: The Past, Present, and Future of a Concept. *Annual Review of Political Science* 5: 305–31.
Mowery DC. 1999. America's Industrial Resurgence (?): An Overview. In *U.S. Industry in 2000. Studies in Competitive Performance*, ed. DC Mowery, pp. 1–16. Washington, DC: National Academy Press.
Müller U, Werle R. 2000. Der Kampf um den Markt: Technische Konvergenz, institutionelle Heterogenität und die Entwicklung von Märkten in der technischen Kommunikation. In *Die politische Konstitution von Märkten*, ed. R Czada, S Lütz, pp. 264–85. Wiesbaden: VS-Verlag.
Munz CM. 2001. Europäisierung und verbandliche Orientierungen: Eine Inhaltsanalyse der Wahrnehmung von Umweltveränderungen durch den Verband der Chemischen Industrie. MA thesis. University of Konstanz.
National Dairy Council. 1996. *Dairy Facts and Figures*. London: NDC.
Nelson RR. 1994. The Coevolution of Technologies and Institutions. In *Evolutionary Concepts in Contemporary Economics*, ed. RW England, pp. 139–56. Ann Arbor, MI: University of Michigan Press.
Nelson RR, Rosenberg N. 1993. Technical Innovation and National Systems. In *National Innovation Systems. A Comparative Analysis*, ed. RR Nelson, pp. 3–21. New York/ Oxford: Oxford University Press.
Noam EM. 2001. *Interconnecting the Network of Networks*. Cambridge, MA: MIT Press.
NTPA. div. *National Trade and Professional Associations of the United States and Canada and Labor Unions*. Washington, DC: Columbia Books.
OECD. div.-a. *National Accounts of OECD Countries*. Paris: OECD.
OECD. div.-b. *The OECD STAN Database for Industrial Analysis. OECD Statistical Compendium*. Paris: OECD.
Offe C, Wiesenthal H. 1980. Two Logics of Collective Action: Theoretical Notes on Social Class and Organizational Form. *Political Power and Social Theory* 1: 67–115.
Olson M. 1970 [1965]. *The Logic of Collective Action. Public Goods and the Theory of Groups*. Cambridge, MA: Harvard University Press.
O'Riain S. 2004. *The Politics of High-Tech Growth*. Cambridge: Cambridge University Press.
Pappi FU, Henning CHCA. 1999. The Organization of Influence on the EC's Common Agricultural Policy: A Network Approach. *European Journal of Political Research* 36: 257–81.
Perrow C. 2002. *Organizing America: Wealth, Power, and the Origins of Corporate Capitalism*. Princeton, NJ: Princeton University Press.

Pestoff V. 1987. The Effect of State Institutions on Associative Action in the Food Processing Industry. In *Business Interests, Organizational Development and Private Interest Government*, ed. W Grant, pp. 93–116. Berlin/New York: de Gruyter.

Pierson P. 2003. Big, Slow-Moving, and ... Invisible: Macrosocial Processes in the Study of Comparative Politics. In *Comparative Historical Analysis in the Social Sciences*, ed. J Mahoney, D Rueschemeyer, pp. 177–207. Cambridge: Cambridge University Press.

PIRG. 1999. Trust Us, Don't Track Us: Executive Summary. Boston, MA: PIRG.

Pisano GP. 2002. Pharmaceutical Biotechnology. In *Technological Innovation and Economic Performance*, ed. B Steil, DG Victor, RR Nelson, pp. 347–66. Princeton, NJ: Princeton University Press.

Platzer H. 1984. *Industrieverbände im Prozess der Internationalisierung von Wirtschaft und Politik. Die Verbände der chemischen und pharmazeutischen Industrie. Sektorstudie im Rahmen eines DFG-Forschungsprojektes*. Tübingen/Darmstadt:

Plöhn J. 2001. Großbritannien. Interessengruppen im Zeichen von Traditionen, sozialem Wandel und politischen Reformen. In *Verbände und Verbandssysteme in Westeuropa*, ed. W Reutter, P Rütters, pp. 169–96. Opladen: Leske + Budrich.

Pollitt C, Talbot C. 2004. *Unbundled Government: A Critical Analysis of the Global Trend to Agencies, Quangos and Contractualisation*. London: Routledge.

Popp H. 2000. *Das Jahrhundert der Agrarrevolutionen*. Bern: Schweizer Agrarmedien.

Przeworski A, Teune H. 1970. *The Logic of Comparative Social Inquiry*. New York: John Wiley & Sons.

Ragin CC. 2000. *Fuzzy-Set Social Science*. Chicago, IL/London: University of Chicago Press.

Reutter W. 2001. Deutschland. Verbände zwischen Pluralismus, Korporatismus und Lobbyismus. In *Verbände und Verbandssysteme in Westeuropa*, ed. W Reutter, P Rütters, pp. 75–101. Opladen: Leske + Budrich.

Ronit K, Schneider V. 1997. Organisierte Interessen in nationalen und supranationalen Politökologien: Ein Vergleich der G 7-Länder mit der Europäischen Union. In *Verbände in vergleichender Perspektive*, ed. Uv Alemann, B Weßels, pp. 29–62. Berlin: Sigma.

Ronit K, Schneider V. 1999. Global Governance through Private Organizations. *Governance* 12: 243–66.

Ronit K, Schneider V, ed. 2000. *Private Organizations in Global Politics*. London/New York: Routledge.

Rosenkopf L, Tushman ML. 1994. The Coevolution of Technology and Organization. In *Evolutionary Dynamics of Organizations*, ed. JAC Baum, JV Singh, pp. 403–24. New York/Oxford: Oxford University Press.

Salisbury RH. 1969. An Exchange Theory of Interest Groups. *Midwest Journal of Political Science* 13: 1–32.

Salisbury RH. 1984. Interest Representation: The Dominance of Institutions. *American Political Science Review* 78: 64–76.

Sandholtz W. 1993. Institutions and Collective Action: The New Telecommunications in Western Europe. *World Politics* 45: 242–70.

Sandholz W. 1998. The Emergence of a Supranational Telecommunications Regime. In *European Integration and Supranational Governance*, ed. W Sandholz, A Stone-Sweet, pp. 134–63. Oxford: Oxford University Press.

Sargent JA. 1993. The Corporate Benefits of Lobbying: The British Case and its Relevance to the European Community. In *Lobbying in the European*

Community, ed. S Mazey, J Richardson, pp. 230–45. Oxford: Oxford University Press.
Schmedes H-J. 2003. Trade Associations in the US Chemical Industry. An Empirical Assessment of Organizational Change. MA thesis. Konstanz: University of Konstanz.
Schmidt VA. 2006. *Democracy in Europe: The EU and National Polities*. Oxford: Oxford University Press.
Schmitter PC. 1979. Still the Century of Corporatism? In *Trends Toward Corporatist Intermediation*, ed. PC Schmitter, G Lehmbruch, pp. 7–52. Beverly Hills, CA: Sage.
Schmitter PC. 1994. The Future Euro-Polity and its Impact upon Private Interest Governance within Member States. *Droit et société* 28: 659–75.
Schmitter PC. 1997. The Emerging Europolity and its Impact upon National Systems of Production. In *Contemporary Capitalism*, ed. JR Hollingsworth, R Boyer, pp. 395–430. Cambridge: Cambridge University Press.
Schmitter PC. 2000. The Impact of Europeanization and Globalization on National Patterns of Business Interest Intermediation. Unpublished memorandum. Florence: European University Institute.
Schmitter PC, Grote JR. 1997. The Corporatist Sisyphus: Past, Present and Future. Working paper 97/4. Florence: European University Institute.
Schmitter PC, Lehmbruch G, ed. 1979. *Trends toward Corporatist Intermediation*. Beverly Hills, VA: Sage.
Schmitter PC, Streeck W. 1999 [1981]. *The Organization of Business Interests: Studying the Associative Action of Business in Advanced Industrial Societies*. MPIfG Discussion Paper 99/1. Cologne: MPIfG.
Schneiberg MJ, Hollingsworth R. 1998. Can Transaction Cost Economics Explain Trade Associations? In *Institutions and Political Choice. On the Limits of Rationality*, ed. R Czada, A Héritier, H Keman, pp. 191–210. Amsterdam: VU University Press.
Schneider G, Baltz K. 2004. Specialization pays off: Interest Group Influence on Pre-Negotiations in Four Member States. In *Governance in Europe. The Role of Interest Groups*, ed. A Warntjen, A Wonka, pp. 130–47. Baden-Baden: Nomos.
Schneider V. 1985. Corporatist and Pluralist Patterns of Policy-Making for Chemicals Control: A Comparison between West Germany and the USA. In *Organized Interests and the State: Studies in Meso-Corporatism*, ed. A Cawson, pp. 174–94. London/Beverly Hills, CA: Sage.
Schneider V. 1988. *Politiknetzwerke in der Chemikalienkontrolle. Eine Analyse einer transnationalen Politikentwicklung*. Berlin: de Gruyter.
Schneider V. 1992. Organized Interests in the European Telecommunications Sector. In *Organized Interests and the European Community*, ed. J Greenwood, JR Grote, K Ronit, pp. 42–68. London: Sage.
Schneider V. 2001. Institutional Reform in Telecommunications: The European Union in Transnational Policy Diffusion. In *Transforming Europe. Europeanization and Domestic Change*, ed. M Green-Cowles, J Casparo, T Risse, pp. 60–78. Ithaca, NY: Cornell University Press.
Schneider V. 2006. Business in Policy Networks: Estimating the Relative Importance of Corporate Direct Lobbying and Representation by Trade Associations. In *Business and Government: Methods and Practice. International Political Science*

Association 2000 Series, ed. D Coen, W Grant, pp. 109–27. Opladen: Barbara Budrich Publishers.

Schneider V, Bauer JM. 2007. Governance: Prospects of Complexity Theory in Revisiting System Theory. *65th Annual National Conference of the Midwestern Political Science Association*. Chicago, IL, April 12–15.

Schneider V, Grote JR. 2006. Business Associations, Associative Order and Internationalization. In *Governing Interests: Business Associations Facing Internationalization*, ed. W Streeck, JR Grote, V Schneider, J Visser. London: Routledge.

Schneider V, Häge F. 2008. Europeanization and the Retreat of the State. *Journal of European Public Policy* 15: 1–19.

Schneider V, Tenbücken M, ed. 2004. *Der Staat auf dem Rückzug. Die Privatisierung der öffentlichen Infrastruktruren*. Frankfurt: Campus.

Schneider V, Werle R. 1990. International Regime or Corporate Actor? The European Community in Telecommunications Policy. In *The Political Economy of Communications. International and European Dimensions*, ed. K Dyson, H Peter, pp. 77–106. London/New York: Routledge.

Schneider V, Werle R. 1991. Policy Networks in the German Telecommunications Domain. In *Policy Networks. Empirical Evidence and Theoretical Considerations*, ed. B Marin, R Mayntz, pp. 97–136. Frankfurt: Campus.

Schneider V, Werle R. 2007. Telecommunications Policy. In *Europeanization: New Research Agendas*, ed. P Graziano, M Vink, pp. 266–80. London: Palgrave Macmillan.

Schneider V, Fink S, Tenbücken M. 2005. Buying Out the State: A Comparative Perspective on the Privatization of Infrastructures. *Comparative Political Studies* 38: 704–27.

Schneider V, Janning F, Leifeld P, Malang T. 2008. *Politiknetzwerke. Modelle, Anwendungen und Visualisierungen*. Wiesbaden: VS-Verlag.

Scott WR. 1998. *Organizations: Rational, Natural, and Open Systems*. Upper Saddle River, NJ: Prentice Hall.

Sebaldt M. 1997. *Organisierter Pluralismus: Kräftefeld, Selbstverständnis und politische Arbeit deutscher Interessengruppen*. Opladen: Westdeutscher Verlag.

Siaroff A. 1999. Corporatism in 24 Industrial Democracies. *European Journal of Political Research* 36: 175–205.

Simmons BA, Elkins Z. 2004. The Globalization of Liberalization: Policy Diffusion in the International Political Economy. *American Political Science Review* 98: 171–89.

Staber U, Aldrich H. 1986. Government Regulation and the Expansion of Trade Associations. In *Population Perspectives on Organizations*, ed. H Aldrich, pp. 77–93. Uppsala: Uppsala University Press.

Steil B, Victor DG, Nelson RR. 2002. *Technological Innovation and Economic Performance*. Princeton, NJ: Princeton University Press.

Stokman FN, van Assen M, van der Knoop J, van Oosten RCH. 1999. *Strategic Decision Making*. Unpublished manuscript. Groningen: University of Groningen.

Stopford J, Strange S. 1991. *Rival States, Rival Firms*. Cambridge: Cambridge University Press.

Streeck W. 1989. The Territorial Organization of Interests and the Logics of Associative Action: The case of Handwerk Organization in West Germany.

In *Regionalism, Business Interests and Public Policy*, ed. WD Coleman, HJ Jacek, pp. 59–94. London: Sage.

Streeck W. 1992. Preface. In *Social Institutions and Economic Performance: Studies of Industrial Relations in Advanced Capitalist Economies*, ed. W Streeck, pp. vii–xi. London: Sage.

Streeck W. 1998. The Internationalization of Industrial Relations in Europe: Prospects and Problems. *Politics and Society* 26: 429–59.

Streeck W, Kenworthy L. 2005. Theories and Practices of Neocorporatism. In *The Handbook of Political Sociology*, ed. T Janoski, RR Alford, AM Hicks, MA Schwartz, pp. 441–60. Cambridge: Cambridge University Press.

Streeck W, Schmitter PC. 1985a. Community, Market, State – and Associations? The Prospective Contribution of Interest Governance to Social Order. In *Private Interest Governments*, ed. W Streeck, PC Schmitter, pp. 1–29. London: Sage.

Streeck W, Schmitter PC, ed. 1985b. *Private Interest Government: Beyond Market and State*. Beverly Hills, CA: Sage.

Streeck W, Schmitter PC. 1994. From National Corporatism to Transnational Pluralism. Organized Interests in the Single European Market. In *Europäische Integration und verbandliche Interessenvermittlung*, ed. V Eichener, H Voelzkow, pp. 181–215. Marburg: Metropolis-Verlag.

Streeck W, Grote JR, Schneider V, Visser J, ed. 2006. *Governing Interests: Business Associations Facing Internationalization*. London/New York: Routledge.

Temin P, Galambos L. 1987. *The Fall of the Bell System: A Study in Prices and Politics*. Cambridge/New York: Cambridge University Press.

Tenbücken M. 2002. *Corporate Lobbying in the European Union: Strategies of Multinational Companies*. Frankfurt am Main: Peter Lang.

Tenbücken M, Schneider V. 2004. Divergent Convergence: Structures and Functions of National Regulatory Authorities in the Telecommunications Sector. In *The Politics of Regulation: Examining Regulatory Institutions and Instruments in the Age of Governance*, ed. J Jordana, D Levi-Faur, pp. 245–72. Cheltenham: Elgar.

Thatcher M, Sweet AS. 2002. Theory and Practice of Delegation to Non-Majoritarian Institutions. *West European Politics* 25: 1–22.

Thomson R, van der Knoop J, Stokman FN. 1999. *Collecting Data for Models of Decision Makin*. Unpublished manuscript. Groningen: University of Groningen.

Tollison RD. 1997. Rent Seeking. In *Perspectives on Public Choice: a Handbook*, ed. DC Mueller, pp. 506–25. Cambridge: Cambridge University Press.

Trade Association Forum. 2002. *Trade Association Performance: A Five-Year View*. London: Trade Association Forum.

Traxler F. 1985. Prerequisites, Problem-Solving Capacity and Limits of Neo-Corporatist Regulation: A Case Study of Private Interest Governance and Economic Performance in Austria. In *Private Interest Governments*, ed. W Streeck, PC Schmitter, pp. 150–67. London: Sage.

Traxler F. 2006. Economic Internationalization and the Organizational Dilemma of Employer Associations. In *Governing Interests: Business Associations Facing Internationalization*, ed. W Streeck, JR Grote, V Schneider, J Visser, pp. 93–114. London: Routledge.

Traxler F, Huemer G, ed. 2007. *Handbook of Business Interest Associations, Firm Size and Governance: A Comparative Analytical Approach*. London/New York: Routledge.

Traxler F, Unger B. 1994. Industry or Infrastructure? A Cross-National Comparison of Governance: Its Determinants and Economic Consequences in the Dairy Sector. In *Governing Capitalist Economies*, ed. JR Hollingsworth, pp. 183–214. New York/Oxford: Oxford University Press.
Truman DB. 1968 [1951]. *The Governmental Process. Political Interests and Public Opinion.* New York: Knopf.
Ullmann H-P. 1988. *Interessenverbände in Deutschland.* Frankfurt am Main: Suhrkamp.
Van Waarden F. 1987. Sector Structure, Interests and Associative Action in the Food Processing Industry. In *Business Interests, Organizational Development and Private Interest Government*, ed. W Grant, pp. 63–92. Berlin/New York: de Gruyter.
VCI. 2000. *Facts, Analyses, Perspectives: The Chemical Industry 2000, Annual Report.* Frankfurt am Main: Verband der Chemischen Industrie.
VCI. 2003. *Chemiewirtschaft in Zahlen.* Frankfurt am Main: Verband der Chemischen Industrie.
Voelzkow, H. 2000. Korporatismus in Deutschland: Chancen, Risiken und Perspektiven. In *Zwischen Wettbewerbs- und Verhandlungsdemokratie. Analysen zum Regierungssystem der Bundesrepublik Deutschland*, ed. E Holtmann, H. Voelzkow, pp.186–212. Opladen: Westdeutscher Verlag.
Waesche NM. 2003. *Internet Entrepreneurship in Europe: Venture Failure and the Timing of Telecommunications Reform.* Cheltenham: Elgar.
Wagemann C. 2005a. *Organizational Change in Business Associations of the Dairy Industry. Lessons from PIGs for COWs and Beyond.* Florence: European University Institute.
Wagemann C. 2005b. Private Interest Governments Are Dead. Long Live Private Interest Governments? Lessons from Swiss Cows. *Schweizerische Zeitschrift für Politikwissenschaft* 11: 1–25.
Wasserman S, Faust K. 1994. *Social Network Analysis. Methods and Applications.* Cambridge: Cambridge University Press.
Wepler C. 1999. *Europäische Umweltpolitik.* Marburg: Metropolis-Verlag.
Williamson OE. 1991. Comparative Economic Organization: The Analysis of Discrete Structural Alternatives. *Administrative Science Quarterly* 36: 269–96.
Wilson GK. 1990. *Interest Groups.* Oxford: Blackwell.
Witko C, Newmark A. 2005. Business Mobilization and Public Policy in the U.S. States. *Social Science Quarterly*: 356–67.
Woll C. 2005. *Learning to Act on World Trade. Preference Formation of Large Firms in the United States and the European Union.* MPIfG Discussion Paper. Cologne: MPIfG.
Wonka A, Warntjen A. 2004. The Making of Public Policies in the European Union: Linking Theories of Formal Decision-making and Informal Interest Intermediation. In *Governance in Europe. The role of interest groups*, ed. A Warntjen, A Wonka, pp. 9–24. Baden-Baden: Nomos.
Young and Partners. 2003a. *Mergers and Acquisitions Biotechnology Industry: Summary.* www.pharmaindustry.com/bmat.html. Accessed 13 March 2003.
Young and Partners. 2003b. *Mergers and Acquisitions Chemical Industry: Summary.* www.chemicalindustry.com/mat.html. Accessed 13 March 2003.
Young and Partners. 2003c. *Mergers and Acquisitions Pharmaceutical Industry: Summary.* www.pharmaindustry.com/pmat.html. Accessed 13 March 2003.

Author Index

Abromeit, H., 157
Aftalion, F., 90, 93
Aldrich, H., 31, 32, 48, 49, 50
Alexander, J.C., 4
Allen, C.S., 86
Almond, G.A., 7, 26, 27, 40, 45, 136
Amburgey, T.L., 18, 32, 35, 236
Anderson, D., 160, 161, 165
Anderson, P., 5, 54
Armingeon, K., 157
Arora, A., 90, 92, 93
Arthur D. Little, 186
Austen-Smith, D., 23
Averyt, W.F., 206
Axelrod, R., 183

Baggott, R., 110
Baglioni, S., 170
Baltz, K., 198
Banks, J., 160
Bartolini, S., 182
Bauer, J.M., 10, 130, 131
Baum, J.A.C., 18, 32, 35, 158, 222, 236
Baumgartner, F.R., 17, 40
Baumol, W.J., 53
Beck, U., 3, 4
Beer, S.H., 7
Bennett, R.J., 49, 126
Bentley, A.F., 19, 21
Benz, A., 91
Berry, J.M., 88
Beyers, J., 182, 193, 198, 233
Blau, P., 24
Boleat, M., 50, 52, 75
Börzel, T.A., 4, 41, 182
Bouwen, P., 66, 198
Brandes. U., 13, 98
Brickman, R., 65, 67, 92
Brittain, J.W., 38
Brock, G.W., 134
Brophy, J., 75
Broscheid, A., 86
Brose, H.G., 171

Buchanan, J.M., 2
Bunge, M., 35, 42

Campbell, D.T., 36
Cawson, A., 7, 28, 154, 208
Clark, K.B., 54
Clarkson, S., 92
Coen, D., 86, 200, 203, 207, 219, 220
Coleman, J.S., 24, 25, 136
Coleman, W.D., 156
Colomy, P., 4
Conlan, T., 91
Cowles, M., 200, 204, 207
Crouch, C., 156, 171
Cutler, A.C., 30
Czada, R., 7, 27, 154

Dannreuther, C., 86
DiMaggio, P.J., 171, 236
Dolata, U., 53
Dosi, G., 53
Downs, A., 22, 23

Ebers, M., 33
Egeberg, M., 193
Ehrmann, H.W., 7
Eising, R., 31, 46, 86, 109, 122, 182, 233
Elkins, Z., 237
Evans, P., 2
Evenson, R.E., 54

Farago, P., 155, 158, 174
Featherstone, K., 4
Fleischer, M., 185
Fouilleux, E., 174
Freeman, C., 53
Freeman, L.C., 31, 53, 98
Furlong, S.R., 45

Gais, T.L., 45
Galambos, L., 134

Galunic, D.C., 35, 39
Gotsch, W., 33
Grant, A., 91
Grant, W., 8, 65, 71, 73, 75, 86, 100, 110, 155, 156, 159, 174, 175, 194, 205
Gray, V., 17, 32, 34, 38, 49, 50, 235, 236
Greenwood J., 7, 8, 31, 181, 201, 204, 205, 207
Grier, K.B., 51
Grote, J.R., v, x, xi, xii, xiii, xiv, xv, 1, 9, 47, 50, 65, 86, 106, 131, 180, 182, 187, 193, 197, 198, 201

Habermas, J., 3
Haege, F., 57
Hall, P.A., 53, 156
Hannan, M., 31
Henderson, R.M., 54
Henning, C.H.C.A., 182, 198
Hesse, J.J., 91
Hix, S., 181
Holland, J.H., 5
Hollingsworth, R., 33, 34, 51, 136
Hooghe, L., 201
Hörl, B., 180
Huemer, G., 8
Hull, D.L., 37

Jacek, H.J., 7, 104, 154, 155, 156, 160
Jordan, G., 204, 208, 220

Karlhofer, F., 154, 159
Kenis, P., 3, 41
Kennelly, B., 49, 50, 51
Kenworthy, L., 28
Kerremans, B., 182, 193
Kerwin, C.M., 45
King, A.A., 105
Kirke, A., 160, 161, 165
Kittel, B., 159
Knill, C., 48
Knoke, D., 17, 40, 184
Kohler-Koch, B., x, 157, 182, 207
Kriesi, H., 46, 170
Kux, S., 157

Landau, R., 92, 93
Lang, A., v, vi, x, xi, xii, xiii, xiv, 1, 8, 9, 10, 12, 17, 42, 50, 86, 106, 108, 110, 131, 137, 182, 187, 197, 198, 221, 232
Langlois, R.N., 54
Latzer, M., 58, 108, 132
Laumann, E.O., 73, 128
Layard, R., 109
Leech, B.L., 17, 23, 40
Lehmbruch, G., ix, x, 7, 27, 47
Lehmkuhl, D., xii, 46, 48, 198
Levi-Faur, D., 109
Lodge, G.C., 207
Lowery, D., 17, 32, 34, 38, 49, 50, 235, 236

Mach, A., 156
Mahoney, J., 173
Majone, G., 48.
Marin, B., 46
Marks, G., 30, 31
Marsden, P.V., 160
Marx, K., 19, 20
Mathews, J.T., 46
May, T., 110, 114
Mayntz, R., 46
Mayr, E., 29
McFarland, A.S., 17, 21, 22, 34, 222
McLaughlin, A., 200, 204, 208, 220
Moe, T.M., 24
Molina, O., 7
Mowery, D.C., 90
Müller, U., 57
Munz, C.M., 68
Murrell, P., 49, 50, 51

Nelson, R.R., 52, 53
Newmark, A., 22
Noam, E.M., 134

Offe, C., 20, 43, 50
Olson, M., 23, 24, 43, 50, 198
O'Riain, S., 47

Pappi, F.U., 182, 198
Perez, C., 53
Perrow, C., 136

Author Index

Pestoff, V., 174
Pierson, P., 3
Pisano, G.P., 54
Platzer, H., 73
Plöhn, J., 109
Pollitt, C., 45
Popp, H., 158, 160
Powell, G.B., 27, 136
Powell, W.W., 171, 236
Przeworski, A., 157

Quittkat, C., 207

Radaelli, C.M., 4
Ragin, C.C., 162
Reutter, W., 110
Rhodes, M., 7
Risse, T., 4
Ronit, K., 3, 7, 8, 17, 48, 67, 157, 201
Rosenberg, N., 53, 90
Rosenkopf, L., 54

Salisbury, R.H., 24, 41, 204
Sandholtz, W., 58, 132
Sargent, J.A., 205
Schmedes, H.J., v, xi, xiv, 9, 88, 92, 107, 142
Schmidt, V.A., 65
Schmitter, P.C., ix, x, xii, 2, 7, 27, 28, 30, 33, 47, 49, 50, 51, 66, 89, 94, 99, 103, 104, 136, 154, 155, 161, 168, 169, 171, 174, 175, 182, 183, 197, 198, 222, 234, 239
Schneiberg, M.J., 33, 34, 51, 136
Schneider, G., 198
Schneider, V., v, vi, x, xi, xiv, xv, 1, 3, 7, 8, 10, 12, 17, 28, 41, 42, 45, 46, 47, 48, 57, 67, 86, 92, 106, 109, 110, 117, 130, 131, 157, 187, 197, 198, 201, 221, 228, 237
Scott, W.R., 31, 236
Sebaldt, M., 110
Siaroff, A., 109, 154, 157
Simmons, B.A., 237
Soskice, D.W., 53, 156
Staber, U., 32, 48
Steil, B., 52

Stokman, F.N., 213
Stopford, J., 30
Strange, S., 30
Streeck, W., ix, x, xii, xiii, xv, 2, 7, 8, 28, 30, 33, 38, 49, 50, 51, 66, 89, 94, 99, 103, 104, 136, 154, 155, 156, 168, 169, 171, 173, 175, 182, 183, 222, 234, 239
Sverdrup, U., 157
Sweet, A.S., 45

Talbot, C., 45
Tálos, E., 159
Temin, P., 134
Tenbücken, M., vi, xi, xv, 11, 45, 109, 200, 206, 232
Teune, H., 157
Thatcher, M., 45
Thomson, R., 214
Tollison, R.D., 2
Traxler, F., 8, 11, 50, 52, 153, 155, 159, 160, 161, 228
Truman, D.B., 7, 21, 22, 24
Tushman, M.L., 54

Ullmann, H.P., 108, 110
Unger, B., 155, 159, 160, 161, 228

van Waarden, F., 34, 157, 160
Visser, J., xiii, xv
Voelzkow, H., 154, 155, 171

Waesche, N.M., 54
Wagemann, C., vi, xi, xv, 11, 153, 162, 174, 175, 228, 232, 234
Warntjen, A., 184
Weeks, J.R., 35, 39
Wepler, C., 185
Werle, R., v, xi, xv, 9, 42, 46, 53, 57, 117, 228
Wholey, D.R., 38
Wiesenthal, H., 20, 43, 50
Williamson, O.E., 33, 37
Wilson, G.K., 90, 91
Witko, C., 22
Woll, C., 41
Wonka, A., vi, xi, xvi, 11, 46, 106, 179, 184, 225

Young and Partners, 66, 67, 106

Subject Index

AA (Advertising Association), 112–13, 115–20, 124
AAP (Association of American Publishers), 138–9, 142, 144, 147, 149–50
ABC (Association of Biotechnology Companies), 95
ABPI (Association of the British Pharmaceutical Industry), 70, 72, 74–5, 78–9, 81, 84–5, 87
ACC (American Chemistry Council), 95–8, 102–5, 107, 225–6
access, 20, 22, 28, 31, 68, 82, 183, 198, 200–1, 214, 219, 241–2; broker, 197; channel, 85, 195, 207, 233, 239; point, 91, 140, 193; route, 125, 206, 230, 232; strategy, 12, 124; institutionalized, 29, 40; internet, 133, 134
ACEA (Association des Constructeurs Européens de l'Automobile), 204, 205, 211, 214–18, 220
ACM (Association for Computing Machinery), 137–9, 142, 144, 147
ACPA (American Crop Protection Association), 95
actor-centered approach, 17, 40
adaptation, 4–7, 9, 12, 17–8, 32, 39–40, 42, 45, 47–8, 59, 69–79, 85, 99, 108, 111, 119, 131, 145, 150, 165, 221, 230, 233–4, 241–2; behavioral, 182; institutional, 173; pressure, 6, 36, 62, 152, 236; process, 9–11, 38, 42–3, 50, 58, 93; 110, 125, 127, 141, 236, 239; strategies of, 8, 44, 236
AEA (American Electronics Association), 138–9, 142, 144, 147, 149, 232
agencification, 45
agriculture, 9, 43, 50, 57–9, 82, 167, 174

AIA (Alliance of Industry Associations), 71, 75–7, 79, 85, 87
alliance, 75–6, 79, 95, 143, 203; cross-national, 207, 218–19; firm, 68; global, 48; horizontal, 219; network, 79; vertical, 203
ALTS (Association for Local Telecommunication Services), 137–9, 142, 144, 147, 149, 150
ALTV (The Association of Local Television Stations), 138–9, 142, 144
AMA (AgrarMarkt Austria), 161
American; Congress, 90, 91, 102, 147; Digital Millennium Copyright Act, 146; federalism, 27, 44, 140; Free Trade Agreement, 92; interest system, 91, 141, 150; Senate, 102, 147–8; system of business associations, 10, 142–3; trade associations, 139–40; White House, 102, 148
Amsterdam Treaty, 211, 219, 251
ANGA (Verband privater Netzbetreiber – Satelliten- und Kabelkommunikation), 112, 114–15, 117–19
APC (American Plastics Council), 95–7, 103, 107, 225
APR (Arbeitsgemeinschaft Privater Rundfunk), 112, 115, 118, 120–1
arena, 205; bargaining, 31; domestic, 46, 146; European, 31, 124, 179; issue, 201; lobbying, 182; national, 179, 182; policy, 6, 47, 82, 201; political, 19, 31, 46, 60, 143, 147, 200; supranational, 45; two level, 179, 181
associability, 17, 19, 25, 29–31, 38, 40–1, 88–9, 174, 235
association; branch, 70–1, 73, 82, 85, 117, 179, 181–2, 189, 194, 196,

Subject Index 259

224–5, 229, 238; encompassing, 47, 117, 120, 125–6, 160; established, 12, 55–6, 81, 125, 225–6, 228; European branch, 103, 124, 127, 191–3, 233, 237; focal, 69–71, 73, 80, 84, 86–9, 95–8, 104, 113–14, 116, 119, 137, 148, 151, 182, 223, 225, 228; higher-order, 160, 167; newly-founded, 12, 71, 116, 125, 223, 225–6, 228; particularistic, 125; peak, *see* peak association
associational; access route, 124; adaptation, 9, 236; arrangement, 105, 110; behavior, 9, 32, 42, 141; budget, 100; change, 51–2, 137, 222–3, 233, 237, 239; decision-making, 170; density, 50; domain, 99; dynamic, 62, 238; environment, 9, 38, 105, 163; executive, 99; foundation, 32, 43, 237; goods, 171; governance, 32, 34, 156, 158, 160, 166, 221; hierarchy, 11, 43, 116, 227, 234; income, 100; inertia, 233; landscape, 9, 59, 69, 75, 81, 86, 95, 111, 113, 121, 223, 225, 229; lobbying, 11, 37, 101–2, 202, 217, 239; merger, 75; network, 74, 78, 84, 98, 115, 118, 221, 223, 228, 239; order, 4; output, 97, 100, 103; population, 75, 84–5, 88, 137, 141, 156, 228, 232, 235; price-fixing, 160; program, 10, 105, 106; regulation, 160; relations, 12, 38, 40, 97, 222; representative, 99–100, 106, 147; resource, 77, 80, 90, 94, 99–101, 170; self-regulation, 48, 154, 159, 228; service, 81; space, 131; state, 157; structure, 9–10, 28–9, 42–3, 62, 96, 126–7, 131, 169, 193, 222, 227, 234–5; subsystem, 3, 169; task, 79, 119, 145; theory, 222, 239
Austria, 11, 153–4, 157, 159, 161, 163, 166, 171, 174, 227–8, 231, 253
Austrian; associations, 153; dairy sector, 159–61; interest system,

PIG, 161; social partnership, 157; Sozialpartnerschaft, 167
automobile; company, 204–5, 214, 217, 218 industry, 7, 11, 202 209, 211–12, 218, 249; producer, 204, 205, 212–13, 217; production, 205; sector, 212, 232; summit, 212

BACS (British Association for Chemical Specialities), 72, 74–6, 78, 84, 87
BAMA (British Aerosol Manufacturers Association), 72, 74–6, 78, 84, 86, 87
BAU (Deutsche Bauchemie), 72, 74, 78, 84
BCDTA (British Chemical Distributors & Traders Association), 72–4, 76, 78, 84, 86–7
BCF (British Coatings Federation), 71–2, 74, 76, 78, 84, 87
BDA (Bundesvereinigung der Deutschen Arbeitgeberverbände), 110–11
BDI (Bundesverband der Deutschen Industrie), 83, 110–11, 116, 123–4, 126, 128, 199, 215, 235, 239
BDZV (Bundesverband der Deutschen Zeitungsverleger), 112, 114–15, 117–18, 120, 124
belief system, 47
Bell System, 136, 253
betweenness centrality, 78, 98, 144–5
BIMA (British Interactive Multimedia Association), 112–13, 115–16, 118, 120
BIO (Biotechnology Industry Organisation), 94–7, 107
BITKOM (Bundesverband der Informationswirtschaft, Telekommunikation und neue Medien), 112–13, 115–18, 123, 124–6
BLF (British Lubricants Federation), 72, 74, 77–8
BmG (Bundesministeriums für Gesundheit), 82–3

260 Subject Index

BmUNR (Bundesministerium für Umwelt, Naturschutz und Reaktorsicherheit), 82–3
BmVEL (Bundesministerium für Ernährung, Landwirtschaft und Verbraucherschutz), 82–3
BMW, 205, 212–13, 215
BmWT (Bundesministerium für Wirtschaft und Technologie), 82–3
bottom-up; explanation, 19; process, 26; theory, 40
boundary specification, 73, 248
BPF (British Plastics Federation), 72, 74, 78, 84, 87
BPI (Bundesverband der Pharmazeutischen Industrie), 70, 72, 74, 78, 84
BPIF (British Printing Industries Federation), 112–13, 115, 118, 124
breakdown; of associational governance, 168; of companies, 175; of organizational community, 164; of PIGs, 163, 174
Breko (Bundesverband der regionalen und lokalen Telekommunikationsgesellschaften), 112, 115, 117–18
British; associational landscape, 81, 121, 225; associational system, 10, 65–6, 72, 108–9, 111–13, 120–1, 125–7, 164, 166, 180, 182, 194, 226, 229, 232, 245–6, 251; car producer, 212; firm, 166, 27; focal association, 80; government, 169, 172, 212; interest population, 79, 164, 228; milk, 165; milkmen, 170; network, 74, 77–8, 115–19, 223, 228; policy-making, 109; respondents, 69, 119; representatives, 69; Westminster democracy, 44
BRMA (British Rubber Manufacturers Association), 72, 74, 78, 84, 87

Brussels, 11, 84, 124, 127, 180, 185, 188, 194, 196, 200, 203, 208, 212–14, 219, 237, 243–4
Bundeskanzleramt, 216
business dialogue, 200
BVA (British Video Association), 112–13, 115, 118–21, 124

CAA (Clean Air Act), 92
campaign, 22, 121, 143, 171, 183, 185, 202–3, 207, 218
capital, 1, 20–1, 24, 36, 38, 52, 55, 66, 71, 90, 185, 244
capitalism 8, 20, 156, 241, 243, 248, 250–1; varieties of, 5, 48, 111, 180, 197, 237, 246
capitalist, 19–21, 43; class, 21; collective action, 21; diversity, 243; economy, 253–4; society, 20
CCC (Chlorine Chemistry Council), 95–7, 103–4, 107, 225
CCIA (Computer & Communications Industry Association), 138–9, 142, 144, 146–7, 150
CCPA (Canadian Chemical Producers' Association), 104
CEA (Consumer Electronics Association), 138–9, 142, 144–5, 147, 149–50, 152, 228
CEFIC (European Chemical Industry Council), 59, 68, 82–3, 189, 191–2, 194–6, 199, 205, 225, 229
centrality, 98; actor, 8; betweenness, 78, 98, 144–5; in interest intermediation, 193; network, 77, 244
centralization; degree of, 237; of information flows, 229
CEO, 73, 207, 211
CERCLA (Comprehensive Environmental Response, Compensation and Liability Act), 92
CESM model, 35
challenge; economic, 17, 66, 69, 89, 132–3; environmental, 38, 69, 88, 93, 106, 131–2, 137, 150–1; European, 67, 111; external, 125,

128, 131, 140; international, 168; perception of, 69; political, 67–9, 90, 128, 132, 134, 140, 197; technological, 52, 66, 69, 92, 128, 132; trade union, 36; societal, 86
change; economic, 60, 151, 153; holistic, 5; political, 132, 151, 225; technological, 9, 12, 43, 52–3, 57–8, 60, 113, 160, 240
cheese, 158, 165, 174; exporters, 158; market, 174; marketing, 158; producing industry, 165; product, 158; production, 165; sub-sector, 158
chemical; associational network, 84; associational system, 192; branches, *see* segments; industry, 7, 11, 57–8, 60–2, 65–8, 85–90, 92–3, 95, 98, 103, 105–7, 179–80, 182, 184–5, 187, 189, 194–5, 198, 205, 222, 226, 229, 233, 235, 240, 243, 245–7, 251, 254; industry lobbying, 194; Industry Archives, 107, 244; industry peak organizations, 195; innovations, 92; interest population, 77, 79; output, 66, 93; products, 58, 90; Safety and Hazard Investigation Board, 92; sector, 9, 57–8, 61–2, 66–7, 70, 75–6, 91, 92–5, 142, 186, 222, 225–6, 228–30, 236; specialties, 87; specialty association, 75; subsector, 95; substance, 92, 179
chemicals, 9, 43, 58–9, 61, 67, 70, 73, 75, 104, 185, 224, 227, 231, 240, 242, 247; competitiveness, 186; control, 251; domain, 62; industrial, 73; legislation, 184, 191, 193, 198; policy, 76, 179, 180, 183–8, 191–2, 194, 244; policy-making process, 188; producer, 75, 90; production, 66, 107; regulation, 67, 185–6, 195; regulatory regime, 185; turnover, 184–5; users, 73; White Paper, *see* REACH

CHEMNET (Chemical Industry's Mutual Aid Emergency Response Network), 104
CHEMTREC (Chemical Transportation Emergency Center), 104
CHLOREP (Chlorine Emergency Plan), 104
CHPA (Consumer Healthcare Products Association), 95–97, 107
CI (Chlorine Institute), 95–7, 104, 107
CIA (Chemical Industries Association), 71–79, 81, 83–7, 107, 182, 191–3, 223, 226
CIR (Cosmetic Ingredient Review), 104
CLA (CropLife America), 95–7, 104
class; antagonism, 20; capitalist, 21; division, 19–20, 86; dominant, 20; dominated, 20; proletarian, 21; social, 249; theory, 18–9, 21, 36; working, 20–1
CLEPA (Comité de Liaison de la Construction d'Équipements et de Pièces d'Automobile), 218
cluster; analysis, 81, 101, 121–2, 126, 147, 149, 230; of business associations, 81; lobbying, 122; theory, 19,
CMA (Chemical Manufacturers Association), 95, 104
co-decision procedure, 180, 187, 213
cognitive mimicry, 236
collapse; of associational system, 238; of PIG, 162; of regulatory system, 162
collective; actor, 53, 193, 247; agreement 30, 34; bargaining, 28; body, 208; choice, 34; commitment, 46; goods, 23, 155; evolution, 19; interest, 168; interest representation, 208; self-regulation, 34
collective action, 12, 18, 20, 22–4, 26, 29–30, 34, 36, 39, 43, 50–1, 86, 164, 198, 243, 246, 249–50; capitalist, 21; form of, 20; logics of, 20, 23; theories of, 23, 37; third logic of, 86

committee; conciliation, 213, 220; EP, 191–3; EP Environment, 188; Joint, 159; PIG Joint, 164; political action, 51, 143; standing, 76
Common Agricultural Policy, 172, 241, 244–5, 249
company; car, 204; headquarter, 207; member, 49, 61; mentality, 86; merger, 75; size, 85
competition 6, 8, 12, 224, 234; full, 38, 74, 96, 115, 142; global, 222; harmful, 74, 96, 115; interest group, 24; intra-industry, 33–4, 49; partial, 74, 96, 115, 142; party, 22
competitive; advantage, 53, 191; links, 223; network, 125; population, 37, 39, 235; pressure, 50–3, 128; relations, 9, 34, 73, 76, 86, 96, 114, 116, 126, 128, 133, 141–2, 221, 223, 235, 238–9; sub-network, 229; ties, 225–6
competitiveness, 171, 179, 186
complex; adaptation, 11; adaptive systems, 246; adaptive systems literature, 5; adaptive systems theory, 38, 39; association theory, 5, 18, 38, 40; associational systems, 9; associations, 153, 172, 173; associative action theory, 34; evolution, 18; system approach, 35, 131
complexity; compositional, 35; ecological, 35; mechanismic, 35; of adaptation, 7, 221, 233; of consultation system, 200; of multilevel system, 201; of social structure, 22; perspective, 8, 239; relational, 203; theory, 5, 18, 132, 151–2, 236, 240, 252
compliance, 29; company, 104; members, 103, 190; non-, 183,
composition; of associations, 69, 111, 131; of associational landscape, 9, 86, 229; of associational system, 12, 43, 49, 114, 121, 126, 238; of member firms, 6, 9, 39, 105; of network, 84; of organizational population, 32; of sector, 49, 67, 90, 93
concertation 47, 248
conservative; perspective, 2; view, 2; thinking, 110,
constitutional; distribution of powers, 27, 44, model, 134
consultation, 241; internet, 187; and information services, 56, 184; member, 80, 99, 120, 146; system, 200
contact portfolio, 77, 81
convergence, 242, 253; economic, 131; Europeanized, 179; full; partial, 65; technological, 131; view, 156; of associational activities, 128; of economic governance, 173; of branches, 62, 132; of industries, 57; of policy-making styles, 156
cooperation; dense, 223; partial, 73–4, 96, 115, 142; and competition, 6, 32, 38, 71, 94, 95, 96, 114, 131, 141, 226
COPA (Comité des Organisations Professionnelles Agricoles), 205
COREPER (Comité des Représentants Permanents), 181
corporate actor, 25, 52, 170, 252; theory, 8, 24–5,
corporation; MNC, 11, 200–4, 206–11, 213–20, 233; multinational, 1; transnational, 30; global, 30
corporatism, 89, 110, 154, 240, 242, 247, 249, 251–2; concept of, 27; literature, 43; macro, 154; meso, 251; micro, 208; national, 253; neo-, 7–8, 11, 18, 26–9, 36–8, 40–1, 43–4, 142, 153, 222–3, 253; societal, 44; state, 41, 44
corporatist; adaptation, 165; arrangement, 37, 154, 157; association, 70; closure, 47; configuration, 71, 188; country, 68, 109, 237; governance, 28; intermediation, 251; nature, 65; network, 248; pattern, 28, 85, 251; pact, 47; policy-making, 248; regulation, 253; research

agenda, 27; set-up, 70; state, 157; Sisyphus, 251; system, 77, 157, 174
CRCA (Commercial Radio Companies Association), 112–13, 115–18, 124
CSB (Chemical Safety and Hazard Investigation Board), 92
CSMA (Chemical Specialties Manufacturers Association), 95
CSPA (Consumer Specialty Products Association), 95–7, 107
CTFA (Cosmetic Toiletry and Fragrance Association), 95–7, 104, 107
CTIA (Cellular Telecommunications & Internet Association), 137–9, 142, 144, 149, 226
CTPA (Cosmetic Toiletry & Perfumery Association), 72, 74, 76, 78, 84, 87

Daimler-Chrysler, 205, 213, 215–16
dairy, 61, 227, 231; business, 164–5, 174–5; domain, 62; farm, 159; governance, 162; industry, 7, 11, 57–8, 61, 167, 169–70, 172, 222, 228–9, 232, 234, 238, 241, 245, 247, 254; interest association, 160; interests, 160, 168, 172; manufacturer, 158; manufacturing, 164; merger, 164; PIG, 165; producer, 158, 164; product, 156, 158–9, 161, 163, 175, 247; production, 169; sector, 11, 57, 61–2, 153–61, 165, 167–8, 171–5, 254
DCAT (Drug, Chemical and Allied Trades Association), 95–7, 107
deep impact; diagnoses, 4, 130; hypothesis, 137; idea, 3; perspective, 6; theory, 150
DEFRA (UK Department for Environment, Food and Rural Affairs), 82–3
density, 8, 32, 43, 81, 216–217, 224; associational, 50; network, 77; regulatory, 68; of associational system, 50; of information exchange, 226; of relations, 128
Department of Commerce, 148

determinants, 15, 244, 246, 254; decisive, 208; economic, 9, 42; key, 100; technological, 9, 42
DG Enterprise, 82, 186
DG Environment, 82, 185–6
DIAL (Dairy Industry Association Limited), 164
DIB (Deutsche Industrievereinigung Biotechnologie), 70–2, 74, 78, 81, 84, 223
DIF (Dairy Industry Federation), 164
differentiation, 240; functional, 4, 91; internal, 28, 55; regional, 164; structural, 26; subnational, 171; theory, 4; of associational system, 26; of firms, 50; of interest domain, 168; of organizational population, 163; of political systems, of society, 27
digital age, 136
digitization, 54, 58, 132, 134, 146
direct; lobbying, see lobbying; democracy, 157; representation, 201
directive; end-of-life vehicles, 11, 202, 204–5, 207, 209, 210–4, 218–19, 244; EU, 68, 122, 198, 220, 233; liberalization, 109,
disintegration of interest system, 65, 79, 85
distance; Euclidian, 149; geographic, 166; walking, 165
divergence; persistent, 65; in lobbying activities, 122; of economic governance, 173; of national adaptation processes, 173
diversification; market, 234–5, 238; within business associations, 28; of political arenas, 60
division of labor, 1, 12, 28, 50, 109, 163, 195
DMMV (Deutscher Multimediaverband), 113, 116–17, 120, 122, 124, 232
DoJ (U.S. Department of Justice), 134
domain, 28, 39; activity, 145; associational, 62, 99, 141; broad, 120; communication, 227; dairy, 62; chemicals, 62;

264 Subject Index

information, 224, 227; interest, 23, 28, 32, 37, 67, 114, 125–7, 151, 167–8, 171, 233, 235, 238; internet, 113; membership, 163; narrow, 116; policy, 68; organizational, 6; overlap, 116, 235; societal, 143; telecommunications, 252
double-assignment, 186, 187
DTF (Dairy Trade Federation), 159, 164
DTI (Department of Trade and Industry), 82–3, 122–4
DTLR (UK Department of Transport, Local Government and Regions), 82–3

Eco (Electronic Commerce Forum – Verband der deutschen Internetwirtschaft), 112, 113, 115–19, 124
ecology; organizational, 9, 34–9, 43, 77, 84, 152, 241, 245–6; population, 9, 18, 31–2, 35, 50, 61, 245–6; sector, 70
economic; adaptation, 47; agreement, 38; challenge, 17, 66, 69, 89, 128, 132–3; change, 12, 60, 132, 151, 153, 225; consolidation, 9, 105; constraint, 9, 137; convergence, 131; crisis, 136, 162; determinant, 9, 42; development, 4, 20, 32, 49, 58, 61, 66, 85–6, 93, 136; dynamic, 61; environment, 10, 43, 48, 57, 59, 182, 184, 207, 221–2; exostructure, 42; factor, 9, 12, 42, 43, 49, 51, 57, 61, 69, 86, 93, 106, 128, 132, 140, 238; figures, 90, 93; globalization, 46, 153, 156; governance, 34, 38, 154, 156, 173; growth, 32, 50, 60, 113, 125, 234–5, 240, 247; incentive, 184–5; institution, 52, 173; integration, 90; interdependence, 172; interest, 50; internationalization, 47, 253; life cycle, 7, 58; ministry, 122, 124; performance, 53, 57, 61, 244, 248, 250, 252–3; perspective, 24, 195; perturbation, 11; policy, 47, 159, 160; potential, 58; pressure, 140; process, 1, 106, 108–9, 136, 155, 172; sector, 9, 39, 43, 49, 51, 57–8, 222, 230, 237; segment, 125; setting, 59; sociology, 173; stability, 234–5; stress, 140; theory, 244; transaction, 1, 33; transformation, 111; turbulence, 48; turmoil, 108, 229; variables, 32, 43, 50, 59
embeddedness, 243; environmental, 35; historical, 7; network, 223; social, 17, 172
emergency, 11, 104, 135, 202, 206, 209, 213, 215, 217, 218, 231, 233
employer association, 36, 52, 111, 253
encompassing; association, 47, 72, 91, 117, 120, 125–6, 160; interest domain, 37; organization, 32; organizational community, 79; theory, 34
endostructure, 35, 37, 38
environment; changing, 1, 3, 4, 6, 18, 42, 242; competitive, 53; external, 62, 81; policy, 44, 48; political, 10, 43–4, 47, 137, 147, 222, 230; politics, 44, 47; polity, 44; technological, 57, 59, 151, 221
environmental; adaptation, 36, 152; change, 36, 42, 62, 140–1; challenge, 38, 69, 88, 93, 106, 131–2, 137, 150–1; complexity, 239; constraint, 38, 40; Council, 185; demand, 6, 39, 230; effect, 55; factor, 31–2, 62, 89, 172; force, 9, 39, 222; groups, 215; interest, 50; interest group, 186; issue, 81, 91; law, 91; legislation, 211; movement, 39, 86; NGO, 188; politics, 68; pressure, 151; protection, 204; Protection Agency, 82, 92, 102; regulation, 90; quality, 104; sector, 43; selection, 38; shock, 3; transformation, 130; turmoil, 33
EPA (Environmental Protection Agency), 92, 102

Subject Index 265

equilibrium; in interest group system, 21; of pressure groups, 21
EU, 3, 67, 83, 92, 123, 156–7, 161–2, 179–80, 182, 185, 196, 201, 206–9, 211, 220, 224, 231, 240, 246–8, 251; accession, 161; activity, 60; arena, 179; association, 68, 84, 181, 184, 186, 189, 191–4, 225, 229, 242, 245; chemical industry, 184–185; chemical policy, 179, 183–8, 191, 194; chemicals legislation, 191, 193, 198; chemicals regulation, 185, 195; Commission, 68, 82, 148, 181; Council, 92; Council meeting in Weimar, 185; decision-making, 181, 202, 246; demands, 217; Directives, 220; Directorate General, 122, 185; institution, 30, 60, 85, 124, 201, 206–8, 211, 225; interest intermediation, 11, 180–1, 187–90, 193–7; law, 161, 174, 179–80; level, 11, 44, 68, 82, 180, 189–90, 196–8, 201–9, 215, 218–20, 237; legislation, 207; level activities, 182; lobbying, 182, 187, 192, 194–5, 198; member state, 60, 184–5, 191, 193, 196, 207, 237; multi-level system, 183, 201; policy arena, 82; policy-making, 30–1, 180–1, 198; policy-process, 179, 243; politics, 198; polity, 198; precautionary principle, 185; public actor, 186, 193, 195; quota system, 161, 174; representation, 181; two-level system, 180–1; White Paper, *see* REACH
European; Union, 4, 45–7, 92, 147, 157, 180, 184–5, 191, 200, 218, 220, 222, 241–8, 251, 253–4; Commission, 47, 68, 82, 92, 109, 122, 125, 148, 152, 179–80, 185–8, 191–2, 209, 215–16, 244; Court of Justice, 47, 109; business association, 180, 192, 194, 197; lobbying, *see* lobbying;

Parliament, 92, 122, 180–1, 187–8, 191–2, 198–9, 201, 209, 215–16, 244; regulatory agency, 185; regulatory state, 48
European integration, 4, 9, 60, 86, 109, 156, 157, 162, 172, 174, 197, 201, 237, 242, 248, 250; theory, 20, 29–30; research, 30
Europeanization, 4, 6–10, 39, 60, 66, 68, 84–6, 108–9, 111, 127, 153, 172–3, 180, 197–8, 206, 222, 228, 233, 236–8, 241–4, 246, 248, 251–2; hypothesis, 180; literature, 4, 237; of interest groups, 241; of politics, 9, 68, 84
evolution, 1, 7, 18–21, 31, 44, 54, 131–2, 136–7, 139, 153, 163, 240–3, 247–50; biological theory of, 29; biotech, 62, 67, 85; organizational, 86; technological, 125, 222; of associational landscape, 95; of associational structures, 131; of associational system, 141; of I&C industry, 134; of new sectors, 56; of new industry, 57
evolutionary; concepts, 35; dynamics, 240; sketch, 17; thinking, 34; path, 10, 111, 127, 225; perspective, 35; process, 31, 35–8; traits, 18; trajectory, 125
EWG (Environmental Working Group), 104, 107
exchange; theory, 18, 24–5, 40, 250; relation, 24–5, 33, 66, 77; information, *see* information exchange
exostructure, 35–7, 42
expertise, 36, 106, 156; lack of, 155; technical, 189–90, 195, 198
exports, 51, 59, 61–2, 66, 90, 158

FCC (Federal Communications Commission), 134, 148
FCS (Federation of Communication Services), 112–13, 115–16, 118, 121
FDA (Food and Drug Administration), 92, 102

FEA (Federation of European Aerosols), 103
Federalism, 174; New, 91, 243, 246
FEI (Federation of the Electronics Industry), 112–16, 118, 120, 124, 128
FIA (Fibreoptic Industry Association), 112–13, 115, 118
firm; member, 6, 10, 12, 20–1, 28–9, 35–6, 39, 49, 55, 59–60, 66, 87, 127, 143, 194, 222, 238–9; size, 50, 253; small, 20, 53, 243; small and medium-sized, 57, 71, 194–5, 203, 246; large, 4, 53, 186, 200, 203, 206, 243, 254
flexibility, 173, 234; adaptational, 108; internal, 11
FMA (Fertiliser Manufacturers Association), 72–4, 77–8, 84, 87, 112
focal; association, *see* association; organization, 113, 119; organization set, 89, 96–8, 131, 138, 141, 144; population, 128
food; chain, 160; processing, 250, 254; quality of, 174; supply, 158–9
foreign; competitor, 108; investment, 140; direct investment, 52, 90; trade, 39, 58–61, 109
foundation; associational, 43, 50, 62, 71, 223, 235, 237; sector, 58; of organization, 100
fragmentation; organizational, 71; pluralistic, 85; of associational system, 91; of governmental institutions, 91; of institutional framework, 132–3; of political arena, 60; of power, 91, 140
free-rider; behavior, 23; effect, 24; free-riding, 169; problem, 50
FTC (Federal Trade Commission), 102, 134
functional and territorial dimension, 201

General Motors Europe, 215
generic medicines, 70–1
geodesic, 145; path, 28
geographic closeness, 166

German; associational landscape, 81, 111, 121, 225; associational network, 73–4, 76, 78–9, 115, 117–18, 126, 223, 226, 228–9; associational system, 10, 65, 69, 72, 77, 85, 108–12, 114, 119, 121, 125, 127–8, 180, 192–3, 226, 232, 239; business association, 10–11, 66, 68–9, 81–4, 108, 119, 122–8, 153, 179–80, 182–5, 187–93, 197–9, 225–6, 229–30, 232, 246; car company, 204; car producer, 205; car industry, 212; case, 70, 77, 80, 119–22, 226; Chancellor, 207, 211, 216; company, 66, 205, 217; dairy sector, 160, 167; economy, 110; Empire, 110; federalism, government, 212; interest population; 79, 113; interest system, 117; Minister, 211; Ministry, 215, 217; regulatory agency, 122; representative, 69; respondents, 69; voting behavior, 212
Germany, 7, 9, 11, 13, 57–60, 62, 65–7, 69–70, 73, 79–80, 82, 84–6, 93, 106, 109, 114, 119, 122, 124, 128, 153, 157, 160–2, 166–8, 171, 182, 185, 188, 192, 211–2, 215, 220, 223–4, 227–31, 240, 245, 247, 251–2
global; adaptation, 48; alliances, 48; association, 197; challenge, 111; competition, 222; corporation, 30; development, 69, 106–7; firm, 90, 245–6; governance, 48, 233, 238, 250; influence, 93, 140; institution, 46, 146; level, 6, 11, 29, 44, 46, 69, 128, 140, 152–3, 233; lobbying, 233; order, 245; organization, 152; perspective, 66, 195; policy network, 48; politics, 30, 250; polity, 44, 46; problem, 130; process, 44, 172; regulation, 48; scale, 40, 128, 130, 237; structure, 7; technological development, 151; threat, 150; transfers, 46; transformation, 5, 151; trend, 250

Subject Index 267

globalization, 7–8, 10, 39, 44, 46, 66, 108–9, 111, 141, 150, 152–3, 156, 171, 206, 222, 251–2; hypothesis, 140, 146; literature, 3, 4
glocalization, 171, 172
GML (Gemeinschaft der milchwirtschaftlichen Landesvereinigungen), 160
governance, 6, 33, 37, 39, 233, 252–4; arrangement, 28–9; associational, 33–4, 156, 158, 160, 166, 221, 227, 243; associative, 33; dairy, 162; economic, 34, 38, 154, 156, 173; European, 29, 237, 247; global, 48, 233, 238, 250; international, 9, 18, 29, 31, 237; interest, 252; level, 9, 28; literature, 31; mechanisms, 30, 33; mode, 30, 37, 248; multilevel, 9, 30–1, 201, 244, 248; patterns of, 247; perspective, 30, 67; principles; 33; private interest, 251, 253; sectoral, 65, 155–6, 161, 221; self-, 136; societal, 7; style of, 161; supranational, 250; transformation of, 247; of the dairy sector, 159
government; American, 140; British, 169, 172, 212; German, 212; Spanish, 207, 212; Swiss, 165, 172
GPhA (Generic Pharmaceutical Association), 95
GPIA (Generic Pharmaceutical Industry Association), 95
gradual change theories, 150
Great Britain, 62, 157
Green Book, 109
group; size, 23–4, 35, 43, 50; interests, 22, 36; privileged, 22, 156; theory, 18, 21–2, 26, 34
growth, 89, 241; economic, 32, 50, 60, 113, 125, 234–5, 240, 247; GDP, 50; high-tech, 249; long-term, 247; market, 49, 58, 61; membership, 141; production, 109; rate, 10, 58, 62, 125, 127; in regulatory activity, 61; in international policy-making, 233;

of business associations, 135–6; of EU associations, 68
GVC (Global Vinyl Council), 103

harmonization, 109; of art trading, 212
Heads of state and government, 206, 217–18
Heseltine, M., 114
heterogeneity; intra-industry, 51; internal, 32; linguistic, 157; product, 51
hierarchy, 8, 33, 151, 222–3, 226, 228, 234; associational, 116, 234; degree of, 229; formal, 222, 227; increase in, 227; informal, 222, 227–8; medium, 227; low, 227; organizational, 68, 201; perfect, 226; of relations, 77, 117
holistic; perspective, 26; theory, 40, 142
HoR (House of Representatives), 102, 147
House of Lords, 169
hybrid, 33; approach, 131; construct, 140; mode of governance, 37, 38; organization, 33; sector, 132; type, 141
hypothesis, 51, 125, 149, 188–9, 192–3, 197, 202; deep impact, 137; globalization, 140, 146, 150; Europeanization, 180; internationalization, 237; modernization, 236; varieties of capitalism, 111, 180, 237

IBA (Industrial Biotechnology Association), 95
ICCA (International Council of Chemical Associations), 103, 107
ICCTA (International Council of Chemical Trade Associations), 103
identity; product, 171; regional, 171; sector, 67, 76
IFA (International Fertilizer Association), 103
IGPA (International Generic Pharmaceutical Association), 103

268 Subject Index

IHO (Industrieverbandverband Hygiene und Oberfächenschutz für industrielle Anwendung), 70–2, 74, 78, 81, 84
IKW (Industrieverband Körperpflege- und Waschmittel), 72, 74, 78, 84
imports, 51, 59, 61–2, 90
incentive, 21, 24, 29; economic, 185; investment, 93; member, 28–9, 155, 167, 183, 204; political, 204; politico-economic, 184; public, 29; selective, 23, 36, 105; for collective action, 51
inclusiveness of association, 126
industry; boundary, 130, 151; captains of, 143; characteristics, 61, 150, 247; intra-, 33–4, 50–1; process-oriented, 57, 62; specific regulation, 148
inertia; associational, 233; institutional, 150
influence; channel, 206, 216–8, 220; direct, 59; investments, 80, 99–101, 120–1, 145–6, 230–1; logic of, 28–9, 66, 104, 154, 157, 170, 172, 175, 183–4, 239; route, 11, 31, 202, 206–7, 213, 215–20; target, 45, 147–9
Information and Communications sector, 7, 10, 57–8, 60–2, 108, 110–11, 113, 122, 125, 127, 128, 130–1, 135, 222, 225, 228, 230, 235
information; technology, 54, 57, 138, 244; exchange, 8, 38, 55, 77–9, 83, 85, 97–8, 117–19, 123, 131, 143–5, 147–8, 226, 228–9; exchange network, 76, 94–5, 97, 117, 119, 126, 226, 228; broker, 77, 98, 105, 117, 119; services, 131, 134–5, 184; service provider, 134; flow, 87, 97, 119, 126, 129, 134, 144, 221, 226, 228–9
infrastructure; immaterial, 130; material, 130; network, 109, 133; private; public, 47
innovation; cycle, incremental, 53; organizational, process, 238; product, 238; radical, 53–6, 163; rate, 57–8, 61, 125; replacement, 128; slow, 61; system, 249; technical, 42, 52–3, 56, 249; technological, 10, 42, 52, 55–6, 58, 66, 70, 85, 92–4, 108, 127, 136, 234, 237–8, 244–8, 250, 252; types of, 53, 60
institutional; adaptation, 173; challenge, 133; change, 52, 57, 200, 219; configuration, 206, 208, 219; constraint, 25; economics, 33; embeddings, 204; environment, 179; foundation, 246; inertia, 150; isomorphism, 243; legacy, 48; perspective, 236; reform, 57, 251; regulatory setting, 57; rule, 209
institutionalism; historical, 5, 48; sociological, 236; new, 243
institutions; administrative, 48; Community, 200; domestic, 85, 125; dominance of, 250; economic, 52; EU, 30, 60, 85, 122, 124–5, 127, 200–1, 206–208, 211, 220, 225, 242; embeddedness of, 243; global, 46; governmental, 6, 38, 91, 102; historical, 173; national, 31, 103, 124, 220; non-governmental, 137; non-majoritarian, 45, 253; political, 12, 22, 29–30, 101, 200–1, 203–4, 206, 216, 218; public, 82, 214; regional, 147; regulatory, 253; social, 253; state, 98, 250; state-like, 156; supra-national, 94, 219
interest; aggregation, 26–7; articulation, 26–7, 30–1, 37, 136; common, 23, 37; domain, 23, 28, 32, 37, 67, 114, 125–7, 151, 167–8, 171, 233, 235, 238; intermediation, 1, 4, 7, 11, 27–8, 35, 45–6, 65, 91, 94, 98, 103, 109, 156–7, 173–4, 180–3, 187–90, 192–7, 199, 218, 238, 242, 245, 251, 254; members', 5, 9, 33, 37, 44, 101, 126, 150, 195; multiple, 21, 29; objective, 18, 21; organization of, 20, 146, 174,

203, 238, 249, 252; organized business, 1, 7, 17, 21, 23–4, 27, 29, 35, 42, 52, 60, 108, 111, 117, 137; organized, 20, 32, 46–7, 62, 67, 75, 88, 142–3, 242–3, 245–6, 248, 251, 253; particularistic, 27; population, 70, 71, 75, 77, 79, 82; portfolio, 99, 105, 141; representation, 2, 10–11, 17, 23, 27–8, 35, 37, 46–7, 56, 59, 66, 126–7, 200–2, 206, 208–9, 218, 233, 238, 242, 245, 250; subjective, 19; workers', 20
interest group; community, 32; competition, 24; formation, 30, 247; influence, 45, 245, 251; interaction, 21; involvement, 154; literature, 7; niche, 32; penetration, 45; politics, 34; research, 7, 8, 239; society, 88, 241; studies, 9; survival, 32; system, 21, 27, 42, 154, 229, 235; theory, 26, 34, 42
intergovernmentalism, 30–1
intermediary, 25, 225; position, 145, 226; role, 108, 126; structure, 55
international; association, 46–8, 84, 103, 124, 127, 141, 150, 233, 238; bargaining, 31; challenge, 67, 168; company, 52; competitiveness, 179; division of labor, 109; governance, 9, 18, 29–31, 237; governance literature, 31; level, 1–2, 31, 90, 92, 101–3, 146, 150, 230; lobbying, *see* lobbying; merger, 51, 52; organizations, 3, 47, 77, 92, 102, 148, 152, 234; policy-making, 29, 233; political system, 5; political economy, 29, 30; regime, 46, 252; regulation, 37, 207; relations, 30; relations theory, 31; trade, 6, 146, 237
internationalization, 44, 61, 67, 70, 84, 108, 146, 153, 156, 172–3, 228, 236, 238, 246–7, 252–3; economic, 47; hypothesis, 237; political, 233; of economic activity, 156; of governance, 6; of markets, 9, 84, 171; of members, 37
inter-organizational; change, 100; contacts, 166; coordination, 77; links, 169; relation, 10, 35, 221; network, 143; structure, 98, 157
IPA (Institute of Practitioners in Advertising), 112–13, 115–16, 118, 124
IPPIC (International Paint and Printing Ink Council), 103
isomorphism, 165, 236, 243
ISPA (Internet Services Providers Association), 112, 114–15, 118–19, 124
ITAA (Information Technology Association of America), 138–9, 142, 144, 147, 150
IVA (Industrieverband Agrar), 72, 74, 78, 81, 84
IVC (Industrievereinigung Chemiefaser), 72, 74, 78, 84

KLEB (Industrieverband Klebstoffe), 72, 74, 78

labor; capital and, 38; division of, 1, 12, 26, 28, 50, 109, 163, 195; exchange of, 20; movement, 36; relations, 21, 110; union, 32, 249; wage, 20
Lack (Verband der Lackindustrie), 72, 74, 78
legacy, 55; institutional, 48; of the past, 173
level; European, 6–8, 10, 31, 69, 80, 82, 85, 120, 122, 124, 127, 177, 182, 190, 200–1, 203, 205–8, 218, 230, 232, 237; global, *see* global; international, *see* international; national, 7–8, 31, 45–6, 49, 60, 63, 67, 80, 94, 101, 103, 124, 150, 182, 190, 197, 206, 217–18, 220, 232; subnational, 150, 166, 171–2; supranational, 1, 30
liaison office in Brussels, 84, 124, 137
liberalization, 150, 152, 156; Directive, 109; market, 108, 225;

policy, 47, 168, 252; of dairy sector, 162–3; of state monopoly, 237; of telecommunications, 41, 109
LINX (London Internet Exchange), 112, 114–16, 118–19, 124
lobbying; campaign, 185, 202, 218; corporate, 11, 143, 200, 202, 218, 220, 249, 253; direct firm, 200; direct, 11, 46, 68, 127, 143, 200–3, 206–7, 209, 211, 217–19, 233, 251; domestic, 60, 121, 231; European, 69–71, 73, 80, 84, 86–9, 95–8, 104, 113–14, 116, 119, 137, 148, 151, 182, 223, 225, 228; international, 80, 85, 99, 101, 146, 150, 231–3, 280; investment, 145–6, 151, 232; large-firm, 243; path, 181, 194; political, 101, 145; professional, 203; profile, 101, 149; societal, 13, 47, 80–1, 99, 101, 120–2, 146, 222, 230–2; strategy, 188, 206, 209, 213–9; supranational, 11; target, 5, 45, 60, 83, 102, 122–3, 131, 152, 222
lobbyist; domestic, 121, 147, 230–2, 236; multilevel, 121, 127–8, 147, 230–2, 234, 236; chief, 213; sweetener, 220
local; adaptation, 48; association, 241, 247; audience, 171; authority, 134; context, 171; distance service providers, 135; exchange carriers, 135; interaction, 18; level, 91, 140, 171; market, 171; network, 135, 150; state, 134; telephone market, 137; VIP, 171
logic; of effective implementation, 171–2; of goal formation, 171–2; of influence, 28–9, 66, 104, 154, 157, 170, 172, 175, 183–4, 239; of membership, 10, 28, 66, 89, 94, 104–6, 127, 154–5, 157, 170, 172, 175, 183, 239, 241

Maastricht Treaty, 200, 219
majority voting; qualified, 205

management, 100, 170; lean, 170; practice, 104; theory, 169; of associations, 52; of exchange relationships, 25
market; entry, 54, 55, 130; structure, 6, 39, 42, 48, 49, 62, 160, 221, 230, 234, 238, 239, 242, 247
marketing, 80, 155, 170–1, 232; firms, 100; political, 13
Marxism, 8, 43
Marxist, 23; assumption, 19; class theory, 21; idea of objective interests, 21
matrix; dissimilarity, 149; lobbying, 149; rows, 149; structure, 79
member; conferences, 80, 99, 120, 146; consultation, 80, 99, 120, 146; firm, 6, 10, 12, 20–1, 28–9, 35–6, 39, 49, 55, 59, 66, 127, 143, 194, 238–9; information, 80, 99, 120, 126, 146
membership; affiliate, 87; base, 12, 27, 42, 48–9, 53, 76, 113, 120, 126–7, 141; compulsory, 159, 168; declining, 152; demands, 49, 66, 239; diversity, 75; direct firm, 87; domain, 163; dues, 25, 90, 100, 105; EU, 162; fees, 49, 90; growth, 141; heterogeneous, 120, 169; information, 145; investments, 80, 99–100, 120, 145–6, 151, 230; logic of, *see* logic; overlapping, 21, 151; related activity, 80–1; relations, 145; services, 36, 101, 232
MEP, 11, 186, 189, 191–3, 195, 197, 199, 217, 219–20
mergers; associational, 32, 62, 69, 71–2, 75, 95, 110–2, 114, 137, 139, 223–6, 235; and acquisitions, 51–2, 67, 85, 93, 106, 126, 234, 242, 254; company, 75, 140; of sectors, 125, 164
Milchkrise, 162, 166, 1734
milk; farmer, 160, 162, 164, 167–8; marketing, 245; Marketing Board, 158, 164; organic, 163; powder, 161; producer, 158, 163–4, 174; production, 165; raw, 158–9, 161,

Subject Index 271

163–4, 169; supplier, 158–9, 164, 169
MIV (Milchindustrieverband), 167, 169, 171
MMB (Milk Marketing Board), 159, 161, 164, 175
MNC (Multinational corporation), 11, 200–4, 206–9, 211, 213–20, 233
modes of governance; association, 33–4, 156, 158, 160, 166, 221, 227, 243; community, 33; hierarchy, 33; hybrid, 33, 37–8; interest, 253; market, 30, 33; private interest, 10, 11, 88–9, 104, 106, 153–4, 174, 228, 245–6, 250–1, 253–4; self-regulation, 65, 136; state, 30
monopoly; good, 103–4; power, 180; representational, 91, 117, 163, 234; regulated, 151; right, 103
mortality; anxiety, 245; rates, 32
MPA (Music Publishers Association), 112–13, 115, 117–18, 124, 139
MPAA (Motion Picture Association of America), 138, 142, 144, 146–7, 149–50, 232
multilevel; framework, 46; governance, 9, 30–1, 201, 244; interest representation, 47; lobbying, 101, 122, 233; lobbyist, 121, 127–8, 147, 230–2, 234, 236; nature, 7; perspective, 18, 35; system, 183, 201, 206
multinational; company, 3–4, 11, 46, 52, 70, 200, 232, 253; corporation, 1, 30; firm, 46, 194–195
mutualism, 10, 18, 73–4, 76, 96, 115, 130, 142, 240
MWF (Milchwirtschaftsfond), 159, 161

NAA (Newspaper Association of America), 138–9, 142, 144, 147, 149–50
NAB (National Association of Broadcasters), 138–9, 142, 144, 147, 149–50

NACA (National Cosmetology Association), 95
NACD (National Association of Chemical Distributors), 95–7, 103, 107
NAFTA (North America Free Trade Agreement), 92–3, 106
NAM (National Association of Manufacturers), 102–3
nation state, 1, 3–4, 45, 47, 241, 243
NCTA (National Cable & Telecommunications Association), 137–9, 142, 144–5
NDA (National Dairymen's Association), 164
NDMA (Nonprescription Drug Manufacturers Association), 95
neo-corporatism, 7, 11, 18, 26–9, 36–8, 40–1, 44, 142, 153, 222–3, 253
neo-functionalism, 30
neo-liberalism, 47, 110, 248
neo-liberal; arrangement, 156; perspective, 2; policy-model, 47; project, 156
neo-pluralism, 17, 35, 248, 249
network; alliance network, 79; analysis, xi, 8, 13, 147, 248, 254; centrality, 8, 76, 78, 98, 144–5, 244; centralization, 91, 229, 237; density, 8, 50, 77, 81, 128, 224, 226; ecological, 73, 76, 116, 221, 223, 225–6, 229, 235, 239; effect, 62; inter-organizational, 143; operator, 130; organizational, 143; periphery, 226, 228; policy, 3, 41, 46, 48, 242, 247, 248, 251, 252; relation, 55; research, ix, x, xi; spatial, x, xi; of organizations, 79
neutrality; relational, 74, 76, 96, 115, 142, 152
NFTC (National Foreign Trade Council), 103
niche; associational, 39, 49, 116, 128, 235–6; interest, 238; interest group, 32; market, 133; national, 11, 153; overlap, 32;

272 Subject Index

partitioning, 235; product, 51, 235; theory, 29, 245
NPA (National Pharmaceutical Alliance), 95
NPCA (National Paint and Coatings Association), 95–7, 107
NPMA (National Pest Management Association), 95–7, 107
NPRA (National Petrochemical Refiners Association), 95–7, 104, 107
NS (The Newspaper Society), 112–13, 115–16, 118, 124

OFTEL (Office of Telecommunications), 122–3
OPASTCO (Organization for the Promoting & Advancement of Small Telecommunications Companies), 138–9, 142, 144, 147, 149
organization; of business interests, ix, x, 48, 152, 202, 245, 251; theory, 18, 31, 33–4, 39
organizational; adaptation, 93, 99; analysis, 243; behavior, 111, 169; change, 9, 99–100, 105–7, 242, 246, 251, 254; characteristics, 203; community, 5, 11, 79, 153–4, 156, 158, 163–6, 172, 180, 205–6, 242; cohesion, 75; coordination, 77; core, 72; development, 246, 250, 254; dilemma, 28, 253; division, 95, 164; domain, 6; ecology, 34–5, 37–9, 43, 77, 84, 152, 241, 245–6; ecology literature, 9; ecology theory, 35; ecology thinking, 36; ecosystem, 6; evolution, 86; field, 2, 236, 243; form, 31, 68, 75, 108, 136, 249; fragmentation, 71; hierarchy, 68, 201; landscape, 44; learning, 236; level, 4–6, 35, 57, 98, 141, 180, 183; links, 169; members, 25, 170; network, 143; perception, 88; population, 2, 5, 10–1, 73, 136, 153, 163–4, 166–7, 169, 172; property, 6, 28, 35, 38–40, 89, 94, 155–6, 168, 170, 194, 221, 223, 229–31, 235, 239; relations, 10, 35, 221; research, 39; resource, 68, 244; roof, 164; routine, 53; species, 5; split, 70, 169; stability, 137; structure, 6, 28, 39, 88, 98, 157, 171, 196; subunit, 187; support, 55; survival, 105; unit, 55, 94; web, 175
OSHA (Occupational Safety and Health Administration), 92, 102
overlapping; activities, 105; interest domains, 32, 127, 151, 235; interests, 62; membership, 21, 151; missions, 141
ownership; common, 20; limits, 134; private, 130; relations, 207; structure, 70–1, 85

PA (Publishers Association), 112, 115, 118, 120, 124
Parliament, 2, 27, 122–4, 158, 191, 198; European, 92, 122
parliamentarism, 157
partner; association, 104; business, 134; coalition, 193–4, 199; interaction, 190–1; interview, 140, 143; legitimate, 206; lobbying, 192; social, 159; strategic, 192
partnership; association, 104; program, 104; social, 154, 157, 159, 247; strategic, 183
party; competition, 22; discipline, 45; machine, 25; political, 6, 23, 26, 46, 123–4, 181, 191, 241; structure, 45; system, 2, 4, 27, 44
path; break, 66; creation, 65; dependence, 8, 48, 53, 65, 173, 248; evolutionary, 10, 111, 127, 225; geodesic, 98; lobbying, 181, 194; of theory evolution, 18
PBA (Plastic Bag Association), 95
PCIA (Personal Communications Industry Association), 137–9, 142, 144, 147, 149, 152, 226
PDI (Plastic Drum Institute), 95
peak association, 38, 68, 70–1, 73, 75–6, 84, 87, 98, 109–10, 124, 143, 152, 187–8, 192, 204, 224,

Subject Index 273

229; British, 182, 193; domestic, 225; European, 189, 191, 195; German, 193; national, 85, 181, 191, 194, 239; sectoral, 111, 116, 126, 150, 194, 223, 225–6, 235
periphery, 224, 229; network, 77, 223, 226, 228, 229; of population, 85
permanent representative, 207
Peugeot-Citroen group, 219
pharmaceuticals, 57, 61, 67, 69–70, 73, 75, 77, 79, 85, 224; association, 70, 73, 81, 85; biotechnology, 54, 250; company, 84; industry, 58, 70, 254; interests, 84; interest representation, 242; knowledge, 54, 57; manufacturer, 70, 223; producer, 71; products, 67, 93
PhRMA (Pharmaceutical Research and Manufacturers of America), 95
PIG; Private Interest Government, 10–1, 88–9, 104, 106, 153–67, 169–70, 174–5, 228, 245–6, 250, 253–4
piracy; DVD copying, 146; global threat of, 150; music and film, 133; of intellectual property, 130
platform; communication, 116, 134; general-purpose, 133; macro-theoretical, 39; video, 135
pluralist; America, 104; approach, 17, 22, 151–2, 223; associational arrangement, 105; associational system, 28, 94, 96, 98, 142, 143, 174, 229; assumption, 98; character, 103; configuration, 188; environment, 102; feature, 11, 91, 151; fragmentation, 85; group theory, 21–2; image, 10; logic, 89; logic of adaptation, 165; market for influence, 10; market for representation, 27; model, 32, 131, 151; neo-, 248; orientation, 193; pattern of interaction, 65, 106; patterns of policy-making, 252; population ecology, 61; perspective, 145; precinct, 88; pressure politics, 222; role, 26; setting, 89, 145; structure, 141, 143, 239; theory, 35; thinking, 21, 239; tradition, 22
PMA (Pharmaceutical Manufacturers Association), 95
PMA (Polyurethane Manufacturers Association), 95
political; action, 20, 22–3; challenge, 67–9, 90, 128, 132–3, 140, 197; constraints, 9, 137; culture, 47; economy, 8, 29–30, 35, 165; economists, 43; entrepreneur, 22, 24–5, 65; entrepreneurship, 24; environment, 10, 43–4, 47, 59, 137, 147, 182, 221–2, 230; exchange, 25, 207; exostructure, 42; factors, 9, 42–3, 59, 86, 93, 106, 151; gardener, 121, 230–1, 236; gardening, 12, 47, 222, 233; incentive, 204; information, 183, 190–1, 198; inputs, 26; international, institutions, 12, 22, 29–30, 52, 101, 173, 200–1, 203–4, 206, 216, 218; legitimacy, 203; literature, 3; macro-structure, 27, 44, 157; market, 25, 68; order, 1; marketing, 13; outputs, 26; perturbation, 11; process theory, 21; program, 3; regime, 109; research, 1; resource, 29, 207; science, 2, 7, 18, 27, 42, 45; scientists, 2, 12; sociologists, 2; subsystem, 1, 5, system theory, 40; transformation, 111; turmoil, 229; variables, 60–1, 238
Political Action Committee, 51, 143
population; dynamics, 9, 32, 86, 114, 117, 223–5, 227, 229, 234–5, 242; ecology, 9, 18, 31–2, 35, 50, 61, 245–6; structure, 32, 117
Porsche, 205
power; decision-making, 45, 60; delegation of, 85, 154, 234, 238; distribution of, 27, 44; exchange, 241; fragmentation of, 91, 140; market, 34; monopoly, 180; potential, 213–5; resource, 214; separation of, 27, 44, 140; shift, 3, 45–6, 249; structure, 1, 243; withdrawal of, 238

PPA (Periodical Publishers Association), 112–13, 115–20, 124
PPC (Polystyrene Packaging Council), 95
PPI (Plastics Pipe Institute), 95
pressure; adaptation, 12, 36, 39, 40, 62, 152, 236; competitive, 50–1, 53, 128; economic, 140; group, 21, 91, 110, 241, 245; indirect, 59; market, 37; political, 193, 207; selection, 37, 38
price; fixing, 160, 162; negotiation, 161, 170
privatization, 47, 237, 252
producer liability, 209, 211–3
protection; consumer, 82, 134, 204; environmental, 82, 92, 102, 204; food quality, 92; surface, 70, 77; of intellectual property rights, 146, 152
public; choice, 18, 22–4, 40, 221, 241, 253; regulation, 30; affairs manager, 203; department, 203; office, 203, 219

RCRA (Resource Conservation and Recovery Act), 92
R&D, 53–4, 90, 93
REACH (Registration Evaluation Authorisation of Chemicals), 11, 68, 179–80, 183, 184–6, 192, 198
receiving; of information, 76, 144
recovery; energy, 209; quotas, 209; of end-of-life vehicles, 209–10
RegTP (Regulierungsbehörde für Telekomunikation und Post), 122–3
regulation; associational, 160; chemicals, 67, 185–6, 195; software, 148; state, 167
regulatory; agency, 122–3, 185; capacity, 169; framework, 133–4; regime, 48, 57, 149, 185; state, 48, 248
relational; analysis,10; complexity, 203; information, 97; intensity, 144; level, 38–9; network, 145; resources, 77, 81; structure, 224
relations; asymmetric, 114; competitive, 9, 34, 73, 76, 86, 96, 116, 126, 128, 133, 142, 223, 235, 238, 239; cooperative, 76, 97, 114, 126, 141, 221, 229, 239; ecological, 74, 85, 96, 115, 142, 223, 224, 229; inter-associational, 12, 38, 40, 97, 222; multiplex, 131; state-business, 110–11, 201; state-society, 65; symmetric, 38
rent seeking, 23, 221, 253
resource; allocation, 80–1, 99, 101, 119–22, 145–6, 147, 230; exchange, 6, 25; investment, 126; pooling, 25, 38; utilization, 126, 237
reunification, 157, 168
RIAA (Recording Industry Association of America), 138

sampling procedure, 128
SARA (Superfunds Amendments and Reauthorization Act), 92
SBCA (Satellite Broadcasting & Communications Association), 138–9, 142, 144, 147
SDA (Soap and Detergent Association), 95–7, 107
segments of chemicals industry; adhesives, 77, 87; agrochemicals, 57, 61, 67; basics, 67, 93; biotechnology, 9, 54, 56, 61–2, 67, 69, 70–1, 73, 77, 84–6, 93–4, 223–4, 235, 244, 250, 254; coatings, 71, 73, 76, 77, 87, 107; cosmetics, 67, 73, 76, 104; dyes, 67; fertilizers, 67, 73, 103; inorganics, 67; life science, 9, 58, 69, 73, 81, 85, 86, 93; manmade fibers, 67; organics, 67; paints, 67, 73; pigments, 67; plastics, 67, 76, 103, 225; rubber, 67, 73; soaps, 67, 77; surface protection, 70, 77; toiletry, 67, 73, 87; textiles, 77; varnishes, 67
segments of I&C industry; printing, 111, 116, 124, 132; publishing, 111, 114, 131, 134, 135; telematic, 132–3; telephony, 132,

Subject Index 275

133, 134, 136; broadcasting, 58, 131, 132, 133, 138, 147, 149; cable television, 131–5, 149; computing, 131, 138, 148, 151; content provider, 130, 148, 149; electronic equipment, 111, 114, 117; integrated circuits, 54, 58; internet, 46, 57–8, 113, 116, 119, 128, 132–5, 137–8, 142, 254; internet service provision, 114, 117, 134, 149; internet telephony, 119; newspapers, 117, 131; software, 57, 117, 148; telephony, 132, 133, 134, 136
selection; natural, 31–2; forces, 18, 36–8, 40; mechanism, 36–7; pressure, 37–8; process, 36; of associations, 128
selective retention, 31, 36, 242
self-coordination, 136
self-governance, 136
self-interested; corporate actors, 25; political entrepreneur, 24
self-regulation, 2, 3, 30–1, 34, 48, 65, 89, 104, 135–6, 154, 159, 208, 227–8, 234, 247
sending; of information, 76, 144
service; goods, 28; membership, 36, 101, 232; provider, 114, 117, 121–2, 127, 133–5, 147, 170, 230–2, 236; strategy, 37
SIA (Solvent Industries Association), 72, 74, 76, 78, 84, 87
SIIA (Software & Information Industry Association), 138–9, 142, 144, 147, 226
Single European Act, 174, 219
size; company, 85; firm, 50, 253; plant, 163
small and medium-sized enterprise, 57, 71, 194, 195, 204, 246
SMKV (Schweizerischer Milchkäuferverband), 158, 163, 170, 174
SMP (Swiss Milk Producers), 163, 174
SMV (Schweizerischer Milchwirtschaftlicher Verein), 174

social; contract theory, 25; movement, 1, 2, 46; order, 2, 155, 162, 253; partnership, 154, 157, 159, 247
societal; actors, 39, 98; challenge, 86, 128; corporatism, 41, 44; development, 12, 20, 86; governance, 7; groups, 22; interests, 241; lobbying, 13, 47, 80–1, 99, 101, 120–2, 146, 222, 230–2; modernization, 136; order, 31; structures, 7; turmoil, 108
sociology, 18; economic, 173; historical, 248; political, 253
SOCMA (Synthetic Organic Chemical Manufacturers Association), 95–7, 104, 107
SOCSA (Specialised Organic Chemicals Sectors Association), 71–2, 74, 76, 78, 81, 86, 223
solidarity; spontaneous, 155
SPI (Society of the Plastics Industry), 95–7, 107
spillover, 30
split-up, 24, 69–72, 81, 86, 95, 111–12, 114, 139, 169, 223–5, 229, 235
staff; associational, 75, 124, 138, 167, 194; permanent, 33; professional, 27
stakeholder, 130, 135, 149, 151, 186; conference, 186, 188, 195; conflict, 134
standing committee, 76
strategy; access, 124; Commission's, 186; expansion, 213; imperial, 239; lobbying, 188, 196, 202, 206, 209, 211, 213–19; orthodox, 206; political gardening, 12; service, 37
structural; equivalence, 122; functionalism, 7, 26, 44; reform, 170
subordination, 169, 222
substances; new, 185; old, 68; existing, 185; testing of, 185
supranational; actor, 189; association, 195, 197, 203, 206, 218–19; level, 1, 30; governance, 250;

276 Subject Index

lobbying, 11; organization, 238; political system, 45; 4; process, 8; terrain, 47
Swiss Cheese Award, 170
Switzerland, 11, 153, 157–69, 171–2, 174–5, 222, 227–8, 231, 247
system; adaptive, 5, 35, 38–9, 246; complex, 35, 131, 158; most different, 157; theory, 9, 17, 19, 37, 40, 252

take-over, 76
technological; challenge, 52, 66, 69, 92, 128, 132, 140; constraint, 9; development, 61, 93–4, 107, 137, 151; discontinuity, 53, 240; innovation, 10, 42, 52, 55–6, 58, 66, 70, 85, 92–4, 108, 127, 136, 234, 237–8, 244, 248, 250, 252; paradigm, 53, 244; revolution, 125, 222; trajectory, 53, 244
TEGEWA (Verband Textil- u. Lederhilfsmittel u. Gerbstoffe), 84
TFI (The Fertilizer Institute), 95–7, 107
Thatcher, M., 110, 241
theory; association, 8, 17–8, 32, 35, 39, 43, 222, 239; bottom-up, 40; class, 18–21, 36; collective action, 18, 20, 23, 29, 37, 39; complex adaptive systems, 38–9; complex association, 5, 18, 38, 40; of complex associative action, 34; of complex associational systems, 9; complexity, 5, 18, 132, 151–2, 236, 240, 252; corporate actor, 8, 18, 24–5; deep impact, 150; differentiation, 240; ecological, 40; Europeanization, 111; evolution, 18, 29; exchange, 18, 24–5, 37, 40, 250; gradual change, 150; governance, 29; holistic, 142; interest group, 19, 26–7, 34, 42; international relations, 31; integration, 29, 30; management, 169; Marxist, 20–1; modernization, 4, 241; neo-corporatist, 18, 43, 142, 221, 253; neo-functionalist, 30; neo-pluralist, 17; niche, 29;

organization, 18, 31, 33–4, 39; organizational ecology, 35, 37; pluralist, 18, 21–2, 34; political process, 21–2; population ecology, 35; public choice, 18, 34, 37; social contract, 25; structural-functionalist, 7; systems, 9, 17–8, 26–7, 34, 37, 40, 44, 131, 152, 252; top-down, 37, 40; transaction cost, 18, 33–4, 38, 50; two logics, 9
TIA (Telecommunications Industry Association), 136, 138–9, 142, 144–7, 150, 152, 228, 232
TPA (The Proprietary Association), Trade Association Forum, 75, 241, 253
trade and labor union, 19–21, 28, 32, 36, 39, 102–3, 249
trajectory; evolutionary, 125; curvilinear, 50; technological, 53, 244
transaction costs, 33–4, 37–8, 183, 188
tripartism, 27–29, 154
TSCA (Toxic Substances Control Act), 91–2

UK, 7, 57, 59–60, 62, 65–7, 69, 75–6, 80, 84–7, 93, 116, 120, 124, 128, 164, 188, 190, 211–12, 223–4, 227–8, 229, 231
UKCPI (Cleaning Products Industry Association), 72, 74, 85, 87
umbrella association, 38, 82, 143, 164, 167, 169, 175, 226, 235
United States Congress, *see* American Congress
US, 7, 9–11, 27, 32, 41, 44–5, 47–8, 50–1, 57–8, 59, 60, 62, 88–107, 109, 130–152, 222–5, 227–34, 237
USTA (United States Telecom Association), 136–9, 142, 144, 147

VAF (Bundesverband Telekommunikation), 112–15, 117–18, 124
value added, 66, 75; services, 11, 101, 134

Subject Index 277

variables; economic, 28, 32, 43, 50; technological, 43, 59; political, 60, 61, 238
varieties of capitalism, 246; approach, 197; debate, 5, 8, 48; hypothesis, 111, 180, 237
VATM (Verband der Anbieter von Telekommunikations- und Mehrwertdiensten), 111–12, 115, 118, 121, 124
VCI (Verband der Chemischen Industrie), 70, 72–4, 77–8, 81–5, 182, 184–5, 187, 191–3, 223, 225–6
VDA (Verband der Automobilindustrie), 204–5, 214–18
VDM (Verband der deutschen Milchwirtschaft), 160
VDMA (Verband Deutscher Maschinen- und Anlagenbau), 111–18, 124, 126
VDZ (Verband Deutscher Zeitschriftenverleger), 112, 114–15, 117–18, 120, 124
VFA (Verband Forschender Arzneimittelhersteller), 70–2, 74, 77–9, 81, 84–5, 223
VI (Vinyl Institute), 95–7, 103–4, 107, 112
VKE (Verband Kunststofferzeugende Industrie), 72, 74, 78, 84

VÖM (Vereinigung Österreichischer Milchverarbeiter), 166–7
Volkswagen, 204–5, 207, 211–7, 220
VPRT (Verband Privater Rundfunk und Telekommunikation), 111–12, 115–18, 123–4
VSI (Verband der Softwareindustrie Deutschlands), 112, 115, 117–18

Wallström, M., 185
WCC (World Chlorine Council), 103
WHO (World Health Organisation), 92
within-system variation, 81, 121, 147
window of opportunity, 166, 173
workers, 19–20, 108,
World War, 136, 158,
WSMI (World Self-Medication Industry), 103
WTO (World Trade Organisation), 41, 92, 147

ZAW (Zentralverband der deutschen Werbewirtschaft), 112, 114–15, 118, 124
ZVEI (Zentralverband Elektrotechnik- und Elektronikindustrie), 111–18, 120, 122, 124, 126, 232
ZVSM (Zentralverband schweizerischer Milchproduzenten), 158, 163, 174